Get the eBook FREE!

(PDF, ePub, Kindle, and liveBook all included)

We believe that once you buy a book from us, you should be able to read it in any format we have available. To get electronic versions of this book at no additional cost to you, purchase and then register this book at the Manning website.

Go to https://www.manning.com/freebook and follow the instructions to complete your pBook registration.

That's it!
Thanks from Manning!

Real-World Natural Language Processing

MASATO HAGIWARA

MANNING
SHELTER ISLAND

For online information and ordering of this and other Manning books, please visit www.manning.com. The publisher offers discounts on this book when ordered in quantity. For more information, please contact

Special Sales Department
Manning Publications Co.
20 Baldwin Road
PO Box 761
Shelter Island, NY 11964
Email: orders@manning.com

Manning Publications Co.
20 Baldwin Road
PO Box 761
Shelter Island, NY 11964

Development editor: Karen Miller
Technical development editor: Mike Shepard
Review editor: Adriana Sabo
Production editor: Deirdre S. Hiam
Copy editor: Pamela Hunt
Proofreader: Keri Hales
Technical proofreader: Mayur Patil
Typesetter and cover designer: Marija Tudor

ISBN 9781617296420
Printed in the United States of America

To Daphne, Laurel, and Lynn

contents

preface

Having worked at the intersection of machine learning (ML), natural language processing (NLP), and education for the last two decades, I have always been passionate about education and helping people learn new technologies. That's why I didn't think twice when I heard about the opportunity of publishing a book on NLP.

The field of artificial intelligence (AI) went through a lot of changes over the past several years, including the explosive popularization of neural network–based methods and the advent of large, pretrained language models. This change made advanced language technologies possible, many of which you interact with daily—voice-based virtual assistants, speech recognition, and machine translation, to name a few. However, the "technology stack" of NLP, characterized by the use of pretrained models and transfer learning, has finally stabilized in the last few years and is expected to remain so, at least for the next couple of years. This is why I think now is a good time to start learning about NLP.

Developing a book on AI is never easy. It feels like you are chasing a moving target that doesn't slow down and wait for you. When I started writing this book, the Transformer had just been published, and BERT did not yet exist. Over the course of writing, AllenNLP, the main NLP framework we use in this book, went through two major updates. Few people were using Hugging Face Transformer, a widely popular deep NLP library currently used by many practitioners all over the world. Within two years, the landscape of the NLP field changed completely, due to the advent of the Transformer and pretrained language models such as BERT. The good news is that the basics of modern machine learning, including word and sentence embeddings, RNNs, and CNNs, have not become obsolete and remain important. This book intends to capture this "core" of ideas and concepts that help you build real-world NLP applications.

Many great books about ML and deep learning in general are on the market, but some of them focus heavily on math and theories. There's a gap between what's taught in books and what the industry needs. I hope this book will serve to bridge this gap.

acknowledgments

This book would not be possible without the help of many people. I must start by thanking Karen Miller, the development editor at Manning Publications. Thank you for your support and patience during the development of this book. I'm also grateful for the rest of the Manning team: technical development editor Mike Shepard, review editor Adriana Sabo, production editor Deirdre Hiam, copy editor Pamela Hunt, proofreader Keri Hales, and technical proofreader Mayur Patil. Denny (http://www.designsonline.id/) also created some of the high-quality illustrations you see in this book.

I'd also like to thank the reviewers who gave valuable feedback after reading the manuscript of this book: Al Krinker, Alain Lompo, Anutosh Ghosh, Brian S. Cole, Cass Petrus, Charles Soetan, Dan Sheikh, Emmanuel Medina Lopez, Frédéric Flayol, George L. Gaines, James Black, Justin Coulston, Lin Chen, Linda Ristevski, Luis Moux, Marc-Anthony Taylor, Mike Rosencrantz, Nikos Kanakaris, Ninoslav Čerkez, Richard Vaughan, Robert Diana, Roger Meli, Salvatore Campagna, Shanker Janakiraman, Stuart Perks, Taylor Delehanty, and Tom Heiman.

I'd like to acknowledge the AllenNLP team at the Allen Institute for Artificial Intelligence. I've had great discussions with the team, namely, Matt Gardner, Mark Neumann, and Michael Schmitz. I always look up to their great work that makes deep NLP technologies easy and accessible to the world.

Last but not least, I'd like to thank my awesome wife, Lynn. She not only helped me choose the right cover image for this book but has also been understanding and supportive of my work throughout the development of this book.

about this book

Real-World Natural Language Processing is not a typical NLP textbook. We focus on building real-world NLP applications. *Real-world*'s meaning here is twofold: first, we pay attention to what it takes to build real-world NLP applications. As a reader, you will learn not just how to train NLP models but also how to design, develop, deploy, and monitor them. Along the way, you will also learn the basic building blocks of modern NLP models, as well as recent developments in the NLP field that are useful for building NLP applications. Second, unlike most introductory books, we take a top-down approach to teaching. Instead of a bottom-up approach, spending page after page showing neural network theories and mathematical formulae, we focus on quickly building NLP applications that "just work." We then dive deeper into individual concepts and models that make up NLP applications. You'll also learn how to build end-to-end custom NLP applications tailored to your needs using these basic building blocks.

Who should read this book

This book is written mainly for software engineers and programmers who are looking to learn the basics of NLP and how to build NLP applications. We assume that you, the reader, have basic programming and software engineering skills in Python. This book also comes in handy if you are already working on machine learning but would like to move into the NLP field. Either way, you don't need any prior knowledge of ML or NLP. You don't need any math knowledge to read this book, although basic understanding of linear algebra might be helpful. There is not a single mathematical formula in this book.

How this book is organized: A roadmap

This book consists of three parts that span a total of 11 chapters. Part 1 covers the basics of NLP, where we learn how to quickly build an NLP application with AllenNLP for basic tasks such as sentiment analysis and sequence labeling.

- Chapter 1 begins by introducing the "what" and "why" of NLP—what is NLP, what is not NLP, how NLP technologies are used, and how NLP is related to other fields of AI.
- Chapter 2 demonstrates how to build your very first NLP application, a sentiment analyzer, and introduces the basics of modern NLP models—word embeddings and recurrent neural networks (RNNs)—along the way.
- Chapter 3 introduces two important building blocks of NLP applications, word and sentence embeddings, and demonstrates how to use and train them.
- Chapter 4 discusses one of the simplest but most important NLP tasks, sentence classification, and how to use RNNs for this task.
- Chapter 5 covers sequence labeling tasks such as part-of-speech tagging and named entity extraction. It also touches upon a related technique, language modeling.

Part 2 covers advanced NLP topics including sequence-to-sequence models, the Transformer, and how to leverage transfer learning and pretrained language models to build powerful NLP applications.

- Chapter 6 introduces sequence-to-sequence models, which transform one sequence into another. We build a simple machine translation system and a chatbot within an hour.
- Chapter 7 discusses another type of popular neural network architecture, convolutional neural networks (CNNs).
- Chapter 8 provides a deep dive into the Transformer, one of the most important NLP models today. We'll demonstrate how to build an improved machine translation system and a spell-checker using the Transformer.
- Chapter 9 builds upon the previous chapter and discusses transfer learning, a popular technique in modern NLP, with pretrained language models such as BERT.

Part 3 covers topics that become relevant when you develop NLP applications that are robust to real-world data, and deploy and serve them.

- Chapter 10 details best practices when developing NLP applications, including batching and padding, regularization, and hyperparameter optimization.
- Chapter 11 concludes the book by covering how to deploy and serve NLP models. It also covers how to explain and interpret ML models.

About the code

This book contains many examples of source code both in numbered listings and in line with normal text. In both cases, source code is formatted in a `fixed-width font` like this to separate it from ordinary text. Sometimes code is also **in bold** to highlight code that has changed from previous steps in the chapter, such as when a new feature adds to an existing line of code.

In many cases, the original source code has been reformatted; we've added line breaks and reworked indentation to accommodate the available page space in the book. In rare cases, even this was not enough, and listings include line-continuation markers (➥). Additionally, comments in the source code have often been removed from the listings when the code is described in the text. Code annotations accompany many of the listings, highlighting important concepts.

The code for the examples in this book is available for download from the Manning website at https://www.manning.com/books/real-world-natural-language-processing and from GitHub at https://github.com/mhagiwara/realworldnlp.

Most of the code can also be run on Google Colab, which is a free web-based platform where you can run your machine learning code on hardware accelerators, including GPUs.

liveBook discussion forum

Purchase of *Real-World Natural Language Processing* includes free access to a private web forum run by Manning Publications where you can make comments about the book, ask technical questions, and receive help from the author and from other users. To access the forum, go to https://livebook.manning.com/book/real-world-natural-language-processing/discussion. You can also learn more about Manning's forums and the rules of conduct at https://livebook.manning.com/#!/discussion.

Manning's commitment to our readers is to provide a venue where a meaningful dialogue between individual readers and between readers and the author can take place. It is not a commitment to any specific amount of participation on the part of the author, whose contribution to the forum remains voluntary (and unpaid). We suggest you try asking the author some challenging questions lest his interest stray! The forum and the archives of previous discussions will be accessible from the publisher's website as long as the book is in print.

Other online resources

The two NLP frameworks we use heavily in this book, AllenNLP and Hugging Face Transformers, both have great online courses (https://guide.allennlp.org/ and https://huggingface.co/course) where you can learn the basics of NLP and how to use the libraries to solve a variety of NLP tasks.

about the author

MASATO HAGIWARA received a PhD in computer science from Nagoya University in 2009, focusing on natural language processing and machine learning. He has interned at Google and Microsoft Research and worked at Baidu, Rakuten Institute of Technology, and Duolingo, as an engineer and a researcher. He now runs his own research and consultancy company, Octanove Labs, focusing on educational applications of NLP.

about the cover illustration

The figure on the cover of *Real-World Natural Language Processing* is captioned "Bulgare," or a man from Bulgaria. The illustration is taken from a collection of dress costumes from various countries by Jacques Grasset de Saint-Sauveur (1757–1810), titled *Costumes de Différents Pays*, published in France in 1797. Each illustration is finely drawn and colored by hand. The rich variety of Grasset de Saint-Sauveur's collection reminds us vividly of how culturally apart the world's towns and regions were just 200 years ago. Isolated from each other, people spoke different dialects and languages. In the streets or in the countryside, it was easy to identify where they lived and what their trade or station in life was just by their dress.

The way we dress has changed since then and the diversity by region, so rich at the time, has faded away. It is now hard to tell apart the inhabitants of different continents, let alone different towns, regions, or countries. Perhaps we have traded cultural diversity for a more varied personal life—certainly for a more varied and fast-paced technological life.

At a time when it is hard to tell one computer book from another, Manning celebrates the inventiveness and initiative of the computer business with book covers based on the rich diversity of regional life of two centuries ago, brought back to life by Grasset de Saint-Sauveur's pictures.

Part 1

Basics

Welcome to the beautiful and exciting world of natural language processing (NLP)! NLP is a subfield of *artificial intelligence* (AI) that concerns computational approaches to processing, understanding, and generating human languages. NLP is used in many technologies you interact with in your daily life—spam filtering, conversational assistants, search engines, and machine translation. This first part of the book is intended to give you a gentle introduction to the field and bring you up to speed with how to build practical NLP applications.

In chapter 1, we'll begin by introducing the "what" and "why" of NLP—what is NLP, what is not NLP, how NLP technologies are used, and how it's related to other fields of AI.

In chapter 2, you'll build a complete, working NLP application—a sentiment analyzer—within an hour with the help of a powerful NLP framework, Allen-NLP. You'll also learn to use basic machine learning (ML) concepts, including *word embeddings* and *recurrent neural networks* (RNNs). Don't worry if this sounds intimidating—we'll introduce you to the concepts gradually and provide an intuitive explanation.

Chapter 3 provides a deep dive into the one of the most important concepts for deep learning approaches to NLP—word and sentence embeddings. The chapter demonstrates how to use and even train them using your own data.

Chapters 4 and 5 cover fundamental NLP tasks, sentence classification and sequence labeling. Though simple, these tasks have a wide range of applications, including sentiment analysis, part-of-speech tagging, and named entity recognition.

This part familiarizes you with some basic concepts of modern NLP and we'll build useful NLP applications along the way.

Introduction to natural language processing

This chapter covers

- What natural language processing (NLP) is, what it is not, and why it's such an interesting, yet challenging, field
- How NLP relates to other fields, including artificial intelligence (AI) and machine learning (ML)
- What typical NLP applications and tasks are
- How a typical NLP application is developed and structured

This is not an introductory book to machine learning or deep learning. You won't learn how to write neural networks in mathematical terms or how to compute gradients, for example. But don't worry, even if you don't have any idea what they are. I'll explain those concepts as needed, not mathematically but conceptually. In fact, this book contains no mathematical formulae—not a single one. Also, thanks to modern deep learning libraries, you don't really need to understand the math to build practical NLP applications. If you are interested in learning the theories and the math behind machine learning and deep learning, you can find a number of great resources out there.

But you do need to be at least comfortable enough to write in Python and know its ecosystems. However, you don't need to be an expert in software engineering topics. In fact, this book's purpose is to introduce software engineering best practices for developing NLP applications. You also don't need to know NLP in advance. Again, this book is designed to be a gentle introduction to the field.

You need Python version 3.6.1 or higher and AllenNLP 2.5.0 or higher to run the code examples in this book. Note that we do not support Python 2, mainly because AllenNLP (https://allennlp.org/), the deep natural language processing framework I'm going to heavily use in this book, supports only Python 3. If you haven't done so, I strongly recommend upgrading to Python 3 and familiarizing yourself with the latest language features such as type hints and new string-formatting syntax. This will be helpful, even if you are developing non-NLP applications.

Don't worry if you don't have a Python development environment ready. Most of the examples in this book can be run via the Google Colab platform (https://colab.research.google.com). You need only a web browser to build and experiment with NLP models!

This book will use PyTorch (https://pytorch.org/) as its main choice of deep learning framework. This was a difficult decision for me, because several deep learning frameworks are equally great choices for building NLP applications, namely, TensorFlow, Keras, and Chainer. A few factors make PyTorch stand out among those frameworks—it's a flexible and dynamic framework that makes it easier to prototype and debug NLP models; it's becoming increasingly popular within the research community, so it's easy to find open source implementations of major models; and the deep NLP framework AllenNLP mentioned earlier is built on top of PyTorch.

1.1   What is natural language processing (NLP)?

NLP is a principled approach to processing human language. Formally, it is a subfield of artificial intelligence (AI) that refers to computational approaches to process, understand, and generate human language. The reason it is part of AI is because language processing is considered a huge part of human intelligence. The use of language is arguably the most salient skill that separates humans from other animals.

1.1.1   What is NLP?

NLP includes a range of algorithms, tasks, and problems that take human-produced text as an input and produce some useful information, such as labels, semantic representations, and so on, as an output. Other tasks, such as translation, summarization, and text generation, directly produce text as output. In any case, the focus is on producing some output that is useful per se (e.g., a translation) or as input to other downstream tasks (e.g., parsing). I'll touch upon some popular NLP applications and tasks in section 1.3.

You might wonder why NLP explicitly has "natural" in its name. What does it mean for a language to be natural? Are there any *un*natural languages? Is English natural? Which is more natural: Spanish or French?

The word "natural" here is used to contrast natural languages with *formal* languages. In this sense, all the languages humans speak are natural. Many experts believe that language emerged naturally tens of thousands of years ago and has evolved organically ever since. Formal languages, on the other hand, are types of languages that are invented by humans and have strictly and explicitly defined syntax (i.e., what is grammatical) and semantics (i.e., what it means).

Programming languages such as C and Python are good examples of formal languages. These languages are defined in such a strict way that it is always clear what is grammatical and ungrammatical. When you run a compiler or an interpreter on the code you write in those languages, you either get a syntax error or not. The compiler won't say something like, "Hmm, this code is maybe 50% grammatical." Also, the behavior of your program is always the same if it's run on the same code, assuming external factors such as the random seed and the system states remain constant. Your interpreter won't show one result 50% of the time and another the other 50% of the time.

This is not the case for human languages. You can write a sentence that is *maybe* grammatical. For example, do you consider the phrase "The person I spoke to" ungrammatical? There are some grammar topics where even experts disagree with each other. This is what makes human languages interesting but challenging, and why the entire field of NLP even exists. Human languages are *ambiguous*, meaning that their interpretation is often not unique. Both structures (how sentences are formed) and semantics (what sentences mean) can have ambiguities in human language. As an example, let's take a close look at the next sentence:

He saw a girl with a telescope.

When you read this sentence, who do you think has a telescope? Is it the boy, who's using a telescope to see a girl (from somewhere far), or the girl, who has a telescope and is seen by the boy? There seem to be at least two interpretations of this sentence as shown in figure 1.1.

Figure 1.1   Two interpretations of "He saw a girl with a telescope."

The reason you are confused upon reading this sentence is because you don't know what the phrase "with a telescope" is about. More technically, you don't know what this prepositional phrase (PP) modifies. This is called a *PP-attachment* problem and is a classic example of *syntactic ambiguity*. A syntactically ambiguous sentence has more than one interpretation of how the sentence is structured. You can interpret the sentence in multiple ways, depending on which structure of the sentence you believe.

Another type of ambiguity that may arise in natural language is *semantic ambiguity*. This is when the meaning of a word or a sentence, not its structure, is ambiguous. For example, let's look at the following sentence:

I saw a bat.

There is no question how this sentence is structured. The subject of the sentence is "I" and the object is "a bat," connected by the verb "saw." In other words, there is no syntactical ambiguity in it. But how about its meaning? "Saw" has at least two meanings. One is the past tense of the verb "to see." The other is to cut some object with a saw. Similarly, "a bat" can mean two very different things: is it a nocturnal flying mammal or a piece of wood used to hit a ball? All in all, does this sentence mean that I observed a nocturnal flying mammal or that I cut a baseball or cricket bat? Or even (cruelly) that I cut a nocturnal animal with a saw? You never know, at least from this sentence alone.

Ambiguity is what makes natural languages rich but also challenging to process. We can't simply run a compiler or an interpreter on a piece of text and just "get it." We need to face the complexities and subtleties of human languages. We need a scientific, principled approach to deal with them. That's what NLP is all about.

Welcome to the beautiful world of natural languages.

1.1.2   *What is not NLP?*

Now let's consider the following scenario and think how you'd approach this problem: you are working as a junior developer at a midsized company that has a consumer-facing product line. It's 3 p.m. on a Friday. The rest of the team is becoming more and more restless as the weekend approaches. That's when your boss drops by at your cubicle.

"Hey, got a minute? I've got something interesting to show you. I just sent it to you."

Your boss just sent you an email with a huge zip file attached to it.

"OK, so this is a giant TSV file. It contains all the responses to the survey questions about our product. I just got this data from the marketing team."

Obviously, the marketing team has been collecting user opinions about one of the products through a series of survey questions online.

"The survey questions include standard ones like 'How did you know about our product?' and 'How do you like our product?' There is also a free-response question, where our customers can write whatever they feel about our product. The thing is, the marketing team realized there was a bug in the online system and the answers to the second question were not recorded in the database at all."

"Wait, so there's no way to tell how the customers are feeling about our product?" This sounds weirdly familiar. This must be a copy-and-paste error. When you first created an online data-collection interface, you copied and pasted the backend code without modifying the ID parameters, resulting in a loss of some data fields.

"So," your boss continues. "I was wondering if we can recover the lost data somehow. The marketing team is a little desperate now because they need to report the results to the VP early next week."

At this point, your bad feeling has been confirmed. Unless you come up with a way to get this done as quickly as possible, your weekend plans will be ruined.

"Didn't you say you were interested in some machine learning? I think this is a perfect project for you. Anyway, it'd be great if you can give it a stab and let me know what you find. Do you think you can have some results by Monday?"

"Well, I'll give it a try."

You know "no" is not an acceptable answer here. Satisfied with your answer, your boss smiles and walks off.

You start by skimming the TSV file. To your relief, its structure is fairly standard—it has several fields such as timestamps and submission IDs. At the end of each line is a lengthy field for the free-response question. Here they are, you think. At least you know where to look for some clues.

After a quick glance over the field, you find responses such as "A very good product!" and "Very bad. It crashes all the time!" Not too bad, you think. At least you can capture these simple cases. You start by writing the following method that captures those two cases:

```python
def get_sentiment(text):
    """Return 1 if text is positive, -1 if negative.
       Otherwise, return 0."""
    if 'good' in text:
        return 1
    elif 'bad' in text:
        return -1
    return 0
```

Then you run this method on the responses in the file and log the results, along with the original input. As intended, this method seems to be able to capture a dozen or so of the responses that contains "good" or "bad."

But then you start to see something alarming, as shown next:

"I can't think of a single good reason to use this product": positive
"It's not bad.": negative

Oops, you think. *Negation.* Yeah, of course. But this is pretty easy to deal with. You modify the method as follows:

```python
def get_sentiment(text):
    """Return 1 if text is positive, -1 if negative.
       Otherwise, return 0."""
    sentiment = 0
```

```
if 'good' in text:
    sentiment = 1
elif 'bad' in text:
    sentiment = -1
if 'not' in text or "n't" in text:
    sentiment *= -1
return sentiment
```

You run the script again. This time, it seems to be behaving as intended, until you see an even more complicated example:

"The product is not only cheap but also very good!": negative

Hmm, you think. This is probably not as straightforward as I initially thought after all. Maybe the negation has to be somewhere near "good" or "bad" for it to be effective. Wondering what steps you could take next, you scroll down to see more examples, which is when you see responses like these:

"I always wanted this feature badly!": negative
"It's very badly made.": negative

You silently curse to yourself. How could a single word in a language have two completely opposite meanings? At this point, your little hope for enjoying the weekend has already disappeared. You are already wondering what excuses you use with your boss next Monday.

As a reader of this book, you'll know better. You'll know that NLP is not about throwing a bunch of `if`s and `then`s at natural language text. It is a more principled approach to processing natural language. In the following chapters, you'll learn how you should approach this problem before writing a single line of code and how to build a custom-made NLP application just for your task at hand.

1.1.3 AI, ML, DL, and NLP

Before delving into the details of NLP, it'd be useful to clarify how it relates to other, similar fields. Most of you have at least heard about artificial intelligence (AI) and machine learning (ML). You may also have heard of deep learning (DL), because it's generating a lot of buzz in popular media these days. Figure 1.2 illustrates how those different fields overlap with each other.

Artificial intelligence (AI) is a broad umbrella field that is concerned with achieving human-like intelligence using machines. It encompasses a wide range of subfields, including machine learning, natural language processing, computer vision, and speech recognition. The field also includes subfields such as reasoning, planning, and search, which do not fall under either machine learning or natural language processing and are not in the scope of this book.

Machine learning (ML) is usually considered a subfield of artificial intelligence that is about improving computer algorithms through experience and data. This includes learning a general function that maps inputs to outputs based on past experience

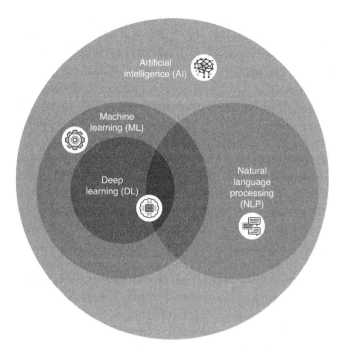

Figure 1.2 The relationship among different fields: AI, ML, DL, and NLP

(supervised learning), drawing hidden patterns and structures from data (unsupervised learning), and learning how to act in a dynamic environment based on indirect rewards (reinforcement learning). Throughout this book, we'll make a heavy use of supervised machine learning, which is the main paradigm for training NLP models.

Deep learning (DL) is a subfield of machine learning that usually uses deep neural networks. These neural network models are called "deep" because they consist of a number of layers. A *layer* is just a fancy word for a substructure of neural networks. By having many stacked layers, deep neural networks can learn complex representations of data and can capture highly complicated relationships between the input and the output.

As the amount of available data and computational resources increases, modern NLP makes a heavier and heavier use of machine learning and deep learning. Modern NLP applications and tasks are usually built on top of machine learning pipelines and trained from data. But also notice in figure 1.2 that a part of NLP does not overlap with machine learning. Traditional methods such as counting words and measuring similarities between text are usually not considered to be machine learning techniques per se, although they can be important building blocks for ML-based models.

I'd also like to mention some other fields that are related to NLP. One such field is *computational linguistics* (CL). As its name suggests, computational linguistics is a subfield of linguistics that uses computational approaches to study human language. The main distinction between CL and NLP is that the former encompasses scientific approaches to study language, whereas the latter is concerned with engineering approaches for making computers perform something useful related to language. People often use those terms interchangeably, partly due to some historical reasons. For example, the most prestigious conference in the field of NLP is called *ACL*, which actually stands for "the Association for Computational Linguistics!"

Another related field is *text mining*. Text mining is a type of data mining targeted at textual data. Its focus is on drawing useful insights from unstructured textual data, which is a type of text data that is not formatted in a form that is easily interpretable by computers. Such data is usually collected from various sources, such as crawling the web and social media. Although its purpose is slightly different from that of NLP, these two fields are similar, and we can use the same tools and algorithms for both.

1.1.4 *Why NLP?*

If you are reading this, you have at least some interest in NLP. Why is NLP exciting? Why is it worth learning more about NLP and, specifically, real-world NLP?

The first reason is that NLP is booming. Even without the recent AI and ML boom, NLP is more important than ever. We are witnessing the advent of practical NLP applications in our daily lives, such as conversational agents (think Apple Siri, Amazon Alexa, and Google Assistant) and near human-level machine translation (think Google Translate). A number of NLP applications are already an integral part of our day-to-day activities, such as spam filtering, search engines, and spelling correction, as we'll discuss later. The number of Stanford students enrolled in NLP classes grew fivefold from 2008 to 2018 (http://realworldnlpbook.com/ch1.html#tweet1). Similarly, the number of attendees for EMNLP (Empirical Methods in Natural Language Processing), one of the top NLP conferences, doubled within just one year (http://realworldnlpbook .com/ch1.html#tweet2). Other major NLP conferences are also experiencing similar increases in participants and paper submissions (http://realworldnlpbook.com/ch1 .html#nivre17).

The second reason is that NLP is an evolving field. The field of NLP itself has a long history. The first experiment to build a machine translation system, called *The Georgetown–IBM Experiment*, was attempted back in 1954. For more than 30 years since this experiment, most NLP systems relied on handwritten rules. Yes, it was not much different from what you just saw in section 1.1.1. The first milestone, which came in the late 1980s, was the use of statistical methods and machine learning for NLP. Many NLP systems started leveraging statistical models trained from data. This led to some recent successes in NLP, including, most notably, IBM Watson. The second milestone was more drastic. Starting around the late 2000s, the use of so-called deep learning, that is, deep neural network models, took the field by storm. By the mid-2010s, deep neural network models became the new standard in the field.

This second milestone was so drastic and fast that it's worth noting here. New neural network–based NLP models are not only more effective but also a lot simpler. For example, it used to take a lot of expertise and effort to replicate even a simple, baseline machine translation model. One of the most popular open source software packages for statistical machine translation, called Moses (http://www.statmt.org/moses/), is a behemoth, consisting of 100,000s of lines of code and dozens of supporting modules and tools. Experts spent hours just installing the software and making it work. On the other hand, as of 2018, anyone with some prior programming experience could run a neural machine translation system more powerful than traditional statistical models with a fraction of the code size—less than a few thousand lines of code (e.g., see Tensor-Flow's neural machine translation tutorial at https://github.com/tensorflow/nmt). Also, the new neural network models are trained "end-to-end," which means that those big, monolithic networks take the input and directly produce the output. Entire models are trained to match the desired output. On the other hand, traditional machine learning models consist of (at least) several submodules. These submodules are trained separately using different machine learning algorithms. In this book, I'll mainly discuss modern neural network–based approaches to NLP but also touch upon some traditional concepts as well.

The third and final reason is that NLP is challenging. Understanding and producing language is the central problem of artificial intelligence, as we saw in the previous section. The accuracy and performance in major NLP tasks such as speech recognition and machine translation got drastically better in the past decade or so. But human-level understanding of language is far from being solved.

To verify this quickly, open up your favorite machine translation service (or simply Google Translate), and type this sentence: "I saw her duck." Try to translate it to Spanish or some other language you understand. You should see words like "*pato*," which means "a duck" in Spanish. But did you notice another interpretation of this sentence? See figure 1.3 for the two interpretations. The word "duck" here could be a verb meaning "to crouch down." Try adding another sentence after this, such as "She tried to avoid a flying ball." Did the machine translation change the first translation in any way? The answer is probably no. You should still see the same "*pato*" in the translation. As you can see, most (if not all) commercial machine translation systems that are available as of today do not understand the context outside of the sentence that is being translated. A lot of research effort is spent on this problem in academia, but this is still one of many problems in NLP that is considered unsolved.

Figure 1.3 Two interpretations of "I saw her duck."

Compared to other AI fields such as robotics and computer vision, language has its own quirks. Unlike images, utterances and sentences have variable length. You can say a very short sentence ("Hello.") or a very long one ("A quick brown fox . . ."). Most machine learning algorithms are not good at dealing with something of variable length, and you need to come up with ways to represent languages with something more fixed. If you look back at the history of the field, NLP is largely concerned with the problem of how to *represent* language mathematically. Vector space models and word embeddings (discussed in chapter 3) are some examples of this.

Another characteristic of language is that it is *discrete*. What this means is that things in languages are separate as concepts. For example, if you take a word "rat" and change its first letter to the next one, you'll have "sat." In computer memory, the difference is just a single bit. However, there is no relationship between those two words except they both end with "at," and maybe a rat can sit. There is no such thing as something that is in between "rat" and "sat." These two are totally discrete, separate concepts that happen to have similar spelling. On the other hand, if you take an image of a car and change the value of a pixel by a single bit, you still have a car that is almost identical to the one before this change. Maybe it has a slightly different color. In other words, images and sounds are continuous, meaning that you can make small modifications without greatly affecting what they are. Many mathematical toolkits, such as vectors, matrices, and functions, are good at dealing with something continuous. The history of NLP is actually a history of challenging this discreteness of language, and only recently have we begun to see some successes on this front, for example, with word embeddings.

1.2   *How NLP is used*

As I mentioned previously, NLP is already an integral part of our daily life. In modern life, a larger and larger portion of our daily communication is done online, and our online communication is still largely conducted in natural language text. Think of your favorite social networking services, such as Facebook and Twitter. Although you can post photos and videos, a large portion of communication is still in text. As long as you are dealing with text, there is a need for NLP. For example, how do you know if a particular post is spam? How do you know which posts are the ones you are most likely to "like?" How do you know which ads you are most likely to click?

Because many large internet companies need to deal with text in one way or another, chances are many of them are already using NLP. You can also confirm this from their "careers" page—you'll see that they are always hiring NLP engineers and data scientists. NLP is also used to a varying extent in many other industries and products including, but not limited to, customer service, e-commerce, education, entertainment, finance, and health care, which all involve text in some ways.

Many NLP systems and services can be classified into or built by combining some major types of NLP applications and tasks. In this section, I'm going to introduce some of the most popular applications of NLP as well as common NLP tasks.

1.2.1 NLP applications

An NLP application is a software application whose main purpose is to process natural language text and draw some useful information from it. Similar to general software applications, it can be implemented in various ways, such as an offline data-processing script, an offline standalone application, a backend service, or a full-stack service with a frontend, depending on its scope and use cases. It can be built for end users to use directly, for other backend services to consume its output, or for other businesses to use as a SaaS (software as a service).

You can use many NLP applications out of the box, such as machine translation software and major SaaS products (e.g., Google Cloud API), if your requirement is generic and doesn't require a high level of customization. You can also build your own NLP applications if you need customizations and/or you need to deal with a specific target domain. This is exactly what you'll learn throughout this book!

MACHINE TRANSLATION

Machine translation is probably one of the most popular and easy-to-understand NLP applications. Machine translation (MT) systems translate a given text from one language to another language. An MT system can be implemented as a full-stack service (e.g., Google Translate), as well as a pure backend service (e.g., NLP SaaS products). The language the input text is written in is called *the source language*, whereas the one for the output is called *the target language*. MT encompasses a wide range of NLP problems, including language understanding and generation, because MT systems need to understand the input and then generate the output. MT is one of the most well-studied areas in NLP, and it was one of the earliest applications of NLP as well.

One challenge in MT is the tradeoff between *fluency* and *adequacy*. Translation needs to be fluent, meaning that the output has to sound natural in the target language. Translation also needs to be adequate, meaning that the output has to reflect the meaning expressed by the input as closely as possible. These two are often in conflict, especially when the source and the target languages are not very similar (e.g., English and Mandarin Chinese). You can write a sentence that is a precise, verbatim translation of the input, but doing so often leads to something that doesn't sound natural in the target language. On the other hand, you can make up something that sounds natural but might not reflect the precise meaning. Good human translators address this tradeoff in a creative way. It's their job to come up with translations that are natural in the target language while reflecting the meaning of the original.

GRAMMATICAL AND SPELLING ERROR CORRECTION

Most major web browsers nowadays support spelling correction. Even if you forget how to spell "Mississippi," you can do your best and type what you remember, and the browser highlights it with a correction. Some word-processing software applications, including recent versions of Microsoft Word, do more than just correct spelling. They point out grammatical errors such as uses of "it's" instead of "its." This is not an easy feat, because both words are, in a sense, "correct" (no mistakes in spelling), and the system needs to infer whether they are used correctly from the context. Some commercial products (most notably, Grammarly, https://www.grammarly.com/) specialize in grammatical error correction. Some products go a long way and point out incorrect usage of punctuation and even writing styles. These products are popular among both native and non-native speakers of the language.

Research into grammatical error correction has been active due to the increasing number of non-native English speakers. Traditionally, grammatical error correction systems for non-native English speakers dealt with individual types of mistakes one by one. For example, you could think of a subcomponent of the system that detects and corrects only incorrect uses of articles (*a, an, the,* etc.), which is very common among non-native English speakers. More recent approaches to grammatical error correction are similar to the ones for machine translation. You can think of the (potentially incorrect) input as one language and the corrected output as another. Then your job is to "translate" between these two languages!

SEARCH ENGINE

Another application of NLP that is already an integral part of our daily lives is search engines. Few people would think of search engines as an NLP application, yet NLP plays such an important role in making search engines useful that they are worth mentioning here.

Page analysis is one area where NLP is heavily used for search engines. Ever wonder why you don't see any "hot dog" pages when you search for "dogs?" If you have any experience building your own full-text search engines using open source software such as Solr and Elasticsearch, and if you simply used a word-based index, your search result pages would be littered with "hot dogs," even when you want just "dogs." Major commercial search engines solve this problem by running the page content being indexed through NLP pipelines that recognize that "hot dogs" are not a type of "dogs." But the extent and types of NLP pipelines that go into page analysis is confidential information for search engines and is difficult to know.

Query analysis is another NLP application in search engines. If you have noticed Google showing a box with pictures and bios when you search for a celebrity or a box with the latest news stories when you search for certain current events, that's query analysis in action. Query analysis identifies the intent (what the user wants) of the query and shows relevant information accordingly. A common way to implement query analysis is to make it a classification problem, where an NLP pipeline classifies queries into classes of intent (e.g., celebrity, news, weather, videos), although again, the details of how commercial search engines run query analysis are usually highly confidential.

Finally, search engines are not only about analyzing pages and classifying queries. They have many other functionalities that make your searches easier, one of which is query correction. This comes into play when you make a spelling or a grammatical mistake when formulating the query, and Google and other major search engines show corrections with labels such as "showing results for:" and "Did you mean." How this works is somewhat similar to grammatical error correction that I mentioned earlier, except it is optimized for the types of mistakes and queries that search engine users use.

DIALOG SYSTEMS

Dialog systems are machines that humans can have conversations with. The field of dialog systems has a long history. One of the earliest dialog systems, ELIZA, was developed in 1966.

But it's only recently that dialog systems have found their ways into our daily lives. We have seen an almost exponential increase in their popularity in recent years, mainly driven by the availability of consumer-facing "conversational AI" products such as Amazon Alexa and Google Assistant. In fact, according to a survey in 2018, 20% of US homes already own a smart speaker. You may also remember being mind-blown watching the keynote at Google IO in 2018, where Google's conversational AI called Google Duplex was shown making a phone call to a hair salon and a restaurant, having natural conversations with the staff at the business, and making an appointment on behalf of its user.

The two main types of dialog systems are task-oriented and chatbots. Task-oriented dialog systems are used to achieve specific goals (for example, reserving a plane ticket), obtaining some information, and, as we saw, making a reservation at a restaurant. Task-oriented dialog systems are usually built as an NLP pipeline consisting of several components, including speech recognition, language understanding, dialog management, response generation, and speech synthesis, which are usually trained separately. Similar to machine translation, though, there are new deep learning approaches where dialog systems (or their subsystems) are trained end-to-end.

The other type of dialog system is chatbots, whose main purpose is to have conversations with humans. Traditional chatbots are usually managed by a set of handwritten rules (e.g., when the human says this, say that). Recently, the use of deep neural networks, particularly sequence-to-sequence models and reinforcement learning, has become increasingly popular. However, because the chatbots do not serve particular purposes, the evaluation of chatbots, that is, assessing how good a particular chatbot is, remains an open question.

1.2.2 NLP tasks

Behind the scenes, many NLP applications are built by combining multiple NLP components that solve different NLP problems. In this section, I introduce some notable NLP tasks that are commonly used in NLP applications.

TEXT CLASSIFICATION

Text classification is the process of classifying pieces of text into different categories. This NLP task is one of the simplest yet most widely used. You might not have heard of the term "text classification" before, but I bet most of you benefit from this NLP task every day. For example, spam filtering is one type of text classification. It classifies emails (or other types of text, such as web pages) into two categories—spam or not spam. This is why you get very few spam emails when you use Gmail and you see so few spammy (low-quality) web pages when you use Google.

Another type of text classification is called *sentiment analysis*, which is what we saw in section 1.1. Sentiment analysis is used to automatically identify subjective information, such as opinions, emotions, and feelings, within text.

PART-OF-SPEECH TAGGING

A *part of speech* (POS) is a category of words that share the similar grammatical properties. In English, for example, nouns describe the names of things like objects, animals, people, and concepts, among many other things. A noun can be used as a subject of a verb, an object of a verb, and an object of a preposition. Verbs, in contrast, describe actions, states, and occurrences. Other English parts of speech include adjectives (*green, furious*), adverbs (*cheerfully, almost*), determiners (*a, the, this, that*), prepositions (*in, from, with*), conjunctions (*and, yet, because*), and many others. Almost all languages have nouns and verbs, but other parts of speech differ from language to language. For example, many languages, such as Hungarian, Turkish, and Japanese, have *postpositions* instead of prepositions, which are placed *after* words to add some extra meaning to them. A group of NLP researchers came up with a set of tags that cover frequent parts of speech that exist in most languages, called a *universal part-of-speech tagset* (http://realworldnlpbook.com/ch1.html#universal-pos). This tagset is widely used for language-independent tasks.

Part-of-speech tagging is the process of tagging each word in a sentence with a corresponding part-of-speech tag. Some of you may have done this at school. As an example, let's take the sentence "I saw a girl with a telescope." The POS tags for this sentence are shown in figure 1.4.

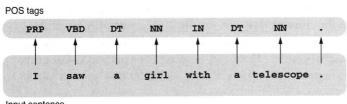

POS tags

| PRP | VBD | DT | NN | IN | DT | NN | . |

| I | saw | a | girl | with | a | telescope | . |

Input sentence

POS tag	Description
DT	Determiner
IN	Preposition
NN	Noun (singular or mass)
PRP	Pronoun
VBD	Verb (past tense)

Figure 1.4   Part-of-speech (POS) tagging

These tags come from the Penn Treebank POS tagset, which is the most popular standard corpus for training and evaluating various NLP tasks such as POS tagging and parsing. Traditionally, POS tagging was solved by sequential labeling algorithms such as hidden Markov models (HMMs) and conditional random fields (CRFs). Recently, recurrent neural networks (RNNs) have become a popular and practical choice for training a POS tagger with high accuracy. The results of POS tagging are often used as the input to other downstream NLP tasks, such as machine translation and parsing. I'll cover part-of-speech tagging in more detail in chapter 5.

PARSING

Parsing is the task of analyzing the structure of a sentence. Broadly speaking, there are two main types of parsing, *constituency parsing* and *dependency parsing,* which we'll discuss in detail next.

Constituency parsing uses *context-free grammars* to represent natural language sentences. (See http://mng.bz/GO5q for a brief introduction to context-free grammars). A context-free grammar is a way to specify how smaller building blocks of a language (e.g., words) are combined to form larger building blocks (e.g., phrases and clauses) and eventually sentences. To put it another way, it specifies how the largest unit (a sentence) is broken down to phrases and clauses and all the way down to words. The ways the linguistic units interact with each other are specified by a set of *production rules* as follows:

```
S -> NP VP

NP -> DT NN | PRN | NP PP
VP -> VBD NP | VBD PN PP
PP -> IN NP

DT -> a
IN -> with
NN -> girl | telescope
PRN -> I
VBD -> saw
```

A production rule describes a transformation from the symbol on the left-hand side (e.g., "S") to the symbols on the right-hand side (e.g., "NP VP"). The first rule means that a sentence is a noun phrase (NP) followed by a verb phrase (VP). Some of the symbols (e.g., DT, NN, VBD) may look familiar to you—yes, they are the POS tags we just saw in the POS tagging section. In fact, you can consider POS tags as the smallest grammatical categories that behave in similar ways (because they are!).

Now the parser's job is to figure out how to reach the final symbol (in this case, "S") starting from the raw words in the sentence. You can think of those rules as transformation rules from the symbols on the right to the ones on the left by traversing the arrow backward. For example, using the rule "DT → a" and "NN → girl," you can convert "a girl" to "DT NN." Then, if you use "NP → DT NN," you can reduce the entire phrase to "NP." If you illustrate this process in a tree-like diagram, you get something like the one shown in figure 1.5.

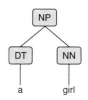

Figure 1.5 Subtree for "a girl"

Tree structures that are created in the process of parsing are called *parse trees*, or simply *parses*. The figure is a subtree because it doesn't cover the entirety of the tree (i.e., it doesn't show all the way from "S" to words). Using the sentence "I saw a girl with a telescope" that we discussed earlier and see if you can parse it by hand. If you keep breaking down the sentence using the production rules until you get the final "S" symbol, you get the tree-like structure shown in figure 1.6.

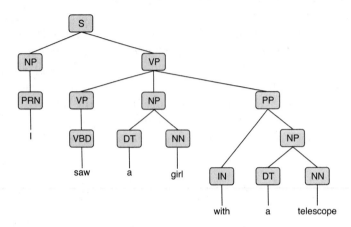

Figure 1.6   Parse tree for "I saw a girl with a telescope."

Don't worry if the tree in figure 1.6 is different from what you got. Actually, there's another parse tree that is a valid parse of this sentence, shown in figure 1.7.

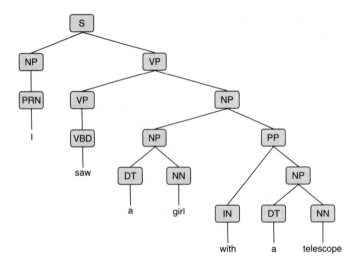

Figure 1.7   Another parse tree for "I saw a girl with a telescope."

If you look at those two trees carefully, you'll notice a difference where the "PP" (prepositional phrase) is located, or attached. In fact, these two parse trees correspond to the two different interpretations of this sentence we discussed in section 1.1. The first tree (figure 1.6), where the PP attaches the verb "saw," corresponds to the interpretation where the boy is using a telescope to see the girl. In the second tree (figure 1.7), where the PP attaches to the noun "a girl," the boy saw the girl who has a telescope. Parsing is a great step forward to reveal the structure and the semantics of a sentence, but in cases like this one, parsing alone cannot uniquely decide what is the single most likely interpretation of a sentence.

The other type of parsing is called *dependency parsing.* Dependency parsing uses dependency grammars to describe the structure of sentences, not in terms of phrases but in terms of words and the binary relations between them. For example, the result of dependency parsing of the earlier sentence is shown in figure 1.8.

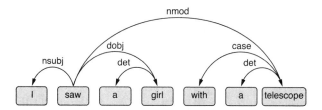

Figure 1.8   Dependency parse for "I saw a girl with a telescope."

Notice that each relation is directional and labeled. A relation specifies which word depends on which word and the type of relationship between the two. For example, the relation connecting "a" to "girl" is labeled "det," meaning the first word is the determiner of the second. If you take the most central word, "saw," and pull it upward, you'll notice that these words and relations form a tree. Such trees are called *dependency trees.*

One advantage of dependency grammars is that they are agnostic regarding some word-order changes, meaning that the order of certain words in the sentence will not change the dependency tree. For example, in English, there is some freedom as to where to put an adverb in a sentence, especially when the adverb describes the manner in which the action referred to by the verb is done. For example, "I carefully painted the house" and "I painted the house carefully" are both acceptable and mean the same thing. If you represent these sentences by a dependency grammar, the word "carefully" always modifies the verb "painted," and the two sentences have completely identical dependency trees. Dependency grammars capture more than just phrasal structures of sentences—they capture something more fundamental about the relationship of the words. Therefore, dependency parsing is considered an important step toward semantic analysis of natural language. A group of researchers is working on a formal language-independent dependency grammar, called *Universal Dependencies*, that is linguistically motivated and applicable to many languages, similar to the universal POS tagset.

TEXT GENERATION

Text generation, also called *natural language generation* (NLG), is the process of generating natural language text from something else. In a broader sense, machine translation, which we discussed previously, involves a text-generation problem, because MT systems need to generate text in the target language. Similarly, summarization, text simplification, and grammatical error correction all produce natural language text as output and are instances of text-generation tasks. Because all of these tasks take natural language text as their input, they are called *text-to-text* generation.

Another class of text-generation task is called *data-to-text* generation. For those tasks, the input is data that is not text. For example, a dialog system needs to generate natural utterances based on the current state of the conversation. A publisher may wish to generate news text based on events such as sports game outcomes and weather. There is also a growing interest in generating natural language text that best describes a given image, called *image captioning*.

Finally, a third class of text classification is unconditional text generation, where natural language text is generated randomly from a model. You can train models so that they can generate random academic papers, Linux source code, or even poems and play scripts. For example, Andrej Karpathy trained an RNN model from all of Shakespeare's works and succeeded in generating pieces of text that look exactly like his work (http://realworldnlpbook.com/ch1.html#karpathy15), as shown next:

```
PANDARUS:
Alas, I think he shall be come approached and the day
When little srain would be attain'd into being never fed,
And who is but a chain and subjects of his death,
I should not sleep.

Second Senator:
They are away this miseries, produced upon my soul,
Breaking and strongly should be buried, when I perish
The earth and thoughts of many states.

DUKE VINCENTIO:
Well, your wit is in the care of side and that.

Second Lord:
They would be ruled after this chamber, and
my fair nues begun out of the fact, to be conveyed,
Whose noble souls I'll have the heart of the wars.

Clown:
Come, sir, I will make did behold your worship.

VIOLA:
I'll drink it.
```

Traditionally, text generation has been solved by handcrafted templates and rules for generating text from some information. You can think of this as the reverse of parsing, where rules are used to infer information about natural language text, as we discussed earlier. In recent years, neural network models are an increasingly popular choice for natural language generation, be it text-to-text generation (sequence-to-sequence models), data-to-text generation (encoder-decoder models), and unconditional text generation (neural language models and generative adversarial networks, or GANs). We'll discuss text generation more in chapter 5.

1.3 Building NLP applications

In this section, I'm going to show you how NLP applications are typically developed and structured. Although details may vary on a case-by-case basis, understanding the typical process helps you plan and budget before you start developing an application. It also goes a long way if you know best practices in developing NLP applications beforehand.

1.3.1 Development of NLP applications

The development of NLP applications is a highly iterative process, consisting of many phases of research, development, and operations (figure 1.9). Most learning materials such as books and online tutorials focus mainly on the training phase, although all the other phases of application development are equally important for real-world NLP

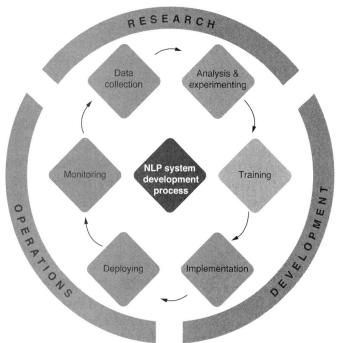

Figure 1.9 The development cycle of NLP applications

applications. In this section, I briefly introduce what each stage involves. Note that no clear boundary exists between these phases. It is not uncommon that application developers (researchers, engineers, managers, and other stakeholders) go back and forth between some of these phases through trial and error.

DATA COLLECTION

Most modern NLP applications are based on machine learning. Machine learning, by definition, requires data on which NLP models are trained (remember the definition of ML we talked about previously—it's about improving algorithms through data). In this phase, NLP application developers discuss how to formulate the application as an NLP/ML problem and what kind of data should be collected. Data can be collected from humans (e.g., by hiring in-house annotators and having them go through a bunch of text instances), crowdsourcing (e.g., using platforms such as Amazon Mechanical Turk), or automated mechanisms (e.g., from application logs or clickstreams).

You may choose not to use machine learning approaches for your NLP application at first, which could totally be the right choice depending on various factors, such as time, budgets, the complexity of the task, and the expected amount of data you might be able to collect. Even in that case, it may be a good idea to collect a small amount of data for validation purposes. I'll talk more about training, validation, and testing of NLP applications in chapter 11.

ANALYSIS AND EXPERIMENTING

After collecting the data, you move on to the next phase where you analyze and run some experiments. For analyses, you usually look for signals such as: What are the characteristics of the text instances? How are the training labels distributed? Can you come up with signals that are correlated with the training labels? Can you come up with some simple rules that can predict the training labels with reasonable accuracy? Should we even use ML? This list goes on and on. This analysis phase includes aspects of data science, where various statistical techniques may come in handy.

You run experiments to try a number of prototypes quickly. The goal in this phase is to narrow down the possible set of approaches to a couple of promising ones, before you go all-in and start training a gigantic model. By running experiments, you wish to answer questions including: What types of NLP tasks and approaches are appropriate for this NLP application? Is this a classification, parsing, sequence labeling, regression, text generation, or some other problem? What is the performance of the baseline approach? What is the performance of the rule-based approach? Should we even use ML? What is the estimate of training and serving time for the promising approaches?

I call these first two phases the "research" phase. The existence of this phase is arguably the biggest difference between NLP applications and other generic software systems. Due to its nature, it is difficult to predict the performance and the behavior of a machine learning system, or an NLP system, for that matter. At this point, you might not have written a single line of production code, and that's totally fine. The point of this research phase is to prevent you from wasting your effort writing production code that turns out to be useless at a later stage.

TRAINING

At this point you have pretty clear ideas what the approaches will be for your NLP application. This is when you start adding more data and computational resources (e.g., GPUs) for training your model. It is not uncommon for modern NLP models to take days if not weeks to train, especially if they are based on neural network models. It is always a good practice to gradually ramp up the amount of the data and the size of the model you train. You don't want to spend weeks training a gigantic neural network model only to find that a smaller and simpler model performs just as well, or even worse, that you introduced a bug in the model and that the model you spent weeks training is simply useless!

It is critical at this phase that you keep your training pipeline reproducible. Chances are, you will need to run this several times with different sets of hyperparameters, which are tuning values set before starting the model's learning process. It is also likely that you will need to run this pipeline several months later, if not years. I'll touch upon some best practices when training NLP/ML models in chapter 10.

IMPLEMENTATION

When you have a model that is working with acceptable performance, you move on to the implementation phase. This is when you start making your application "production ready." This process basically follows software engineering best practices, including: writing unit and integration tests for your NLP modules, refactoring your code, having your code reviewed by other developers, improving the performance of your NLP modules, and dockerizing your application. I'll talk more about this process in chapter 11.

DEPLOYING

Your NLP application is finally ready to deploy. You can deploy your NLP application in many ways—it can be an online service, a recurring batch job, an offline application, or an offline one-off task. If this is an online service that needs to serve its predictions in real time, it is a good idea to make this a *microservice* to make it loosely coupled with other services. In any case, it is a good practice to use continuous integration (CI) for your application, where you run tests and verify that your code and model are working as intended every time you make changes to your application.

MONITORING

An important final step for developing NLP applications is monitoring. This not only includes monitoring the infrastructure such as server CPU, memory, and request latency, but also higher-level ML statistics such as the distributions of the input and the predicted labels. Some of the important questions to ask at this stage are: What do the input instances look like? Are they what you expected when you built your model? What do the predicted labels look like? Does the predicted label distribution match the one in the training data? The purpose of the monitoring is to check that the model you built is behaving as intended. If the incoming text or data instances or the predicted labels do not match your expectation, you may have an out-of-domain problem, meaning that the domain of the natural language data you are receiving is different from the one in which your model is trained. Machine learning models are usually not good at dealing with out-of-domain data, and the prediction accuracy may suffer. If this issue becomes obvious, it may be a good idea to repeat the whole process again, starting from collecting more in-domain data.

1.3.2 Structure of NLP applications

The structures of modern, machine learning–based NLP applications are becoming surprisingly similar for two main reasons—one is that most modern NLP applications rely on machine learning to some degree, and they should follow best practices for machine learning applications. The other is that, due to the advent of neural network models, a number of NLP tasks, including text classification, machine translation, dialog systems, and speech recognition, can now be trained end-to-end, as I mentioned before. Some of these tasks used to be hairy, enormous monsters with dozens of components with complex plumbing. Now, however, some of these tasks can be solved by less than 1,000 lines of Python code, provided that there's enough data to train the model end-to-end.

Figure 1.10 illustrates the typical structure of a modern NLP application. There are two main infrastructures: the training and the serving infrastructure. The training infrastructure is usually offline and serves the purpose of training the machine learning model necessary for the application. It takes the training data, converts it to some data structure that can be handled by the pipeline, and further processes it by transforming the data and extracting the features. This part varies greatly from task to task. Finally,

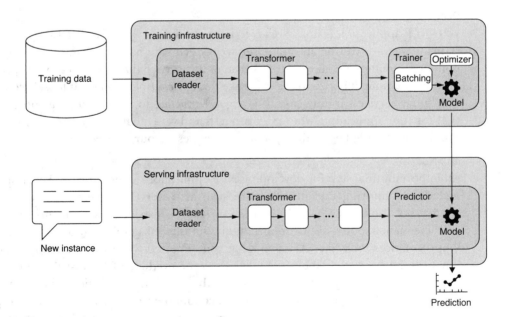

Figure 1.10 Structure of typical NLP applications

if the model is a neural network, data instances are batched and fed to the model, which is optimized to minimize the loss. Don't worry if you don't understand what I'm talking about in that last sentence—we'll talk about those technical terms used with neural networks in chapter 2. The trained model is usually serialized and stored to be passed to the serving infrastructure.

The serving infrastructure's job is to, given a new instance, produce the prediction, such as classes, tags, or translations. The first part of this infrastructure, which reads the instance and transforms it into some numbers, is similar to the one for training. In fact, you must keep the dataset reader and the transformer identical. Otherwise, discrepancies will arise in the way those two process the data, also known as *training-serving skew*. After the instance is processed, it's fed to the pretrained model to produce the prediction. I'll talk more about designing your NLP applications in chapter 11.

Summary

- Natural language processing (NLP) is a subfield of artificial intelligence (AI) that refers to computational approaches to process, understand, and generate human language.
- One of the challenges for NLP is ambiguity in natural languages. There is syntactic and semantic ambiguity.
- Where there is text, there is NLP. Many tech companies use NLP to draw information from a large amount of text. Typical NLP applications include machine translation, grammatical error correction, search engines, and dialog systems.
- NLP applications are developed in an iterative way, with more emphasis on the research phase.
- Many modern NLP applications rely heavily on machine learning (ML) and are structurally similar to ML systems.

Your first NLP application

This chapter covers

- Building a sentiment analyzer using AllenNLP
- Applying basic machine learning concepts (datasets, classification, and regression)
- Employing neural network concepts (word embeddings, recurrent neural networks, linear layers)
- Training the model through reducing loss
- Evaluating and deploying your model

In section 1.1.2, we saw how not to do NLP. In this chapter, we are going to discuss how to do NLP in a more principled, modern way. Specifically, we'd like to build a sentiment analyzer using a neural network. Even though the sentiment analyzer we are going to build is a simple application and the library (AllenNLP) takes care of most heavy lifting, it is a full-fledged NLP application that covers a lot of basic components of modern NLP and machine learning. I'll introduce important terms and concepts along the way. Don't worry if you don't understand some concepts at first. We will revisit most of the concepts introduced here in later chapters.

2.1 Introducing sentiment analysis

In the scenario described in section 1.1.2, you wanted to extract users' subjective opinions from online survey results. You have a collection of textual data in response to a free-response question, but you are missing the answers to the "How do you like our product?" question, which you'd like to recover from the text. This task is called *sentiment analysis*, which is a text analytic technique used in the automatic identification and categorization of subjective information within text. The technique is widely used in quantifying opinions, emotions, and so on that are written in an unstructured way and, thus, hard to quantify otherwise. Sentiment analysis is applied to a wide variety of textual resources such as survey, reviews, and social media posts.

In machine learning, *classification* means categorizing something into a set of predefined, discrete categories. One of the most basic tasks in sentiment analysis is the classification of *polarity*, that is, to classify whether the expressed opinion is positive, negative, or neutral. You could use more than three classes, for example, strongly positive, positive, neutral, negative, or strongly negative. This may sound familiar to you if you have used a website (such as Amazon) where people can review things using a five-point scale expressed by the number of stars.

Classification of polarity is one type of sentence classification task. Another type of sentence classification task is spam filtering, where each sentence is categorized into two classes—spam or not spam. It's called *binary classification* if there are only two classes. If there are more than two classes (the five-star classification system mentioned earlier, for example), it's called *multiclass classification.*

In contrast, when the prediction is a continuous value instead of discrete categories, it's called *regression.* If you'd like to predict the price of a house based on its properties, such as its neighborhood, numbers of bedrooms and bathrooms, and square footage, it's a regression problem. If you attempt to predict stock prices based on the information collected from news articles and social media posts, it's also a regression problem. (Disclaimer: I'm not suggesting this is an appropriate approach to stock price prediction. I'm not even sure if it works.) As I mentioned earlier, most linguistic units such as characters, words, and part-of-speech tags are discrete. For this reason, most uses of machine learning in NLP are classification, not regression.

> **NOTE** *Logistic regression,* a widely used statistical model, is usually used for classification, even though it has "regression" in its name. Yes, I know it's confusing!

Many modern NLP applications, including the sentiment analyzer we are going to build in this chapter (shown in figure 2.1), are built based on the *supervised machine learning* paradigm. Supervised machine learning is one type of machine learning where the algorithm is trained with data that has supervision signals—the desired outcome for individual input. The algorithm is trained in such a way that it reproduces the signals as closely as possible. For sentiment analysis, this means that the system is trained on data that contains the desired labels for each input sentence.

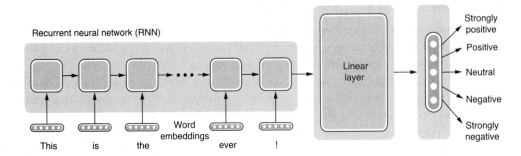

Figure 2.1   Sentiment analysis pipeline

2.2   *Working with NLP datasets*

As we discussed in the previous section, many modern NLP applications are developed using supervised machine learning, where algorithms are trained from data annotated with desired outcomes, instead of using handwritten rules. Almost by definition, data is a critical part for machine learning, and it is important to understand how it is structured and used with machine learning algorithms.

2.2.1   *What is a dataset?*

A *dataset* simply means a collection of data. If you are familiar with relational databases, you can think of a dataset as a dump of one table. It consists of pieces of data that follow the same format. In database terms, each piece of the data corresponds to a record, or a row in a table. A record can have any number of fields, which correspond to columns in a database.

In NLP, records in a dataset are usually some type of linguistic units, such as words, sentences, or documents. A dataset of natural language texts is called a *corpus* (plural: *corpora*). As an example, let's think of a (hypothetical) dataset for spam filtering. Each record in this dataset is a pair of a piece of text and a label, where the text is a sentence or a paragraph (e.g., from an email) and the label specifies whether the text is spam. Both the text and the label are the fields of a record.

Some NLP datasets and corpora have more complex structures. For example, a dataset may contain a collection of sentences, where each sentence is annotated with detailed linguistic information, such as part-of-speech tags, parse trees, dependency structures, and semantic roles. If a dataset contains a collection of sentences annotated with their parse trees, the dataset is called a *treebank*. The most famous example of this is Penn Treebank (PTB) (http://realworldnlpbook.com/ch2.html#ptb), which has been serving as the de facto standard dataset for training and evaluating NLP tasks such as part-of-speech (POS) tagging and parsing.

A closely related term to a record is an *instance*. In machine learning, an instance is a basic unit for which the prediction is made. For example, in the spam-filtering task mentioned earlier, an instance is one piece of text, because predictions (spam or not

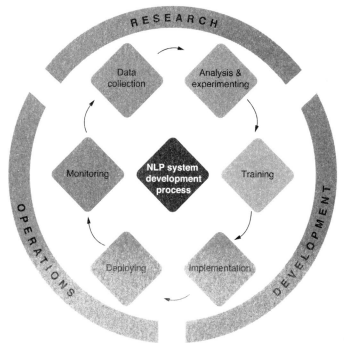

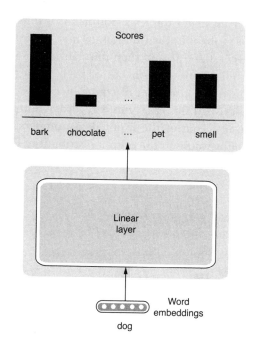

Figure 3.5 Skip-gram model structure

3.4.4 Softmax

Now let's talk about how to "train" the Skip-gram model and learn the word embeddings we want. The key here is to turn this into a classification task, where the model predicts what words appear in the context. The "context" here simply means a window of a fixed size (e.g., 5 + 5 words on both sides) centered around the target word (e.g., "dog"). See figure 3.6 for an illustration when the window size is 2. This is actually a "fake" task because we are not interested in the prediction of the model per se, but rather in the by-product (word embeddings) produced while training the model. In machine learning and NLP, we often make up a fake task to train something else as a by-product.

Figure 3.6 Target word and context words (when window size = 2)

NOTE This setting of machine learning, where the training labels are automatically created from a given dataset, can also be called *self-supervised learning*. Recent popular techniques, such as word embeddings and language modeling, all use self-supervision.

It is relatively easy to make a neural network solve a classification task. You need to do the following two things:

- Modify the network so that it produces a probability distribution.
- Use cross entropy as the loss function (we'll cover this in detail shortly).

You can use something called *softmax* to do the first. Softmax is a function that turns a vector of *K* float numbers to a probability distribution, by first "squashing" the numbers so that they fit a range between 0.0–1.0, and then normalizing them so that the sum equals 1. If you are not familiar with the concept of probabilities, replace them with *confidence*. A probability distribution is a set of confidence values that the network places on individual predictions (in this case, context words). Softmax does all this while preserving the relative ordering of the input float numbers, so large input numbers still have large probability values in the output distribution. Figure 3.7 illustrates this conceptually.

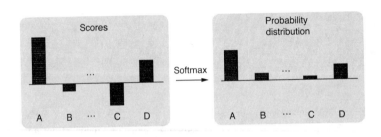

Figure 3.7   Softmax

Another component required to turn a neural network into a classifier is *cross entropy*. Cross entropy is a loss function used to measure the distance between two probability distributions. It returns zero if two distributions match exactly and higher values if the two diverge. For classification tasks, we use cross entropy to compare the following:

- Predicted probability distribution produced by the neural network (output of softmax)
- Target probability distribution, where the probability of the correct class is 1.0 and everything else is 0.0

The predictions made by the Skip-gram model get closer and closer to the actual context words, and word embeddings are learned at the same time.

3.4.5   *Implementing Skip-gram on AllenNLP*

It is relatively straightforward to turn this model into working code using AllenNLP. Note that all the code listed in this section can be executed on the Google Colab notebook (http://realworldnlpbook.com/ch3.html#word2vec-nb). First, you need to implement a dataset reader that reads a plain text corpus and turns it into a set of instances that can be consumed by the Skip-gram model. The details of the dataset reader are not critical to the discussion here, so I'm going to omit the full code listing. You can clone the code repository of this book (https://github.com/mhagiwara/realworldnlp) and import it as follows:

```
from examples.embeddings.word2vec import SkipGramReader
```

Alternatively, if you are interested, you can see the full code from http://realworldnlp-book.com/ch3.html#word2vec. You can use the reader as follows:

```
reader = SkipGramReader()
text8 = reader.read('https://realworldnlpbook.s3.amazonaws.com/data/text8/
    text8')
```

Also, be sure to import all the necessary modules and define some constants in this example, as shown next:

```
from collections import Counter

import torch
import torch.optim as optim
from allennlp.data.data_loaders import SimpleDataLoader
from allennlp.data.vocabulary import Vocabulary
from allennlp.models import Model
from allennlp.modules.token_embedders import Embedding
from allennlp.training.trainer import GradientDescentTrainer
from torch.nn import CosineSimilarity
from torch.nn import functional

EMBEDDING_DIM = 256
BATCH_SIZE = 256
```

We are going to use the text8 (http://mattmahoney.net/dc/textdata) dataset in this example. The dataset is an excerpt from Wikipedia and is often used for training toy word embedding and language models. You can iterate over the instances in the dataset. token_in is the input token to the model, and token_out is the output (the context word):

```
>>> for inst in text8:
>>>     print(inst)
...
Instance with fields:
    token_in: LabelField with label: ideas in namespace: 'token_in'.'
    token_out: LabelField with label: us in namespace: 'token_out'.'

Instance with fields:
    token_in: LabelField with label: ideas in namespace: 'token_in'.'
    token_out: LabelField with label: published in namespace: 'token_out'.'

Instance with fields:
    token_in: LabelField with label: ideas in namespace: 'token_in'.'
    token_out: LabelField with label: journal in namespace: 'token_out'.'

Instance with fields:
    token_in: LabelField with label: in in namespace: 'token_in'.'
    token_out: LabelField with label: nature in namespace: 'token_out'.'

Instance with fields:
    token_in: LabelField with label: in in namespace: 'token_in'.'
    token_out: LabelField with label: he in namespace: 'token_out'.'
```

```
Instance with fields:
    token_in: LabelField with label: in in namespace: 'token_in'.'
    token_out: LabelField with label: announced in namespace: 'token_out'.'
...
```

Then, you can build the vocabulary, as we did in chapter 2, as shown next:

```
vocab = Vocabulary.from_instances(
    text8, min_count={'token_in': 5, 'token_out': 5})
```

Note that we are using `min_count`, which sets the lower bound on the number of occurrences for each token. Also, let's define the data loader we use for training as follows:

```
data_loader = SimpleDataLoader(text8, batch_size=BATCH_SIZE)
data_loader.index_with(vocab)
```

Let's then define an `Embedding` object that holds all the word embeddings we'd like to learn:

```
embedding_in = Embedding(num_embeddings=vocab.get_vocab_size('token_in'),
                         embedding_dim=EMBEDDING_DIM)
```

Here, `EMBEDDING_DIM` is the length of each word vector (number of float numbers). A typical NLP application uses word vectors of a couple hundred dimensions long (in this example, 256), but this value depends greatly on the task and the datasets. It is often suggested that you use longer word vectors as your training data grows.

Finally, you need to implement the body of the Skip-gram model, as shown next.

Listing 3.1   Skip-gram model implemented in AllenNLP

```
class SkipGramModel(Model):                        ◁──┐ AllenNLP requires every model
                                                       │ to be inherited from Model.
    def __init__(self, vocab, embedding_in):
        super().__init__(vocab)

        self.embedding_in = embedding_in          ◁──┐ The embedding object is passed from
                                                      │ outside rather than defined inside.
        self.linear = torch.nn.Linear(
            in_features=EMBEDDING_DIM,
            out_features=vocab.get_vocab_size('token_out'),
            bias=False)

    def forward(self, token_in, token_out):        ◁──┐ The body of neural network computation
                                                       │ is implemented in forward().

        embedded_in = self.embedding_in(token_in)  ◁──┐ Converts input tensors
                                                       │ (word IDs) to word
        logits = self.linear(embedded_in)             │ embeddings

        loss = functional.cross_entropy(logits, token_out)   ◁──┐ Computes
                                                                 │ the loss
        return {'loss': loss}
```

This creates a linear layer (note that we don't need biases). *(annotation pointing to self.linear = torch.nn.Linear)*

Applies the linear layer *(annotation pointing to logits = self.linear(embedded_in))*

A few things to note:

- AllenNLP requires every model to be inherited from `Model`, which can be imported from `allennlp.models`.
- Model's initializer (`__init__`) takes a `Vocabulary` instance and any other parameters or submodels defined externally. It also defines any internal parameters or models.
- The main computation of the model is defined in `forward()`. It takes all the fields from instances (in this example, `token_in` and `token_out`) as tensors (multidimensional arrays) and returns a `dict` that contains the `'loss'` key, which will be used by the optimizer to train the model.

You can train this model using the following code.

Listing 3.2 Code for training the Skip-gram model

```
reader = SkipGramReader()
text8 = reader.read(' https://realworldnlpbook.s3.amazonaws.com/data/text8/
    text8')

vocab = Vocabulary.from_instances(
    text8, min_count={'token_in': 5, 'token_out': 5})

data_loader = SimpleDataLoader(text8, batch_size=BATCH_SIZE)
data_loader.index_with(vocab)

embedding_in = Embedding(num_embeddings=vocab.get_vocab_size('token_in'),
                         embedding_dim=EMBEDDING_DIM)

model = SkipGramModel(vocab=vocab,
                      embedding_in=embedding_in)
optimizer = optim.Adam(model.parameters())

trainer = GradientDescentTrainer(
    model=model,
    optimizer=optimizer,
    data_loader=data_loader,
    num_epochs=5,
    cuda_device=CUDA_DEVICE)
trainer.train()
```

Training takes a while, so I recommend truncating the training data first, say, by using only the first one million tokens. You can do this by inserting `text8 = list(text8)[:1000000]` after `reader.read()`. After the training is finished, you can get related words (words with the same meanings) using the method shown in listing 3.3. This method first obtains the word vector for a given word (`token`), then computes how similar it is to every other word vector in the vocabulary. The similarity is calculated using something called the *cosine similarity*. In simple terms, the cosine similarity is the opposite of the angle between two vectors. If two vectors are identical, the angle between them is zero, and the similarity will be 1, which is the largest possible value. If two vectors are perpendicular, the angle is 90 degrees, and the cosine will be 0. If the vectors are in totally opposite directions, the cosine will be –1.

Listing 3.3 Method to obtain related words using word embeddings

```
def get_related(token: str, embedding: Model, vocab: Vocabulary,
                num_synonyms: int = 10):
    token_id = vocab.get_token_index(token, 'token_in')
    token_vec = embedding.weight[token_id]
    cosine = CosineSimilarity(dim=0)
    sims = Counter()

    for index, token in
      vocab.get_index_to_token_vocabulary('token_in').items():
        sim = cosine(token_vec, embedding.weight[index]).item()
        sims[token] = sim

    return sims.most_common(num_synonyms)
```

If you run this for words "one" and "december," you get the lists of related words shown in table 3.1. Although you can see some words that are not related to the query word, overall, the results look good.

Table 3.1 Related words for "one" and "december"

"one"	"december"
one	december
nine	january
eight	nixus
six	londini
five	plantarum
seven	june
three	smissen
four	february
d	qanuni
actress	october

One final note: you need to implement a couple of techniques if you want to use Skip-gram to train high-quality word vectors in practice, namely, negative sampling and subsampling of high-frequency words. Although they are important concepts, they can be a distraction if you are just starting out and would like to learn the basics of NLP. If you are interested in learning more, check out this blog post that I wrote on this topic: http://realworldnlpbook.com/ch3.html#word2vec-blog.

3.4.6 *Continuous bag of words (CBOW) model*

Another word-embedding model that is often mentioned along with the Skip-gram model is the *continuous bag of words* (CBOW) *model.* As a close sibling of the Skip-gram model, proposed at the same time (http://realworldnlpbook.com/ch3.html# mikolov13), the architecture of the CBOW model looks similar to that of the Skip-gram model but flipped upside down. The "fake" task the model is trying to solve is to predict the target word from a set of its context words. This is also similar to fill-in-the-blank type of questions. For example, if you see a sentence "I heard a ___ barking in the distance," most of you can probably guess the answer "dog" instantly. Figure 3.8 shows the structure of this model.

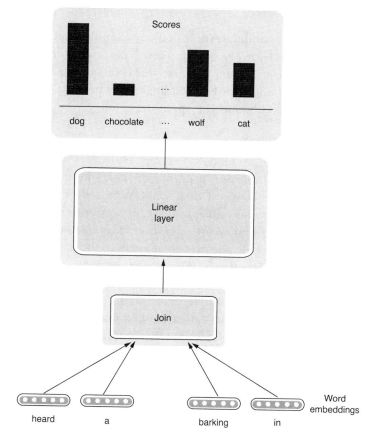

Figure 3.8 Continuous bag of words (CBOW) model

I'm not going to implement the CBOW model from scratch here for a couple of reasons. It should be straightforward to implement if you understand the Skip-gram model. Also, the accuracy of the CBOW model measured on word semantic tasks is usually slightly lower than that of Skip-gram, and CBOW is less often used in NLP than Skip-gram. Both models are implemented in the original Word2vec (https://code .google.com/archive/p/word2vec/) toolkit, if you want to try them yourself, although the vanilla Skip-gram and CBOW models are less and less often used nowadays because of the advent of more recent, powerful word-embedding models (such as GloVe and fastText) that are covered in the rest of this chapter.

3.5   GloVe

In the previous section, I implemented Skip-gram and showed how you can train your word embeddings using large text data. But what if you wanted to build your own NLP applications leveraging high-quality word embeddings while skipping all the hassle? What if you couldn't afford the computation and data required to train word embeddings?

Instead of training word embeddings, you can always download pretrained word embeddings published by somebody else, which many NLP practitioners do. In this section, I'm going to introduce another popular word-embedding model—*GloVe*, named after *Global Vectors*. Pretrained word embeddings generated by GloVe are probably the most widely used embeddings in NLP applications today.

3.5.1   *How GloVe learns word embeddings*

The main difference between the two models described earlier and GloVe is that the former is *local*. To recap, Skip-gram uses a prediction task where a context word ("bark") is predicted from the target word ("dog"). CBOW basically does the opposite of this. This process is repeated as many times as there are word tokens in the dataset. It basically scans the entire dataset and asks the question, "Can this word be predicted from this other word?" for every single occurrence of words in the dataset.

Let's think how efficient this algorithm is. What if there were two or more identical sentences in the dataset? Or very similar sentences? In that case, Skip-gram would repeat the exact same set of updates multiple times. "Can 'bark' be predicted from 'dog'?" you might ask. But chances are you already asked that exact same question a couple of hundred sentences ago. If you know that the words "dog" and "bark" appear together in the context N times in the entire dataset, why repeat this N times? It's as if you were adding "1" N times to something else ($x + 1 + 1 + 1 + \ldots + 1$) when you could simply add N to it ($x + N$). Could we somehow use this *global* information directly?

The design of GloVe is motivated by this insight. Instead of using local word co-occurrences, it uses aggregated word co-occurrence statistics in the entire dataset. Let's say "dog" and "bark" co-occur N times in the dataset. I'm not going into the details of the model, but roughly speaking, the GloVe model tries to predict this number N from the embeddings of both words. Figure 3.9 illustrates this prediction task. It still makes some predictions about word relations, but notice that it makes one prediction per a combination of word *types*, but Skip-gram does so for every combination of word *tokens*!

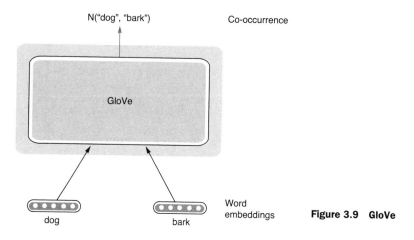

N("dog", "bark") Co-occurrence

GloVe

dog   bark   Word embeddings   **Figure 3.9 GloVe**

TOKEN AND TYPE As mentioned in section 3.3.1, a *token* is an occurrence of a word in text. There may be multiple occurrences of the same word in a corpus. A *type*, on the other hand, is a distinctive, unique word. For example, in the sentence "A rose is a rose is a rose," there are eight tokens but only three types ("a," "rose," and "is"). If you are familiar with object-oriented programming, they are roughly equivalent to instance and class. There can be multiple instances of a class, but there is only one class for a concept.

3.5.2 *Using pretrained GloVe vectors*

In fact, not many NLP practitioners train GloVe vectors from scratch by themselves. More often, we download and use word embeddings, which are pretrained using large text corpora. This is not only quick but usually beneficial in making your NLP applications more accurate, because those pretrained word embeddings (often made public by the inventor of word-embedding algorithms) are usually trained using larger datasets and more computational power than most of us can afford. By using pretrained word embeddings, you can "stand on the shoulders of giants" and quickly leverage high-quality linguistic knowledge distilled from large text corpora.

In the rest of this section, let's see how we can download and search for similar words using pretrained GloVe embeddings. First, you need to download the data file. The official GloVe website (https://nlp.stanford.edu/projects/glove/) provides multiple word-embedding files trained using different datasets and vector sizes. You can pick any one you like (although the file size could be large, depending on which one you choose) and unzip it. In what follows, we assume you save it under the relative path data/glove/.

Most word-embedding files are formatted in a similar way. Each line contains a word, followed by a sequence of numbers that correspond to its word vector. There are as many numbers as there are dimensions (in the GloVe files distributed on the website above, you can tell the dimensionality from the filename suffix in the form of xxxd). Each field is delimited by a space. Here is an excerpt from one of the GloVe word-embedding files:

```
...
if 0.15778 0.17928 -0.45811 -0.12817 0.367 0.18817 -4.5745 0.73647 ...
one 0.38661 0.33503 -0.25923 -0.19389 -0.037111 0.21012 -4.0948 0.68349 ...
has 0.08088 0.32472 0.12472 0.18509 0.49814 -0.27633 -3.6442 1.0011 ...
...
```

As we did in section 3.4.5, what we'd like to do is to take a query word (say, "dog") and find its neighbors in the *N*-dimensional space. One way to do this is to calculate the similarity between the query word and every other word in the vocabulary and sort the words by their similarities, as shown in listing 3.3. Depending on the size of the vocabulary, this approach could be very slow. It's like linearly scanning an array to find an element instead of using binary search.

Instead, we'll use approximate nearest neighbor algorithms to quickly search for similar words. In a nutshell, these algorithms enable us to quickly retrieve nearest neighbors without computing the similarity between every word pair. In particular, we'll use Annoy (https://github.com/spotify/annoy), a library for approximate neighbor search released from Spotify. You can install it by running `pip install annoy`. It implements a popular approximate nearest neighbor algorithm called *locally sensitive hashing* (LSH) using random projection.

To use Annoy to search similar words, you first need to build an index, which can be done as shown in listing 3.4. Note that we are also building a `dict` from word indices to words and saving it to a separate file to facilitate the word lookup later (listing 3.5).

Listing 3.4   Building an Annoy index

```python
from annoy import AnnoyIndex
import pickle

EMBEDDING_DIM = 300
GLOVE_FILE_PREFIX = 'data/glove/glove.42B.300d{}'

def build_index():
    num_trees = 10

    idx = AnnoyIndex(EMBEDDING_DIM)

    index_to_word = {}
    with open(GLOVE_FILE_PREFIX.format('.txt')) as f:
        for i, line in enumerate(f):
            fields = line.rstrip().split(' ')
            vec = [float(x) for x in fields[1:]]
            idx.add_item(i, vec)
            index_to_word[i] = fields[0]

    idx.build(num_trees)
    idx.save(GLOVE_FILE_PREFIX.format('.idx'))
    pickle.dump(index_to_word,
                open(GLOVE_FILE_PREFIX.format('.i2w'), mode='wb'))
```

Reading a GloVe embedding file and building an Annoy index can be quite slow, but once it's built, accessing it and retrieving similar words can be performed very quickly. This configuration is similar to search engines, where an index is built to achieve near real-time retrieval of documents. This is suitable for applications where retrieval of similar items in real time is required but update of the dataset happens less frequently. Examples include search engines and recommendation engines.

Listing 3.5 Using an Annoy index to retrieve similar words

```
def search(query, top_n=10):
    idx = AnnoyIndex(EMBEDDING_DIM)
    idx.load(GLOVE_FILE_PREFIX.format('.idx'))
    index_to_word = pickle.load(open(GLOVE_FILE_PREFIX.format('.i2w'),
                                     mode='rb'))
    word_to_index = {word: index for index, word in index_to_word.items()}

    query_id = word_to_index[query]
    word_ids = idx.get_nns_by_item(query_id, top_n)
    for word_id in word_ids:
        print(index_to_word[word_id])
```

If you run this for the words "dog" and "december," you'll get the lists of the 10 most-related words shown in table 3.2.

Table 3.2 Related words for "dog" and "december"

"dog"	"december"
dog	december
puppy	january
cat	october
cats	november
horse	september
baby	february
bull	august
kid	july
kids	april
monkey	march

You can see that each list contains many related words to the query word. You see the identical words at the top of each list—this is because the cosine similarity of two identical vectors is always 1, its maximum possible value.

3.6   *fastText*

In the previous section, we saw how to download pretrained word embeddings and retrieve related words. In this section, I'll explain how to train word embeddings using your own text data using fastText, a popular word-embedding toolkit. This is handy when your textual data is not in a general domain (e.g., medical, financial, legal, and so on) and/or is not in English.

3.6.1   *Making use of subword information*

All the word-embedding methods we've seen so far in this chapter assign a distinct word vector for each word. For example, word vectors for "dog" and "cat" are treated distinctly and are independently trained at the training time. At first glance, there seems to be nothing wrong about this. After all, they *are* separate words. But what if the words were, say, "dog" and "doggy?" Because "-y" is an English suffix that denotes some familiarity and affection (other examples include "grandma" and "granny" and "kitten" and "kitty"), these pairs of words have some semantic connection. However, word-embedding algorithms that treat words as distinct cannot make this connection. In the eyes of these algorithms, "dog" and "doggy" are nothing more than, say, `word_823` and `word_1719`.

This is obviously limiting. In most languages, there's a strong connection between word orthography (how you write words) and word semantics (what they mean). For example, words that share the same stems (e.g., "study" and "studied," "repeat" and "repeatedly," and "legal" and "illegal") are often related. By treating them as separate words, word-embedding algorithms are losing a lot of information. How can they leverage word structures and reflect the similarities in the learned word embeddings?

fastText, an algorithm and a word-embedding library developed by Facebook, is one such model. It uses *subword information*, which means information about linguistic units that are smaller than words, to train higher-quality word embeddings. Specifically, fastText breaks words down to character n-grams (section 3.2.3) and learns embeddings for them. For example, if the target word is "doggy," it first adds special symbols at the beginning and end of the word and learns embeddings for <do, dog, ogg, ggy, gy>, when n = 3. The vector for "doggy" is simply the sum of all these vectors. The rest of the architecture is quite similar to that of Skip-gram. Figure 3.10 shows the structure of the fastText model.

Another benefit in leveraging subword information is that it can alleviate the *out-of-vocabulary* (OOV) problem. Many NLP applications and models assume a fixed vocabulary. For example, a typical word-embedding algorithm such as Skip-gram learns word vectors only for the words that were encountered in the train set. However, if a test set contains words that did not appear in the train set (which are called *OOV words*), the model would be unable to assign any vectors to them. For example, if you train Skip-gram word embeddings from books published in the 1980s and apply them to modern social media text, how would it know what vectors to assign to "Instagram"? It won't. On the other hand, because fastText uses subword information (character n-grams), it can assign word vectors to any OOV words, as long as they contain character n-grams

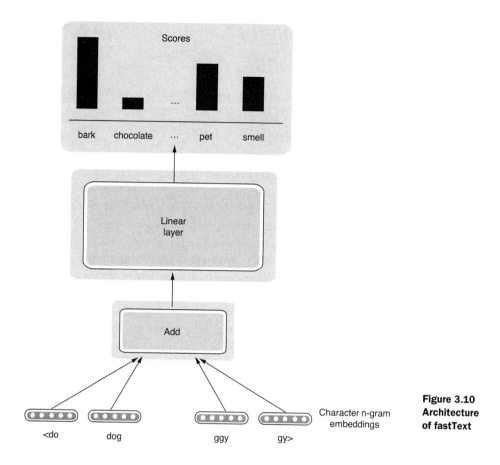

**Figure 3.10
Architecture
of fastText**

seen in the training data (which is almost always the case). It can potentially guess it's related to something quick ("Insta") and pictures ("gram").

3.6.2 *Using the fastText toolkit*

Facebook provides the open source for the fastText toolkit, a library for training the word-embedding model discussed in the previous section. In the remainder of this section, let's see how it feels like to use this library to train word embeddings.

First, go to their official documentation (http://realworldnlpbook.com/ch3.html #fasttext) and follow the instruction to download and compile the library. It is just a matter of cloning the GitHub repository and running make from the command line in most environments. After compilation is finished, you can run the following command to train a Skip-gram-based fastText model:

```
$ ./fasttext skipgram -input ../data/text8 -output model
```

We are assuming there's a text data file under ../data/text8 that you'd like to use as the training data, but change this if necessary. This will create a model.bin file, which is a binary representation of the trained model. After training the model, you can obtain word vectors for any words, even for the ones that you've never seen in the training data, as follows:

```
$ echo "supercalifragilisticexpialidocious" \
| ./fasttext print-word-vectors model.bin
supercalifragilisticexpialidocious 0.032049 0.20626 -0.21628 -0.040391 -
     0.038995 0.088793 -0.0023854 0.41535 -0.17251 0.13115 ...
```

3.7   *Document-level embeddings*

All the models I have described so far learn embeddings for individual words. If you are concerned only with word-level tasks such as inferring word relationships, or if they are combined with more powerful neural network models such as recurrent neural networks (RNNs), they can be very useful tools. However, if you wish to solve NLP tasks that are concerned with larger linguistic structures such as sentences and documents using word embeddings and traditional machine learning tools such as logistic regression and support vector machines (SVMs), word-level embedding methods are still limited. How can you represent larger linguistic units such as sentences using vector representations? How can you use word embeddings for sentiment analysis, for example?

One way to achieve this is to simply use the average of all word vectors in a sentence. You can average vectors by taking the average of first elements, second elements, and so on and make a new vector by combining these averaged numbers. You can use this new vector as an input to traditional machine learning models. Although this method is simple and can be effective, it is also very limiting. The biggest issue is that it cannot take word order into consideration. For example, both sentences "Mary loves John." and "John loves Mary." would have exactly the same vectors if you simply averaged word vectors for each word in the sentence.

NLP researchers have proposed models and algorithms that can specifically address this issue. One of the most popular is *Doc2Vec*, originally proposed by Le and Mikolov in 2014 (https://cs.stanford.edu/~quocle/paragraph_vector.pdf). This model, as its name suggests, learns vector representations for documents. In fact, "document" here simply means any variable-length piece of text that contains multiple words. Similar models are also called under many similar names such as *Sentence2Vec*, *Paragraph2Vec*, *paragraph vectors* (this is what the authors of the original paper used), but in essence, they all refer to the variations of the same model.

In the rest of this section, I'm going to discuss one of the Doc2Vec models called *distributed memory model of paragraph vectors* (PV-DM). The model looks very similar to CBOW, which we studied earlier in this chapter, but with one key difference—one additional vector, called *paragraph vector*, is added as an input. The model predicts the target word from a set of context words *and* the paragraph vector. Each paragraph is assigned a distinct paragraph vector. Figure 3.11 shows the structure of this PV-DM model. Also, PV-DM uses only context words that come before the target word for prediction, but this is a minor difference.

What effect would this paragraph vector have on the prediction task? Now you have some extra information from the paragraph vector for predicting the target word. As the model tries to maximize the prediction accuracy, you can expect that the

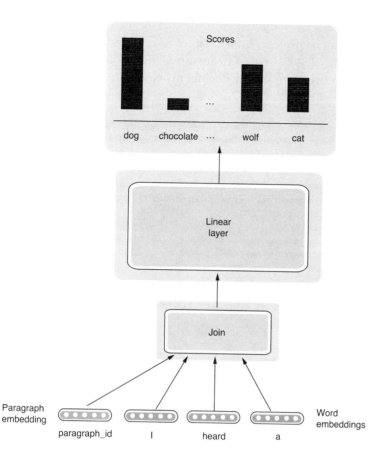

**Figure 3.11
Distributed memory
model of paragraph
vectors**

paragraph vector is updated so that it provides some useful "context" information in the sentence that is not collectively captured by the context word vectors. As a by-product, the model learns something that reflects the overall meaning of each paragraph, along with word vectors.

Several open source libraries and packages support Doc2Vec models, but one of the most widely used is Gensim (https://radimrehurek.com/gensim/), which can be installed by running `pip install gensim`. Gensim is a popular NLP toolkit that supports a wide range of vector and topic models such as TF-IDF (term frequency and inverse document frequency), LDA (latent semantic analysis), and word embeddings.

To train a Doc2Vec model using Gensim, you first need to read a dataset and convert documents to `TaggedDocument`. This can be done using the `read_corpus()` method shown here:

```
from gensim.utils import simple_preprocess
from gensim.models.doc2vec import TaggedDocument

def read_corpus(file_path):
    with open(file_path) as f:
        for i, line in enumerate(f):
            yield TaggedDocument(simple_preprocess(line), [i])
```

We are going to use a small dataset consisting of the first 200,000 English sentences taken from the Tatoeba project (https://tatoeba.org/). You can download the dataset from http://mng.bz/7l0y. Then you can use Gensim's `Doc2Vec` class to train the Doc2Vec model and retrieve similar documents based on the trained paragraph vectors, as demonstrated next.

Listing 3.6   Training a Doc2Vec model and retrieving similar documents

```
from gensim.models.doc2vec import Doc2Vec

train_set = list(read_corpus('data/mt/sentences.eng.200k.txt'))
model = Doc2Vec(vector_size=256, min_count=3, epochs=30)
model.build_vocab(train_set)
model.train(train_set,
            total_examples=model.corpus_count,
            epochs=model.epochs)

query_vec = model.infer_vector(
    ['i', 'heard', 'a', 'dog', 'barking', 'in', 'the', 'distance'])
sims = model.docvecs.most_similar([query_vec], topn=10)
for doc_id, sim in sims:
    print('{:3.2f} {}'.format(sim, train_set[doc_id].words))
```

This will show you a list of documents similar to the input document "I heard a dog barking in the distance," as follows:

```
0.67 ['she', 'was', 'heard', 'playing', 'the', 'violin']
0.65 ['heard', 'the', 'front', 'door', 'slam']
0.61 ['we', 'heard', 'tigers', 'roaring', 'in', 'the', 'distance']
0.61 ['heard', 'dog', 'barking', 'in', 'the', 'distance']
0.60 ['heard', 'the', 'door', 'open']
0.60 ['tom', 'heard', 'the', 'door', 'open']
0.60 ['she', 'heard', 'dog', 'barking', 'in', 'the', 'distance']
0.59 ['heard', 'the', 'door', 'close']
0.59 ['when', 'he', 'heard', 'the', 'whistle', 'he', 'crossed', 'the', 'street']
0.58 ['heard', 'the', 'telephone', 'ringing']
```

Notice that most of the retrieved sentences here are related to hearing sound. In fact, an identical sentence is in the list, because I took the query sentence from Tatoeba in the first place! Gensim's `Doc2Vec` class has a number of hyperparameters that you can use to tweak the model. You can read further about the class on their reference page (https://radimrehurek.com/gensim/models/doc2vec.html).

3.8   *Visualizing embeddings*

In the final section of this chapter, we are going to shift our focus on visualizing word embeddings. As we've done earlier, retrieving similar words given a query word is a great way to quickly check if word embeddings are trained correctly. But it gets tiring and time-consuming if you need to check a number of words to see if the word embeddings are capturing semantic relationships between words as a whole.

As mentioned earlier, word embeddings are simply *N*-dimensional vectors, which are also "points" in an *N*-dimensional space. We were able to see those points visually in a 3-D space in figure 3.1 because *N* was 3. But *N* is typically a couple of hundred in most word embeddings, and we cannot simply plot them on an *N*-dimensional space.

A solution is to reduce the dimension down to something that we can see (two or three dimensions) while preserving relative distances between points. This technique is called *dimensionality reduction*. We have a number of ways to reduce dimensionality, including PCA (principal component analysis) and ICA (independent component analysis), but by far the most widely used visualization technique for word embeddings is called *t-SNE* (t-distributed Stochastic Neighbor Embedding, pronounced "tee-snee). Although the details of t-SNE are outside the scope of this book, the algorithm tries to map points to a lower-dimensional space by preserving the relative neighboring relationship between points in the original high-dimensional space.

The easiest way to use t-SNE is to use Scikit-Learn (https://scikit-learn.org/), a popular Python library for machine learning. After installing it (usually just a matter of running `pip install scikit-learn`), you can use it to visualize the GloVe vectors read from a file as shown next (we use Matplotlib to draw the plot).

Listing 3.7 Using t-SNE to visualize GloVe embeddings

```python
from sklearn.manifold import TSNE
import matplotlib.pyplot as plt

def read_glove(file_path):
    with open(file_path) as f:
        for i, line in enumerate(f):
            fields = line.rstrip().split(' ')
            vec = [float(x) for x in fields[1:]]
            word = fields[0]
            yield (word, vec)

words = []
vectors = []
for word, vec in read_glove('data/glove/glove.42B.300d.txt'):
    words.append(word)
    vectors.append(vec)

model = TSNE(n_components=2, init='pca', random_state=0)
coordinates = model.fit_transform(vectors)

plt.figure(figsize=(8, 8))

for word, xy in zip(words, coordinates):
    plt.scatter(xy[0], xy[1])
    plt.annotate(word,
                 xy=(xy[0], xy[1]),
                 xytext=(2, 2),
                 textcoords='offset points')
plt.xlim(25, 55)
plt.ylim(-15, 15)
plt.show()
```

In listing 3.7, I used `xlim()` and `ylim()` to limit the plotted range to magnify some areas that are of interest to us. You may want to try different values to focus on other areas in the plot.

The code in listing 3.7 generates the plot shown in figure 3.12. There's a lot of interesting stuff going on here, but at a quick glance, you will notice the following clusters of words that are semantically related:

- Bottom-left: web-related words (*posts, article, blog, comments, . . .*).
- Upper-left: time-related words (*day, week, month, year, . . .*).
- Middle: numbers (0, 1, 2, . . .). Surprisingly, these numbers are lined up in an increasing order toward the bottom. GloVe figured out which numbers are larger purely from a large amount of textual data.
- Bottom-right: months (january, february, . . .) and years (2004, 2005, . . .). Again, the years seem to be lined up in an increasing order, almost in parallel with the numbers (0, 1, 2, . . .).

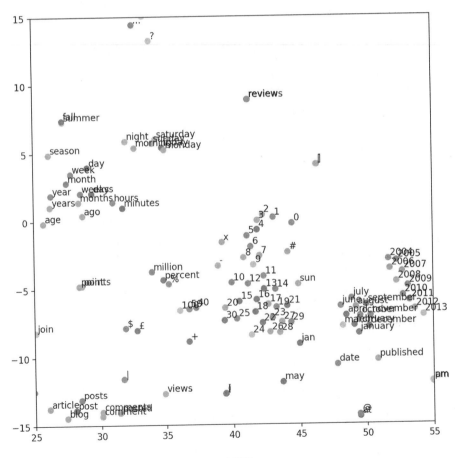

Figure 3.12   GloVe embeddings visualized by t-SNE

If you think about it, it's an incredible feat for a purely mathematical model to figure out these relationships among words, all from a large amount of text data. Hopefully, now you know how much of an advantage it is if the model knows "july" and "june" are closely related compared to needing to figure everything out starting from `word_823` and `word_1719`.

Summary

- Word embeddings are numeric representations of words, and they help convert discrete units (words and sentences) to continuous mathematical objects (vectors).
- The Skip-gram model uses a neural network with a linear layer and softmax to learn word embeddings as a by-product of the "fake" word-association task.
- GloVe makes use of global statistics of word co-occurrence to train word embeddings efficiently.
- Doc2Vec and fastText learn document-level embeddings and word embeddings with subword information, respectively.
- You can use t-SNE to visualize word embeddings.

Sentence classification

In this chapter, we are going to study the task of sentence classification, where an NLP model receives a sentence and assigns some label to it. A spam filter is an application of sentence classification. It receives an email message and assigns whether or not it is spam. If you want to classify news articles into different topics (business, politics, sports, and so on), it's also a sentence-classification task. Sentence classification is one of the simplest NLP tasks that has a wide range of applications, including document classification, spam filtering, and sentiment analysis. Specifically, we are going to revisit the sentiment classifier we introduced in chapter 2 and discuss its components in detail. At the end of this section, we are going to study another application of sentence classification—language detection.

4.1 Recurrent neural networks (RNNs)

The first step in sentence classification is to represent variable-length sentences using neural networks (RNNs). In this section, I'm going to present the concept of recurrent neural networks, one of the most important concepts in deep NLP. Many modern NLP models use RNNs in some way. I'll explain why they are important, what they do, and introduce their simplest variant.

4.1.1 Handling variable-length input

The Skip-gram network structure shown in the previous chapter was simple. It takes a word vector of a fixed size, runs it through a linear layer, and obtains a distribution of scores over all the context words. The structure and the size of the input, output, and the network are all fixed throughout the training.

However, many, if not most, of what we deal with in NLP are sequences of variable lengths. For example, words, which are sequences of characters, can be short ("a," "in") or long ("internationalization"). Sentences (sequences of words) and documents (sequences of sentences) can be of any lengths. Even characters, if you look at them as sequences of strokes, can be simple (e.g., "O" and "L" in English) or more complex (e.g., "鬱" is a Chinese character meaning "depression" which, depressingly, has 29 strokes).

As we discussed in the previous chapter, neural networks can handle only numbers and arithmetic operations. That was why we needed to convert words and documents to numbers through embeddings. We used linear layers to convert a fixed-length vector into another. But to do something similar with variable-length inputs, we need to figure out how to structure the neural networks so that they can handle them.

One idea is to first convert the input (e.g., a sequence of words) to embeddings, that is, a sequence of vectors of floating-point numbers, then average them. Let's assume the input sentence is sentence = ["john", "loves", "mary", "."], and you already know word embeddings for each word in the sentence v("john"), v("loves"), and so on. The average can be obtained with the following code and illustrated in figure 4.1:

```
result = (v("john") + v("loves") + v("mary") + v(".")) / 4
```

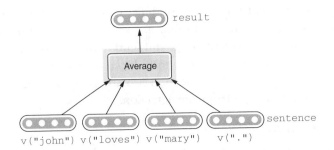

Figure 4.1 Averaging embedding vectors

This method is quite simple and is actually used in many NLP applications. However, it has one critical issue, which is that it cannot take word order into account. Because the order of input elements doesn't affect the result of averaging, you'd get the same vector for both "Mary loves John" and "John loves Mary." Although it's up to the task in hand, it's hard to imagine many NLP applications would want this kind of behavior.

If we step back and reflect how we humans read language, this "averaging" is far from actuality. When we read a sentence, we don't usually read individual words in isolation and remember them first, then move on to figuring out what the sentence means. We usually scan the sentence from the beginning, one word at a time, while holding what the "partial" sentence means up until the part you are reading in our short-term memory. In other words, you maintain some sort of mental representation of the sentence while you read it. When you reach the end of the sentence, the mental representation is its meaning.

Can we design a neural network structure that simulates this incremental reading of the input? The answer is a resounding yes. That structure is called *recurrent neural networks* (RNNs), which I'll explain in detail next.

4.1.2 *RNN abstraction*

If you break down the reading process mentioned earlier, its core is the repetition of the following series of operations:

1 Read a word.
2 Based on what has been read so far (your "mental state"), figure out what the word means.
3 Update the mental state.
4 Move on to the next word.

Let's see how this works using a concrete example. If the input sentence is `sentence = ["john", "loves", "mary", "."]`, and each word is already represented as a word-embedding vector. Also, let's denote your "mental state" as `state`, which is initialized by `init_state()`. Then, the reading process is represented by the following incremental operations:

```
state = init_state()
state = update(state, v("john"))
```

```
state = update(state, v("loves"))
state = update(state, v("mary"))
state = update(state, v("."))
```

The final value of `state` becomes the representation of the entire sentence from this process. Notice that if you change the order in which these words are processed (e.g., by flipping "John" and "Mary"), the final value of state also changes, meaning that the state also encodes some information about the word order.

You can achieve something similar if you can design a network substructure that is applied to each element of the input while updating some internal states. RNNs are neural network structures that do exactly this. In a nutshell, an RNN is a neural network with a loop. At its core is an operation that is applied to every element in the input as they come in. If you wrote what RNNs do in Python pseudocode, it'd be like the following:

```
def rnn(words):
    state = init_state()
    for word in words:
        state = update(state, word)
    return state
```

Notice that there is `state` that gets initialized first and passed around during the iteration. For every input `word`, `state` is updated based on the previous state and the input using the function `update`. The network substructure corresponding to this step (the code block inside the loop) is called a *cell*. This stops when the input is exhausted, and the final value of `state` becomes the result of this RNN. See figure 4.2 for the illustration.

You can see the parallelism here. When you are reading a sentence (sequence of words), your internal mental representation of the sentence, `state`, is updated after reading each word. You can assume that the final state encodes the representation of the entire sentence.

The only remaining work is to design two functions—`init_state()` and `update()`. The state is usually initialized with zero (i.e., a vector filled with zeros), so

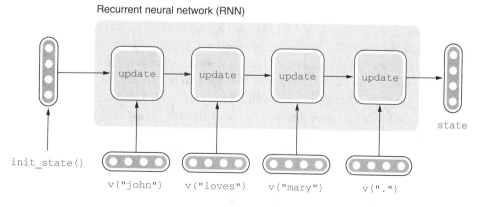

Recurrent neural network (RNN)

Figure 4.2 RNN abstraction

you usually don't have to worry about how to go about defining the former. It's more important how you design update(), which determines the characteristics of the RNN.

4.1.3   *Simple RNNs and nonlinearity*

In section 3.4.3, I talked about how to implement a linear layer with an arbitrary number of inputs and outputs. Can we do something similar and implement update(), which is basically a function that takes two input variables and produces one output variable? After all, a cell is a neural network with its own input and output, right? The answer is yes, and it looks like this:

```
def update_simple(state, word):
    return f(w1 * state + w2 * word + b)
```

Notice that this is strikingly similar to the linear2() function in section 3.4.3. In fact, if you ignore the difference in variable names, it's exactly the same except for the f() function. An RNN defined by this type of the update function is called a *simple RNN* or *Elman RNN*, which is, as its name suggests, one of the simplest RNN structures.

You may be wondering, then, what is this function f() doing here? What does it look like? Do we need it here at all? The function, called an *activation function* or *nonlinearity*, takes a single input (or a vector) and transforms it (or every element of a vector) in a nonlinear fashion. Many kinds of nonlinearities exist, and they play an indispensable role in making neural networks truly powerful. What they exactly do and why they are important requires some math to understand, which is outside the scope of this book, but I'll attempt an intuitive explanation with a simple example next.

Imagine you are building an RNN that recognizes "grammatical" English sentences. Differentiating grammatical sentences from ungrammatical ones is itself a difficult NLP problem, which is, in fact, a well-established research area (see section 1.2.1), but here, let's simplify it and consider agreement only between the subject and the verb. Let's further simplify it and assume that there are only four words in this "language"—"I," "you," "am," and "are." If the sentence is either "I am" or "you are," it's grammatically correct. The other two combinations, "I are" and "you am," are incorrect. What you want to build is an RNN that outputs 1 for the correct sentences while producing 0 for the incorrect ones. How would you go about building such a neural network?

The first step in almost every modern NLP model is to represent words with embeddings. As mentioned in the previous chapter, they are usually learned from a large dataset of natural language text, but here, we are simply going to give them some predefined values, as shown in figure 4.3.

Now, let's imagine there was no activation function. The previous update_simple() function simplifies to the following:

```
def update_simple_linear(state, word):
    return w1 * state + w2 * word + b
```

We will assume the initial value of state is simply [0, 0], because the specific initial values are not relevant to the discussion here. The RNN takes the first word embedding,

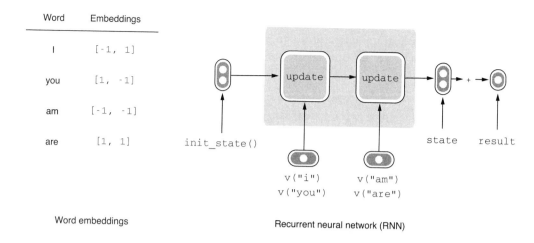

Figure 4.3   Recognizing grammatical English sentences using an RNN

x1, updates state, takes the second word embedding, x2, then produces the final state, which is a two-dimensional vector. Finally, the two elements in this vector are summed and converted to result. If result is close to 1, the sentence is grammatical. Otherwise, it is not. If you apply the update_simple_linear() function twice and simplify it a little bit, you get the following function, which is all this RNN does, after all:

```
w1 * w2 * x1 + w2 * x2 + w1 * b + b
```

Remember, w1, w2, and b are parameters of the model (aka "magic constants") that need to be trained (adjusted). Here, instead of adjusting these parameters using a training dataset, let's assign some arbitrary values and see what happens. For example, when w1 = [1, 0], w2 = [0, 1], and b = [0, 0], the input and the output of this RNN will be as shown in figure 4.4.

Word 1	Word 2	x1	x2	state	result	Desired
I	am	[-1, 1]	[-1, -1]	[0, -1]	-1	1
I	are	[-1, 1]	[1, 1]	[0, 1]	1	0
you	am	[1, -1]	[-1, -1]	[0, -1]	-1	0
you	are	[1, -1]	[1, 1]	[0, 1]	1	1

w1 = [1, 0], w2 = [0, 1], b = [0, 0]

Figure 4.4   Input and output when w1 = [1, 0], w2 = [0, 1], and b = [0, 0] **without an activation function**

If you look at the values of `result`, this RNN groups ungrammatical sentences (e.g., "I are") with grammatical ones (e.g., "you are"), which is not the desired behavior. How about we try another set of values for the parameters? Let's use `w1 = [1, 0]`, `w2 = [-1, 0]`, and `b = [0, 0]` and see what happens (see figure 4.5 for the result).

Word 1	Word 2	x1	x2	state	result	Desired
I	am	[-1, 1]	[-1, -1]	[2, 0]	2	1
I	are	[-1, 1]	[1, 1]	[0, 0]	0	0
you	am	[1, -1]	[-1, -1]	[0, 0]	0	0
you	are	[1, -1]	[1, 1]	[-2, 0]	-2	1

w1 = [1, 0], w2 = [-1, 0], b = [0, 0]

Figure 4.5 Input and output when `w1 = [1, 0]`, `w2 = [-1, 0]`, and `b = [0, 0]` without an activation function

This is much better, because the RNN is successful in grouping ungrammatical sentences by assigning 0 to both "I are" and "you am." However, it also assigns completely opposite values (2 and –2) to grammatical sentences ("I am" and "you are").

I'm going to stop here, but as it turns out, you cannot use this neural network to differentiate grammatical sentences from ungrammatical ones, no matter how hard you try. Despite the values you assign to the parameters, this RNN cannot produce results that are close enough to the desired values and, thus, are able to group sentences by their grammaticality.

Let's step back and think why this is the case. If you look at the previous update function, all it does is multiply the input by some value and add them up. In more specific terms, it only transforms the input *in a linear fashion*. The result of this neural network always changes by some constant amount when you change the value of the input by some amount. But this is obviously not desirable—you want the result to be 1 only when the input variables are some specific values. In other words, you don't want this RNN to be linear; you want it to be nonlinear.

To use an analogy, imagine you can use only assignment ("="), addition ("+"), and multiplication ("*") in your programming language. You can tweak the input values to some degree to come up with the result, but you can't write more complex logic in such a restricted setting.

Now let's put the activation function `f()` back and see what happens. The specific activation function we are going to use is called *the hyperbolic tangent function*, or more commonly, *tanh*, which is one of the most commonly used activation functions in neural networks. The details of this function are not important in this discussion, but in a nutshell, it behaves as follows: tanh doesn't do much to the input when it is close to zero, for example, 0.3 or –0.2. In other words, the input passes through the function almost unchanged. When the input is far from zero, tanh tries to squeeze it between –1 and 1. For example, when the input is large (say, 10.0), the output becomes very close to 1.0, whereas when it is small (say, –10.0), the output becomes almost –1.0. This creates an effect similar to the OR logical gate (or an AND gate, depending on the weights) if two or more variables are fed into the activation function. The output of the gate becomes ON (~1) and OFF (~–1) depending on the input.

When `w1 = [-1, 2]`, `w2 = [-1, 2]`, `b = [0, 1]`, and the tanh activation function is used, the result of the RNN becomes a lot closer to what we desire (see figure 4.6). If you round them to the closest integers, the RNN successfully groups sentences by their grammaticality.

Word 1	Word 2	x1	x2	state	result	Desired
I	am	[-1, 1]	[-1, -1]	[0.23, 0.75]	0.99	1
I	are	[-1, 1]	[1, 1]	[-0.94, 0.99]	0.06	0
you	am	[1, -1]	[-1, -1]	[0.94, -0.98]	-0.04	0
you	are	[1, -1]	[1, 1]	[-0.23, 0.90]	0.67	1

w1 = [-1, 2], w2 = [-1, 2], b = [0, 1]

Figure 4.6   Input and output when `w1 = [-1, 2]`, `w2 = [-1, 2]`, **and** `b = [0, 1]` **with an activation function**

To use the same analogy, using activation functions in your neural networks is like using ANDs and ORs and IFs in your programming language, in addition to basic math operations like addition and multiplication. In this way, you can write complex logic and model complex interactions between input variables, like the example in this section.

> **NOTE**   This example I use in this section is a slightly modified version of the popular XOR (or *exclusive-or*) example commonly seen in deep learning textbooks. This is the most basic and simplest example that can be solved by neural networks but not by other linear models.

Some final notes on RNNs—they are trained just like any other neural networks. The final outcome is compared with the desired outcome using the loss function, then the difference between the two—the loss—is used for updating the "magic constants." The magic constants are, in this case, w1, w2, and b in the `update_simple()` function. Note that the update function and its magic constants are identical across all the timesteps in the loop. This means that what RNNs are learning is a general form of updates that can be applied to any situation.

4.2 Long short-term memory units (LSTMs) and gated recurrent units (GRUs)

In fact, the simple RNNs that we discussed earlier are rarely used in real-world NLP applications due to one problem called the *vanishing gradients problem*. In this section, I'll show the issue associated with simple RNNs and how more popular RNN architectures, namely LSTMs and GRUs, solve this particular problem.

4.2.1 Vanishing gradients problem

Just like any programming language, if you know the length of the input, you can rewrite a loop without using one. An RNN can also be rewritten without using a loop, which makes it look just like a regular neural network with many layers. For example, if you know that there are only six words in the input, the rnn() from earlier can be rewritten as follows:

```
def rnn(sentence):
    word1, word2, word3, word4, word5, word6 = sentence
    state = init_state()

    state = update(state, word1)
    state = update(state, word2)
    state = update(state, word3)
    state = update(state, word4)
    state = update(state, word5)
    state = update(state, word6)

    return state
```

Representing RNNs without loops is called *unrolling*. Now we know what update() looks like for a simple RNN (update_simple), so we can replace the function calls with their bodies, as shown here:

```
def rnn_simple(sentence):
    word1, word2, word3, word4, word5, word6 = sentence
    state = init_state()

    state = f(w1 * f(w1 * f(w1 * f(w1 * f(w1 * f(w1 * state + w2 * word1 + b)
      + w2 * word2 + b) + w2 * word3 + b) + w2 * word4 + b) + w2 * word5 + b)
      + w2 * word6 + b)
    return state
```

This is getting a bit ugly, but I just want you to notice the very deeply nested function calls and multiplications. Now, recall the task we wanted to accomplish in the previous section—classifying grammatical English sentences by recognizing subject-verb agreement. Let's say the input is sentence = ["The", "books", "I", "read", "yesterday", "were"]. In this case, the innermost function call processes the first word

"The," the next one processes the second word "books," and so on, all the way to the outermost function call, which processes "were." If we rewrite the previous pseudocode slightly, as shown in the next code snippet, you can understand it more intuitively:

```
def is_grammatical(sentence):
    word1, word2, word3, word4, word5, word6 = sentence
    state = init_state()

    state = process_main_verb(w1 *
        process_adverb(w1 *
            process_relative_clause_verb(w1 *
                process_relative_clause_subject(w1 *
                    process_main_subject(w1 *
                        process_article(w1 * state + w2 * word1 + b) +
                    w2 * word2 + b) +
                w2 * word3 + b) +
            w2 * word4 + b) +
        w2 * word5 + b) +
    w2 * word6 + b)

    return state
```

To recognize that the input is indeed a grammatical English sentence (or a prefix of a sentence), the RNN needs to retain the information about the subject ("the books") in `state` until it sees the verb ("were") without being distracted by anything in between ("I read yesterday"). In the previous pseudocode, the states are represented by the return values of function calls, so the information about the subject (return value of `process_main_subject`) needs to propagate all the way up in this chain until it reaches the outermost function (`process_main_verb`). This is starting to sound like a difficult task.

Things don't look any better when it comes to training this RNN. RNNs, as well as any other neural networks, are trained using an algorithm called *backpropagation*. Back-propagation is a process where the components of a neural network communicate with previous components on how to adjust the parameters to minimize the loss. This is how it works for this particular case. First, you look at the outcome, that is, the return value of `is_grammatical()` and compare it with what you desire. The difference between these two is called the *loss*. The outermost function, `is_grammatical()`, basically has four ways to decrease the loss to make its output closer to what is desired—1) adjust `w1` while fixing the return value of the nested function `process_adverb()`, 2) adjust `w2`, 3) adjust `b`, or 4) adjust the return value of `process_adverb()` while fixing the parameters. Adjusting the parameters (`w1`, `w2`, and `b`) is the easy part because the function knows the exact effect of adjusting each parameter to its return value. Adjusting the return value of the previous function, however, is not easy, because the caller has no idea about the inner workings of the function. Because of this, the caller tells the previous function (callee) to adjust its return values to minimize the loss. See figure 4.7 for how the loss is propagated back to the parameters and previous functions.

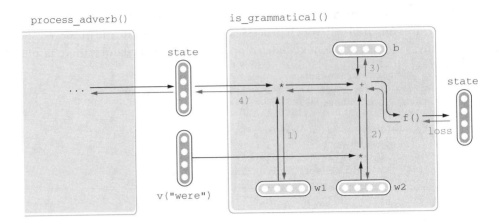

Figure 4.7   Backpropagation of loss

The nested function calls repeat this process and plays the Telephone game until the message reaches the innermost function. By that time, because the message needs to pass through many layers, it becomes so weak and obscure (or so strong and skewed because of some misunderstanding) that the inner functions have a difficult time figuring out what they did wrong.

Technically, the deep learning literature calls this the *vanishing gradients problem*. A *gradient* is a mathematical term that corresponds to the message signal that each function receives from the next one that states how exactly they should improve their process (how to change their magic constants). The reverse Telephone game, where messages are passed backward from the final function (= loss function), is called backpropagation. I'm not going into the mathematical details of these terms, but it is useful to understand them at least conceptually.

Because of the vanishing gradients problem, simple RNNs are difficult to train and rarely used in practice nowadays.

4.2.2   *Long short-term memory (LSTM)*

The way the nested functions mentioned earlier process information about grammar seems too inefficient. After all, why doesn't the outermost function (is_grammatical) tell the particular function in charge (e.g., process_main_subject) what went wrong directly, instead of playing the Telephone game? It can't, because the message can change its shape entirely after each function call because of w2 and f(). The outermost function cannot tell which function was responsible for which part of the message from only the final output.

How could we address this inefficiency? Instead of passing the information through an activation function every time and changing its shape completely, how about adding and subtracting information relevant to the part of the sentence being processed at each step? For example, if process_main_subject() can directly add information about the subject to some type of "memory," and the network can make sure the memory passes through the intermediate functions intact, `is_grammatical()` will have a much easier time telling the previous functions what to do to adjust its output.

Long short-term memory units (LSTMs) are a type of RNN cell that is proposed based on this insight. Instead of passing around states, LSTM cells share a "memory" that each cell can remove old information from and/or add new information to, something like an assembly line in a manufacturing factory. Specifically, LSTM RNNs use the following function for updating states:

```
def update_lstm(state, word):
    cell_state, hidden_state = state

    cell_state *= forget(hidden_state, word)
    cell_state += add(hidden_state, word)

    hidden_state = update_hidden(hidden_state, cell_state, word)

    return (cell_state, hidden_state)
```

Although this looks relatively complicated compared to its simple version, if you break it down to subcomponents, it's not that difficult to understand what is going on here, as described next and shown in figure 4.8:

- The LSTM states comprise two halves—the cell state (the "memory" part) and the hidden state (the "mental representation" part).
- The function `forget()` returns a value between 0 and 1, so multiplying by this number means erasing old memory from `cell_state`. How much to erase is

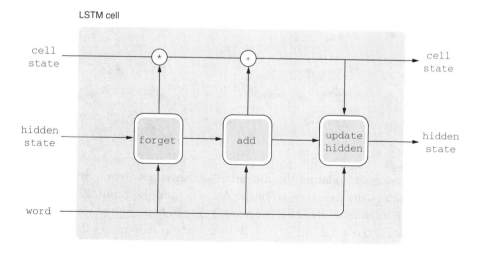

Figure 4.8 LSTM update function

determined from `hidden_state` and `word` (input). Controlling the flow of information by multiplying by a value between 0 and 1 is called *gating*. LSTMs are the first RNN architecture that uses this gating mechanism.

■ The function `add()` returns a new value added to the memory. The value again is determined from `hidden_state` and `word`.

■ Finally, `hidden_state` is updated using a function, whose value is computed from the previous hidden state, the updated memory, and the input `word`.

I abstracted the update function by hiding some mathematical details in the functions `forget()`, `add()`, and `update_hidden()`, which are not important for the discussion here. If you are interested in understanding LSTMs more deeply, I refer you to a wonderful blog post Chris Olah wrote on this topic (http://colah.github.io/posts/2015-08-Understanding-LSTMs/).

Because LSTMs have this cell state that stays constant across different timesteps unless explicitly modified, they are easier to train and relatively well behaved. Because you have a shared "memory" and functions are adding and removing information related to different parts of the input sentence, it is easier to pinpoint which function did what and what went wrong. The error signal from the outermost function can reach responsible functions more directly.

A word on the terminology—LSTM refers to one particular type of architecture mentioned here, but people use "LSTMs" to mean RNNs with LSTM cells. Also, "RNN" is often used to mean "simple RNN," introduced in section 4.1.3. When you see "RNNs" in the literature, you need to be aware of which exact architectures they are using.

4.2.3   *Gated recurrent units (GRUs)*

Another RNN architecture, called *Gated Recurrent Units* (GRUs), uses the gating mechanism. The philosophy behind GRUs is similar to that of LSTMs, but GRUs use only one set of states instead of two halves. The update function for GRUs is shown next:

```
def update_gru(state, word):
    new_state = update_hidden(state, word)

    switch = get_switch(state, word)

    state = swtich * new_state + (1 - switch) * state

    return state
```

Instead of erasing or updating the memory, GRUs use a switching mechanism. The cell first computes the new state from the old state and the input. It then computes `switch`, a value between 0 and 1. The state is chosen between the new state and the old one based on the value of `switch`. If it's 0, the old state passes through intact. If it's 1, it's overwritten by the new state. If it's somewhere in between, the state will be a mix of two. See figure 4.9 for an illustration of the GRU update function.

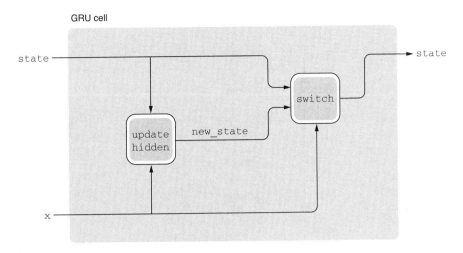

Figure 4.9   GRU update function

Notice that the update function for GRUs is much simpler than that for the LSTMs. Indeed, it has fewer parameters (magic constants) that need to be trained compared to LSTMs. Because of this, GRUs are faster to train than LSTMs.

Finally, although we introduced two different types of RNN architecture, LSTM and GRU, there's no consensus in the community on which type of architecture is the best for all applications. You often need to treat them as a hyperparameter and experiment with different configurations. Fortunately, it is easy to experiment with different types of RNN cells as long as you are using modern deep learning frameworks such as PyTorch and TensorFlow.

4.3   Accuracy, precision, recall, and F-measure

In section 2.7, I briefly talked about some metrics that we use for evaluating the performance of a classification task. Before we move on to actually building a sentence classifier, I'd like to further discuss the evaluation metrics we are going to use—what they mean and what they actually measure.

4.3.1   Accuracy

Accuracy is probably the simplest of all the evaluation metrics that we talk about here. In a classification setting, accuracy is the fraction of instances that your model got right. For example, if there are 10 emails and your spam-filtering model got 8 of them correct, the accuracy of your prediction is 0.8, or 80% (see figure 4.10).

Though simple, accuracy is not without its limitations. Specifically, accuracy can be misleading when the test set is imbalanced. An *imbalanced* dataset contains multiple class labels that greatly differ in their numbers. For example, if a spam-filtering dataset is imbalanced, it may contain 90% nonspam emails and 10% spams. In such a case,

Instances	Labels	Predictions	Correct?
Email 1	Spam	Spam	✓
Email 2	Nonspam	Nonspam	✓
Email 3	Nonspam	Nonspam	✓
Email 4	Spam	Nonspam	✗
Email 5	Nonspam	Nonspam	✓
Email 6	Nonspam	Nonspam	✓
Email 7	Nonspam	Nonspam	✓
Email 8	Nonspam	Spam	✗
Email 9	Spam	Spam	✓
Email 10	Nonspam	Nonspam	✓ Accuracy = 8/10 = 80%

Figure 4.10   Calculating accuracy

even a stupid classifier that labels everything as nonspam would be able to achieve an accuracy of 90%. As an example, if a "stupid" classifier classifies everything as "nonspam" in figure 4.10, it would still achieve an accuracy of 70% (7 out of 10 instances). If you look at this number in isolation, you might be fooled into thinking the performance of the classifier is actually great. When you are using accuracy as a metric, it is always a good idea to compare with the hypothetical, stupid classifier (*majority vote*) as a baseline.

4.3.2   *Precision and recall*

The rest of the metrics—precision, recall, and F-measure—are used in a binary classification setting. The goal of a binary classification task is to identify one class (called a *positive class*) from the other (called a *negative class*). In the spam-filtering setting, the positive class is spam, whereas the negative class is nonspam.

The Venn diagram in figure 4.11 contains four subregions: true positives, false positives, false negatives, and true negatives. True positives (TP) are instances that are predicted as positive (= spam) and are indeed in the positive class. False positives (FP) are instances that are predicted as positive (= spam) but are actually not in the positive class. These are noises in the prediction, that is, innocent nonspam emails that are mistakenly caught by the spam filter and end up in the spam folder of your email client.

On the other hand, false negatives (FN) are instances that are predicted as negative but are actually in the positive class. These are spam emails that slip through the spam filter and end up in your inbox. Finally, true negatives (TN) are instances that are predicted as negative and are indeed in the negative class (nonspam emails in your inbox).

Precision is the fraction of instances that the model classifies as positive that are indeed correct. For example, if your spam filter identifies three emails as spam, and two of them are indeed spam, the precision will be 2/3, or about 66%.

Recall is somewhat opposite of precision. It is the fraction of positive instances in your dataset that are identified as positive by your model. Again, using spam filtering as an example, if your dataset contains three spam emails and your model identifies two of them as spam successfully, the recall will be 2/3, or about 66%.

Figure 4.11 shows the relationship between predicted and true labels as well as recall and precision.

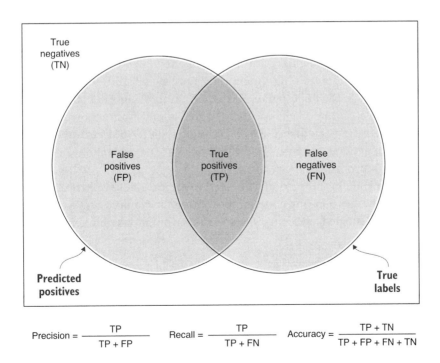

$$Precision = \frac{TP}{TP + FP} \qquad Recall = \frac{TP}{TP + FN} \qquad Accuracy = \frac{TP + TN}{TP + FP + FN + TN}$$

Figure 4.11   Precision and recall

4.3.3   *F-measure*

You may have noticed a tradeoff between precision and recall. Imagine there's a spam filter that is very, very careful in classifying emails. It outputs only one out of several thousand emails as spam, but when it does, it is always correct. This is not a difficult task, because some spam emails are pretty obvious—if they contain a word "vl@gra" in the text and it's sent from someone in the spam blacklist, it should be pretty safe to mark it as a spam. What would the precision of this spam filter be? 100%. Similarly, there's another spam filter that is very, very careless in classifying emails. It classifies every single email as spam, including the ones from your colleagues and friends. Its recall? 100%. Would any of these two spam filters be useful? Hardly!

As you've seen, improving precision or recall alone while ignoring the other is not a good practice, because of the tradeoff between them. It's like you were looking only at your body weight when you are on a diet. You lost 10 pounds? Great! But what if you are seven feet tall? Not so much. You need to take into account both your height and weight—how much is too much depends on the other variable. That's why there are measures like BMI (body mass index) that take both measures into account. Similarly, researchers came up with this metric called *F-measure*, which is an average (or, more precisely speaking, a harmonic mean) of precision and recall. Most often, a special case called *F1-measure* is used, which is the equally weighted version of F-measure. In a classification setting, it is a good practice to measure and try to maximize the F-measure.

4.4   *Building AllenNLP training pipelines*

In this section, we are going to revisit the sentiment analyzer we built in chapter 2 and discuss how to build its training pipeline in more detail. Although I already showed the important steps for building an NLP application using AllenNLP, in this section we will dive deep into some important concepts and abstractions. Understanding these concepts is important not just in using AllenNLP but also in designing NLP applications in general, because NLP applications are usually built using these abstractions in some way or the other.

To run the code in this section, you need to import the necessary classes and modules, as shown in the following code snippet (the code examples in this section can also be accessed via Google Colab, http://www.realworldnlpbook.com/ch2.html#sst-nb):

```
from itertools import chain
from typing import Dict

import numpy as np
import torch
import torch.optim as optim
from allennlp.data.data_loaders import MultiProcessDataLoader
from allennlp.data.samplers import BucketBatchSampler
from allennlp.data.vocabulary import Vocabulary
from allennlp.models import Model
from allennlp.modules.seq2vec_encoders import Seq2VecEncoder,
    PytorchSeq2VecWrapper
```

```
from allennlp.modules.text_field_embedders import TextFieldEmbedder,
    BasicTextFieldEmbedder
from allennlp.modules.token_embedders import Embedding
from allennlp.nn.util import get_text_field_mask
from allennlp.training.metrics import CategoricalAccuracy, F1Measure
from allennlp.training.trainer import GradientDescentTrainer
from allennlp_models.classification.dataset_readers.stanford_sentiment_tree_
    bank import \
    StanfordSentimentTreeBankDatasetReader
```

4.4.1 *Instances and fields*

As mentioned in section 2.2.1, an instance is the atomic unit for which a prediction is made by a machine learning algorithm. A dataset is a collection of instances of the same form. The first step in most NLP applications is to read in or receive some data (e.g., from a file or via network requests) and convert them to instances so that the NLP/ML algorithm can consume them.

AllenNLP supports an abstraction called `DatasetReader` whose job is to read in some input (raw strings, CSV files, JSON data structures from network requests, and so on) and convert it to instances. AllenNLP already provides a wide range of dataset readers for major formats used in NLP, such as the CoNLL format (used in popular shared tasks for language analysis) and the Penn Treebank (a popular dataset for syntactic parsing). To read the Standard Sentiment Treebank, you can use the built-in `StanfordSentimentTreeBankDatasetReader`, which we used earlier in chapter 2. You can also write your own dataset reader just by overriding some core methods from `DatasetReader`.

The AllenNLP class `Instance` represents a single instance. An instance can have one or more fields, which hold some type of data. For example, an instance for the sentiment analysis task has two fields—the text body and the label—which can be created by passing a dictionary of fields to its constructor as follows:

```
Instance({'tokens': TextField(tokens),
          'label': LabelField(sentiment)})
```

Here we assumed that you already created `tokens`, which is a list of tokens, and `sentiment`, a string label corresponding to the sentiment class, from reading the input file. AllenNLP supports other types of fields, depending on the task.

The `read()` method of `DatasetReader` returns an iterator over instances, which enables you to enumerate the generated instances and visually check them, as shown in the following snippet:

```
reader = StanfordSentimentTreeBankDatasetReader()

train_dataset = reader.read('path/to/sst/dataset/train.txt')
dev_dataset = reader.read('path/to/sst/dataset/dev.txt')

for inst in train_dataset + dev_dataset:
    print(inst)
```

In many cases, you access your dataset readers through data loaders. A data loader is an AllenNLP abstraction (which is really a thin wrapper around PyTorch's data loaders) that handles the data and iterates over batched instances. You can specify how instances are sorted, grouped into batches, and fed to the training algorithm by supplying a batch sampler. Here, we are using a `BucketBatchSampler`, which does this by sorting instances by their length and grouping instances with similar lengths into a single batch, as shown next:

```
reader = StanfordSentimentTreeBankDatasetReader()

sampler = BucketBatchSampler(batch_size=32, sorting_keys=["tokens"])
train_data_loader = MultiProcessDataLoader(
    reader, train_path, batch_sampler=sampler)
dev_data_loader = MultiProcessDataLoader(
    reader, dev_path, batch_sampler=sampler)
```

4.4.2 *Vocabulary and token indexers*

The second step in many NLP applications is to build the vocabulary. In computer science, vocabulary is a theoretical concept that represents the set of *all* possible words in a language. In NLP, though, it often means just the set of all unique tokens that appeared in a dataset. It is simply impossible to know all the possible words in a language, nor is it necessary for an NLP application. What is stored in a vocabulary is called a *vocabulary item* (or just an *item*). A vocabulary item is usually a word, although depending on the task at hand, it can be any form of linguistic units, including characters, character n-grams, and labels for linguistic annotation.

AllenNLP provides a class called `Vocabulary`. It not only takes care of storing vocabulary items that appeared in a dataset, but it also holds mappings between vocabulary items and their IDs. As mentioned earlier, neural networks and machine learning models in general can deal only with numbers, and there needs to be a way to map discrete items such as words to some numerical representations such as word IDs. The vocabulary is also used to map the results of an NLP model back to the original words and labels so that humans can actually read them.

You can create a `Vocabulary` object from instances as follows:

```
vocab = Vocabulary.from_instances(chain(train_data_loader.iter_instances(),
                                        dev_data_loader.iter_instances()),
                                  min_count={'tokens': 3})
```

A couple of things to note here: first, because we are dealing with iterators (returned by the data loaders' `iter_instances()` method), we need to use the chain method from `itertools` to enumerate all the instances in both datasets.

Second, AllenNLP's `Vocabulary` class supports *namespaces*, which are a system to separate different sets of items so that they don't get mixed up. Here's why they are useful—say you are building a machine translation system, and you just read a dataset that contains English and French translations. Without namespaces, you'd have just one set that contains all words in English and French. This is usually not a big issue because English words ("hi," "thank you," "language") and French words ("bonjour," "merci, "langue") look quite different in most cases. However, a number of words look exactly the same in both languages. For example, "chat" means "talk" in English and "cat" in French, but it's hard to imagine anybody wanting to mix those two words and assign the same ID (and embeddings). To avoid this conflict, `Vocabulary` implements namespaces and assigns separate sets of items of different types.

You may have noticed the `form_instances()` function call has a `min_count` argument. For each namespace, this specifies the minimum number of occurrences in the dataset that is necessary for an item to be included in the vocabulary. All the items that appear less frequently than this threshold are treated as "unknown" items. Here's why this is a good idea: in a typical language, a very small number of words appear a lot (in English: "the," "a," "of") and a very large number of words appear very infrequently. This usually exhibits a long tail distribution of word frequencies. But it is not likely that these super infrequent words add anything useful to the model, and precisely because they appear infrequently, it is difficult to learn any useful patterns from them anyway. Also, because there are so many of them, they inflate the size of the vocabulary and the number of model parameters. In such a case, a common practice in NLP is to cut this long tail and collapse all the infrequent words to a single entity <UNK> (for "unknown" words).

Finally, a *token indexer* is an AllenNLP abstraction that takes in a token and returns its index, or a list of indices that represent the token. In most cases, there's a one-to-one mapping between unique tokens and their indices, but depending on your model, you may need more advanced ways to index the tokens (such as using character n-grams).

After you create a vocabulary, you can tell the data loaders to index the tokens with the specified vocabulary, as shown in the next code snippet. This means that the tokens that the data loaders read from the datasets are converted to integer IDs according to the vocabulary's mappings:

```
train_data_loader.index_with(vocab)
dev_data_loader.index_with(vocab)
```

4.4.3 Token embedders and RNNs

After you index words using a vocabulary and token indexers, you need to convert them to embeddings. An AllenNLP abstraction called `TokenEmbedder` takes word indices as an input and produces word embedding vectors as an output. You can embed words using continuous vectors in many ways, but if all you want is to map unique tokens to embedding vectors one-to-one, you can use the `Embedding` class as follows:

```
token_embedding = Embedding(
    num_embeddings=vocab.get_vocab_size('tokens'),
    embedding_dim=EMBEDDING_DIM)
```

This will create an `Embedding` instance that takes word IDs and converts them to fixed-length vectors in a one-to-one fashion. The number of unique words this instance can support is given by num_embeddings, which is equal to the size of the tokens vocabulary namespace. The dimensionality of embeddings (i.e., the length of embedded vectors) is given by embedding_dim.

Next, let's define our RNN and convert a variable-length input (a list of embedded words) to a fixed-length vector representation of the input. As we discussed in section 4.1, you can think of an RNN as a neural network structure that consumes a sequence of things (words) and returns a fixed-length vector. AllenNLP abstracts such models into the Seq2VecEncoder class, and you can create an LSTM RNN by using PytorchSeq2VecWrapper as follows:

```
encoder = PytorchSeq2VecWrapper(
    torch.nn.LSTM(EMBEDDING_DIM, HIDDEN_DIM, batch_first=True))
```

A lot is happening here, but essentially this wraps PyTorch's LSTM implementation (torch.nn.LSTM) and makes it pluggable to the rest of the AllenNLP pipeline. The first argument to torch.nn.LSTM() is the dimensionality of the input vector, and the second one is that of LSTM's internal state. The last one, batch_first, specifies the structure of the input/output tensors for batching, but you usually don't have to worry about its details as long as you are using AllenNLP.

> **NOTE** In AllenNLP, everything is batch first, meaning that the first dimension of any tensor is always equal to the number of instances in a batch.

4.4.4 *Building your own model*

Now that we defined all the subcomponents, we are ready to build the model that executes the prediction. Thanks to AllenNLP's well-designed abstractions, you can easily build your model by inheriting AllenNLP's Model class and overriding the forward() method. You don't usually need to be aware of details such as the shapes and dimensions of tensors. The following listing defines the LSTM RNN used for classifying sentences.

Listing 4.1 LSTM sentence classifier

```
@Model.register("lstm_classifier")
class LstmClassifier(Model):                          ◁─┐ AllenNLP models
    def __init__(self,                                   │ inherit Model.
                 embedder: TextFieldEmbedder,
                 encoder: Seq2VecEncoder,
                 vocab: Vocabulary,
                 positive_label: str = '4') -> None:
        super().__init__(vocab)
        self.embedder = embedder
        self.encoder = encoder
                                                    ┌ Creates a linear layer to convert the RNN
        self.linear = torch.nn.Linear(           ◁─┘ output to a vector of another length
            in_features=encoder.get_output_dim(),
            out_features=vocab.get_vocab_size('labels')))
```

```
                    positive_index = vocab.get_token_index(
                        positive_label, namespace='labels')
                    self.accuracy = CategoricalAccuracy()
                    self.f1_measure = F1Measure(positive_index)  ◀─┐

                    self.loss_function = torch.nn.CrossEntropyLoss()  ◀─┐

            def forward(self,
                        tokens: Dict[str, torch.Tensor],
                        label: torch.Tensor = None) -> torch.Tensor:
                mask = get_text_field_mask(tokens)

                embeddings = self.embedder(tokens)
                encoder_out = self.encoder(embeddings, mask)
                logits = self.linear(encoder_out)

                output = {"logits": logits}       ◀─┐
                if label is not None:
                    self.accuracy(logits, label)
                    self.f1_measure(logits, label)
                    output["loss"] = self.loss_function(logits, label)

                return output

        def get_metrics(self, reset: bool = False) -> Dict[str, float]:
            return {'accuracy': self.accuracy.get_metric(reset),   ◀─┐
                    **self.f1_measure.get_metric(reset)}
```

Instances are destructed to individual fields and passed to forward().

F1Measure() requires the label ID for the positive class. '4' means "very positive."

Cross-entropy loss is used for classification tasks. CrossEntropyLoss directly takes logits (no softmax needed).

Output of forward() is a dict, which contains a "loss" key.

Returns accuracy, precision, recall, and F1-measure as the metrics

Every AllenNLP `Model` inherits from PyTorch's `Module` class, meaning you can use PyTorch's low-level operations if necessary. This gives you a lot of flexibility in defining your model while leveraging AllenNLP's high-level abstractions.

4.4.5 Putting it all together

Finally, we finish this section by implementing the entire pipeline to train the sentiment analyzer, as shown next.

Listing 4.2 Training pipeline for the sentiment analyzer

```
EMBEDDING_DIM = 128
HIDDEN_DIM = 128

reader = StanfordSentimentTreeBankDatasetReader()

train_path = 'path/to/sst/dataset/train.txt'
dev_path = 'path/to/sst/dataset/dev.txt'

sampler = BucketBatchSampler(batch_size=32, sorting_keys=["tokens"])
train_data_loader = MultiProcessDataLoader(          ◀─┐
    reader, train_path, batch_sampler=sampler)
dev_data_loader = MultiProcessDataLoader(
    reader, dev_path, batch_sampler=sampler)
```

Defines how to construct the data loaders

```
vocab = Vocabulary.from_instances(chain(train_data_loader.iter_instances(),
                                        dev_data_loader.iter_instances()),
                                  min_count={'tokens': 3})

train_data_loader.index_with(vocab)
dev_data_loader.index_with(vocab)

token_embedding = Embedding(
    num_embeddings=vocab.get_vocab_size('tokens'),
    embedding_dim=EMBEDDING_DIM)

word_embeddings = BasicTextFieldEmbedder({"tokens": token_embedding})

encoder = PytorchSeq2VecWrapper(
    torch.nn.LSTM(EMBEDDING_DIM, HIDDEN_DIM, batch_first=True))

model = LstmClassifier(word_embeddings, encoder, vocab)      ◁──┐ Initializes
                                                                │ the model
optimizer = optim.Adam(model.parameters())          ◁──┐ Defines the
                                                        │ optimizer
trainer = GradientDescentTrainer(               ◁──┐ Initializes
    model=model,                                    │ the trainer
    optimizer=optimizer,
    data_loader=train_data_loader,
    validation_data_loader=dev_data_loader,
    patience=10,
    num_epochs=20,
    cuda_device=-1)

trainer.train()
```

The training pipeline completes when the Trainer instance is created and invoked
with `train()`. You pass all the ingredients that you need for training—the model,
optimizer, data loaders, datasets, and a bunch of hyperparameters.

An optimizer implements an algorithm for adjusting the parameters of the model
to minimize the loss. Here, we are using one type of optimizer called *Adam*, which is a
good "default" optimizer to use as your first option. However, as I mentioned in chapter 2, you often need to experiment with many different optimizers that work best for
your model.

4.5   *Configuring AllenNLP training pipelines*

You may have noticed that very little of listing 4.2 is actually specific to the sentence-
classification problem. Indeed, loading datasets, initializing a model, and plugging an
iterator and an optimizer into the trainer are all common steps across almost every
NLP training pipeline. What if you want to reuse the same training pipeline for many
related tasks without writing the training script from scratch? Also, what if you want to
experiment with different sets of configurations (e.g., different hyperparameters, neural network architectures) and save the exact configurations you tried?

For those problems, AllenNLP provides a convenient framework where you can
write configuration files in the JSON format. The idea is that you write the specifics of
your training pipeline—for example, which dataset reader to use, which models and

their subcomponents to use, and what hyper-parameters to use for training—in a JSON-formatted file (more precisely, AllenNLP uses a format called *Jsonnet*, which is a superset of JSON). Instead of rewriting your model file or the training script, you feed the configuration file to the AllenNLP executable, and the framework takes care of running the training pipeline. If you want to try a different configuration for your model, you simply change the configuration file (or make a new one) and run the pipeline again, without changing the Python code. This is a great practice for making your experiment manageable and reproducible. You need to manage only the configuration files and their results—the same configuration always yields the same result.

A typical AllenNLP configuration file consists of three main parts—the dataset, your model, and the training pipeline. The first part, shown next, specifies which dataset files to use and how:

```
"dataset_reader": {
    "type": "sst_tokens"
  },
  "train_data_path": "https://s3.amazonaws.com/realworldnlpbook/data/
    stanfordSentimentTreebank/trees/train.txt",
  "validation_data_path": "https://s3.amazonaws.com/realworldnlpbook/data/
    stanfordSentimentTreebank/trees/dev.txt"
```

Three keys are in this part: `dataset_reader`, `train_data_path`, and `validation_data_path`. The first key, `dataset_reader`, specifies which `DatasetReader` to use to read the files. Dataset readers, models, and predictors, as well as many other types of modules in AllenNLP, can be registered using the decorator syntax and be referred to from configuration files. For example, if you peek at the following code where `StanfordSentimentTreeBankDatasetReader` is defined

```
@DatasetReader.register("sst_tokens")
class StanfordSentimentTreeBankDatasetReader(DatasetReader):
    ...
```

you notice that it is decorated by `@DatasetReader.register("sst_tokens")`. This registers `StanfordSentimentTreeBankDatasetReader` under the name `sst_tokens`, which allows you to refer it by `"type": "sst_tokens"` from the configuration files.

In the second part of the configuration file, you specify the main model to be trained as follows:

```
"model": {
    "type": "lstm_classifier",

    "embedder": {
      "token_embedders": {
        "tokens": {
          "type": "embedding",
          "embedding_dim": embedding_dim
        }
      }
    },
```

```
  "encoder": {
    "type": "lstm",
    "input_size": embedding_dim,
    "hidden_size": hidden_dim
  }
}
```

As mentioned before, models in AllenNLP can be registered using the decorator syntax and be referred from the configuration files via the `type` key. For example, the `LstmClassifier` class referred here is defined as follows:

```
@Model.register("lstm_classifier")
class LstmClassifier(Model):
    def __init__(self,
                 embedder: TextFieldEmbedder,
                 encoder: Seq2VecEncoder,
                 vocab: Vocabulary,
                 positive_label: str = '4') -> None:
```

Other keys in the model definition JSON `dict` correspond to the names of the parameters of the model constructor. In the previous definition, because `Lstm-Classifier`'s constructor takes two parameters, `word_embeddings` and `encoder` (in addition to `vocab`, which is passed by default and can be omitted, and `positive_label`, for which we are going to use the default value), the model definition has two corresponding keys, the values of which are also model definitions and follow the same convention.

In the final part of the configuration file, the data loader and the trainer are specified. The convention here is similar to the model definition—you specify the type of the class along with other parameters passed to the constructor as follows:

```
"data_loader": {
  "batch_sampler": {
    "type": "bucket",
    "sorting_keys": ["tokens"],
    "padding_noise": 0.1,
    "batch_size" : 32
  }
},
"trainer": {
  "optimizer": "adam",
  "num_epochs": 20,
  "patience": 10
}
```

You can see the full JSON configuration file in the code repository (http://realworld-nlpbook.com/ch4.html#sst-json). Once you define the JSON configuration file, you can simply feed it to the `allennlp` command as follows:

```
allennlp train examples/sentiment/sst_classifier.jsonnet \
    --serialization-dir sst-model \
    --include-package examples.sentiment.sst_classifier
```

The `--serialization-dir` specifies where the trained model (along with additional information such as serialized vocabulary data) is going to be stored. You also need to specify the module path to `LstmClassifier` using `--include-package` so that the configuration file can find the registered class.

As we saw in chapter 2, when the training is finished, you can launch a simple web-based demo interface using the following command:

```
$ allennlp serve \
    --archive-path sst-model/model.tar.gz \
    --include-package examples.sentiment.sst_classifier \
    --predictor sentence_classifier_predictor \
    --field-name sentence
```

4.6 *Case study: Language detection*

In this final section of the chapter, we are going to discuss another scenario—language detection—which can also be formulated as a sentence-classification task. A language-detection system, given a piece of text, detects the language the text is written in. It has a wide range of uses in other NLP applications. For example, a web search engine may want to detect the language a web page is written in before processing and indexing it. Google Translate also switches the source language automatically based on what is typed in the input textbox.

Let's see what this actually looks like. Can you tell the language of each of the following lines? These sentences are all taken from the Tatoeba project (https://tatoeba.org/).

> Contamos con tu ayuda.
>
> Bitte überleg es dir.
>
> Parti için planları tartıştılar.
>
> Je ne sais pas si je peux le faire.
>
> Você estava em casa ontem, não estava?
>
> Ĝi estas rapida kaj efika komunikilo.
>
> Ha parlato per un'ora.
>
> Szeretnék elmenni és meginni egy italt.
>
> Ttwaliɣ nezmer ad nili d imeddukal.

The answer is: Spanish, German, Turkish, French, Portuguese, Esperanto, Italian, Hungarian, and Berber. I chose them from the top 10 most popular languages on Tatoeba that are written in the roman alphabet. You may not be familiar with some of the languages listed here. For those of you who are not, Esperanto is a constructed auxiliary language invented in the late 19th century. Berber is actually a group of related languages spoken in some parts of North Africa that are cousins of Semitic languages such as Arabic.

Maybe you were able to recognize some of these languages, even though you don't actually speak them. I'd like you to step back and think *how* you did it. It's quite interesting that people can do this without actually being able to speak the language, because these languages are all written in the roman alphabet and could look quite similar to each other. You may have recognized some unique diacritic marks (accents) for some of the languages—for example, "ü" for German and "ã" for Portuguese. These are a strong clue for these languages. Or you just knew some words—for example, "ayuda" for Spanish (meaning "help") and "pas" in French ("ne . . . pas" is a French negation syntax). It appears that every language has its own characteristics— be it some unique characters or words—that makes it easy to tell it apart from others. This is starting to sound a lot like a kind of problem that machine learning is good at solving. Can we build an NLP system that can do this automatically? How should we go about building it?

4.6.1   *Using characters as input*

A language detector can also be built in a similar way to the sentiment analyzer. You can use an RNN to read the input text and convert it to some internal representation (hidden states). You can then use a linear layer to convert them to a set of scores corresponding to how likely the text is written in each language. Finally, you can use cross-entropy loss to train the model.

One major difference between the sentiment analyzer and the language detector is how you feed the input into an RNN. When building the sentiment analyzer, we used the Stanford Sentiment Treebank and were able to assume that the input text is always English and already tokenized. But this is not the case for language detection. In fact, you don't even know whether the input text is written in a language that can be tokenized easily—what if the sentence is written in Chinese? Or in Finnish, which is infamous for its complex morphology? You could use a tokenizer that is specific to the language if you know what language it is, but we are building the language detector because we don't know what language it is in the first place. This sounds like a typical chicken-and-egg problem.

To address this issue, we are going to use characters instead of tokens as the input to an RNN. The idea is to break down the input into individual characters, even including whitespace and punctuation, and feed them to the RNN one at a time. Using characters is a common practice used when the input can be better represented as a sequence of characters (such as Chinese, or of an unknown origin), or when you'd like to make the best use of internal structures of words (such as the fastText model we mentioned in chapter 3). The RNN's powerful representational power can still capture interactions between characters and some common words and n-grams mentioned earlier.

4.6.2   *Creating a dataset reader*

For this language-detection task, I created the train and the validation datasets from the Tatoeba project by taking the 10 most popular languages on Tatoeba that use the roman alphabet and by sampling 10,000 sentences for the train set and 1,000 for the validation set. An excerpt of this dataset follows:

```
por   De entre os designers, ele escolheu um jovem ilustrador e deu-lhe a
      tarefa.
por   A apresentação me fez chorar.
tur   Bunu denememize gerek var mı?
tur   O korkutucu bir parçaydı.
ber   Tebḍamt aɣrum-nni ɣef sin, naɣ?
ber   Ad teddud ad twalid taqbuct n umaḍal n tkurt n uḍar deg Brizil?
eng   Tom works at Harvard.
eng   They fixed the flat tire by themselves.
hun   Az arca hirtelen elpirult.
hun   Miért aggodalmaskodsz? Hiszen még csak egy óra van!
epo   Sidiĝu sur la benko.
epo   Tiu ĉi kutime funkcias.
fra   Vu d'avion, cette île a l'air très belle.
fra   Nous boirons à ta santé.
deu   Das Abnehmen fällt ihm schwer.
deu   Tom war etwas besorgt um Maria.
ita   Sono rimasto a casa per potermi riposare.
ita   Le due più grandi invenzioni dell'uomo sono il letto e la bomba atomica:
      il primo ti tiene lontano dalle noie, la seconda le elimina.
spa   He visto la película.
spa   Has hecho los deberes.
```

The first field is a three-letter language code that describes which language the text is written in. The second field is the text itself. The fields are delimited by a tab character. You can obtain the datasets from the code repository (https://github.com/mhagiwara/realworldnlp/tree/master/data/tatoeba).

The first step in building a language detector is to prepare a dataset reader that can read datasets in this format. In the previous example (the sentiment analyzer), because AllenNLP already provides `StanfordSentimentTreeBankDatasetReader`, you just needed to import and use it. In this scenario, however, you need to write your own. Fortunately, writing a dataset reader that can read this particular format is not that difficult. To write a dataset reader, you just need to do the following three things:

- Create your own dataset reader class by inheriting `DatasetReader`.
- Override the `text_to_instance()` method that takes raw text and converts it to an instance object.
- Override the `_read()` method that reads the content of a file and yields instances, by calling `text_to_instance()` above.

The complete dataset reader for the language detector is shown in listing 4.3. We also assume that you already imported necessary modules and classes as follows:

```
from typing import Dict

import numpy as np
import torch
import torch.optim as optim
from allennlp.common.file_utils import cached_path
from allennlp.data.data_loaders import MultiProcessDataLoader
```

```
from allennlp.data.dataset_readers import DatasetReader
from allennlp.data.fields import LabelField, TextField
from allennlp.data.instance import Instance
from allennlp.data.samplers import BucketBatchSampler
from allennlp.data.token_indexers import TokenIndexer, SingleIdTokenIndexer
from allennlp.data.tokenizers.character_tokenizer import CharacterTokenizer
from allennlp.data.vocabulary import Vocabulary
from allennlp.modules.seq2vec_encoders import PytorchSeq2VecWrapper
from allennlp.modules.text_field_embedders import BasicTextFieldEmbedder
from allennlp.modules.token_embedders import Embedding
from allennlp.training import GradientDescentTrainer
from overrides import overrides

from examples.sentiment.sst_classifier import LstmClassifier
```

Listing 4.3   Dataset reader for the language detector

```
class TatoebaSentenceReader(DatasetReader):                     Every new dataset
    def __init__(self,                                          reader inherits
                 token_indexers: Dict[str, TokenIndexer]=None): DatasetReader.
        super().__init__()
        self.tokenizer = CharacterTokenizer()              Uses CharacterTokenizer()
        self.token_indexers = token_indexers or {'tokens': to tokenize text into
    SingleIdTokenIndexer()}                                characters

    @overrides
    def text_to_instance(self, tokens, label=None):      Label will be None
        fields = {}                                       at test time.

        fields['tokens'] = TextField(tokens, self.token_indexers)
        if label:
            fields['label'] = LabelField(label)

        return Instance(fields)

    @overrides
    def _read(self, file_path: str):              If file_path is an URL, returns the
        file_path = cached_path(file_path)        actual path to a cached file on disk
        with open(file_path, "r") as text_file:
            for line in text_file:
                lang_id, sent = line.rstrip().split('\t')
```

Yields instances using
text_to_instance(),   `tokens = self.tokenizer.tokenize(sent)`
defined earlier   ⟶   `yield self.text_to_instance(tokens, lang_id)`

Note that the dataset reader in listing 4.3 uses `CharacterTokenizer()` to tokenize text into characters. Its `tokenize()` method returns a list of tokens, which are AllenNLP objects that represent tokens but actually contain characters in this scenario.

4.6.3   *Building the training pipeline*

Once you build the dataset reader, the rest of the training pipeline looks similar to that of the sentiment analyzer. In fact, we can reuse the `LstmClassifier` class we defined previously without any modification. The entire training pipeline is shown in listing 4.4. You can access the Google Colab notebook of the entire code from here: http://realworldnlpbook.com/ch4.html#langdetect.

Listing 4.4   Training pipeline for the language detector

```
EMBEDDING_DIM = 16
HIDDEN_DIM = 16

reader = TatoebaSentenceReader()
train_path = 'https://s3.amazonaws.com/realworldnlpbook/data/tatoeba/
    sentences.top10langs.train.tsv'
dev_path = 'https://s3.amazonaws.com/realworldnlpbook/data/tatoeba/
    sentences.top10langs.dev.tsv'

sampler = BucketBatchSampler(batch_size=32, sorting_keys=["tokens"])
train_data_loader = MultiProcessDataLoader(
    reader, train_path, batch_sampler=sampler)
dev_data_loader = MultiProcessDataLoader(
    reader, dev_path, batch_sampler=sampler)

vocab = Vocabulary.from_instances(train_data_loader.iter_instances(),
                                  min_count={'tokens': 3})
train_data_loader.index_with(vocab)
dev_data_loader.index_with(vocab)

token_embedding = Embedding(num_embeddings=vocab.get_vocab_size('tokens'),
                            embedding_dim=EMBEDDING_DIM)
word_embeddings = BasicTextFieldEmbedder({"tokens": token_embedding})
encoder = PytorchSeq2VecWrapper(
    torch.nn.LSTM(EMBEDDING_DIM, HIDDEN_DIM, batch_first=True))

model = LstmClassifier(word_embeddings,
                       encoder,
                       vocab,
                       positive_label='eng')

train_dataset.index_with(vocab)
dev_dataset.index_with(vocab)

optimizer = optim.Adam(model.parameters())

trainer = GradientDescentTrainer(
    model=model,
    optimizer=optimizer,
    data_loader=train_data_loader,
    validation_data_loader=dev_data_loader,
    patience=10,
    num_epochs=20,
    cuda_device=-1)

trainer.train()
```

When you run this training pipeline, you'll get the metrics on the dev set that are in the ballpark of the following:

```
accuracy: 0.9461, precision: 0.9481, recall: 0.9490, f1_measure: 0.9485,
    loss: 0.1560
```

This is not bad at all! This means that the trained detector makes only one mistake out of about 20 sentences. Precision of 0.9481 means there's only one false positive (non-English sentence) out of 20 instances that are classified as English. Recall of 0.9490 means there's only one false negative (English sentence that was missed by the detector) out of 20 true English instances.

4.6.4   *Running the detector on unseen instances*

Finally, let's try running the detector we just trained on a set of unseen instances (instances that didn't appear either in the train or the validation sets). It is always a good idea to try feeding a small number of instances to your model and observe how it behaves.

The recommended way for feeding instances into a trained AllenNLP model is to use a predictor, as we did in chapter 2. But here I'd like to do something simpler and instead write a method that, given a piece of text and a model, runs the prediction pipeline. To run a model on arbitrary instances, you can call the model's `forward_on_instances()` method, as shown in the following snippet:

```
def classify(text: str, model: LstmClassifier):
    tokenizer = CharacterTokenizer()
    token_indexers = {'tokens': SingleIdTokenIndexer()}

    tokens = tokenizer.tokenize(text)
    instance = Instance({'tokens': TextField(tokens, token_indexers)})
    logits = model.forward_on_instance(instance)['logits']
    label_id = np.argmax(logits)
    label = model.vocab.get_token_from_index(label_id, 'labels')

    print('text: {}, label: {}'.format(text, label))
```

This method first takes the input (`text` and `model`) and passes it through a tokenizer to create an instance object. Then it calls model's `forward_on_instance()` method to retrieve the logits, the scores for target labels (languages). It gets the label ID that corresponds to the maximum logit value by calling `np.argmax` and then converts it to the label text by using the vocabulary object associated with the model.

When I ran this method on some sentences that are not in the two datasets, I got the following results. Note that the result you get may be different from mine due to some randomness:

```
text: Take your raincoat in case it rains., label: fra
text: Tu me recuerdas a mi padre., label: spa
text: Wie organisierst du das Essen am Mittag?, label: deu
text: Il est des cas où cette règle ne s'applique pas., label: fra
text: Estou fazendo um passeio em um parque., label: por
```

```
text: Ve, postmorgaŭ jam estas la limdato., label: epo
text: Credevo che sarebbe venuto., label: ita
text: Nem tudja, hogy én egy macska vagyok., label: hun
text: Nella ur nli qrib acemma deg tenwalt., label: ber
text: Kurşun kalemin yok, değil mi?, label: tur
```

These predictions are almost perfect, except the very first sentence—it is English, not French. It is surprising that the model makes a mistake on such a seemingly easy sentence while it predicts more difficult languages (such as Hungarian) perfectly. But remember, how difficult the language is for English speakers has nothing to do with how difficult it is for a computer to classify. In fact, some of the "difficult" languages such as Hungarian and Turkish here have very clear signals (accent marks and unique words) that make it easy to detect them. On the other hand, lack of clear signals in the first sentence may have made it more difficult to classify it from other languages.

As a next step, you could try a couple of things: for example, you can tweak some of the hyperparameters to see how the evaluation metrics and the final prediction results change. You can also try a larger number of test instances to see how exactly the mistakes are distributed (e.g., between which two languages). You can also zero in on some of the instances and see why the model made such mistakes. These are all important practices when you are working on real-world NLP applications. I'll discuss these topics in detail in chapter 10.

Summary

- A recurrent neural network (RNN) is a neural network with a loop. It can transform a variable-length input to a fixed-length vector.
- Nonlinearity is a crucial component that makes neural networks truly powerful.
- LSTMs and GRUs are two variants of RNN cells and are easier to train than vanilla RNNs.
- You use accuracy, precision, recall, and F-measure for classification problems.
- AllenNLP provides useful NLP abstractions such as dataset readers, instances, and vocabulary. It also provides a way to configure the training pipeline in the JSON format.
- You can build a language detector as a sentence-classification application similar to the sentiment analyzer.

5

Sequential labeling and language modeling

This chapter covers

- Solving part-of-speech (POS) tagging and named entity recognition (NER) using sequential labeling
- Making RNNs more powerful—multilayer and bidirectional recurrent neural networks (RNNs)
- Capturing statistical properties of language using language models
- Using language models to evaluate and generate natural language text

In this chapter, we are going to discuss sequential labeling—an important NLP framework where systems tag individual words with corresponding labels. Many NLP applications, such as part-of-speech tagging and named entity recognition, can be framed as sequential-labeling tasks. In the second half of the chapter, I'll introduce the concept of language models, one of the most fundamental yet exciting topics in NLP. I'll talk about why they are important and how to use them to evaluate and even generate some natural language text.

5.1   *Introducing sequential labeling*

In the previous chapter, we discussed sentence classification, where the task is to assign some label to a given sentence. Spam filtering, sentiment analysis, and language detection are some concrete examples of sentence classification. Although many real-world NLP problems can be formulated as a sentence-classification task, this method can also be quite limited, because the model, by definition, allows us to assign only a single label to the whole sentence. But what if you wanted something more granular? For example, what if you wanted to do something with individual words, not just with the sentence? The most typical scenario you encounter is when you want to extract something from the sentence, which cannot be easily solved by sentence classification. This is where sequential labeling comes into play.

5.1.1   *What is sequential labeling?*

Sequential labeling is an NLP task where, given a sequence such as a sentence, the NLP system assigns a label to each element (e.g., word) of the input sequence. This contrasts with sentence classification, where a label is assigned just to the input *sentence*. Figure 5.1 illustrates this contrast.

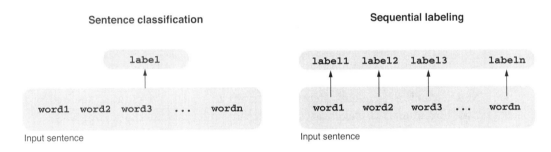

Figure 5.1   Sentence classification vs. sequential labeling

But why is this even a good idea? When do we need a label per word? A typical scenario where sequential labeling comes in handy is when you want to analyze a sentence and produce some linguistic information per word. For example, part-of-speech (POS) tagging, which I mentioned in chapter 1, produces a POS tag such as nouns, verbs, and prepositions for each word in the input sentence and is a perfect match for sequential labeling. See figure 5.2 for an illustration.

POS tagging is one of the most fundamental, important NLP tasks. Many English words (and words in many other languages as well) are ambiguous, meaning that they have multiple possible interpretations. For example, the word "book" can be used to describe a physical or electronic object consisting of pages ("I read a book") or an

Part-of-speech (POS) tagging

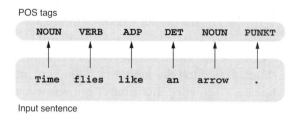

Figure 5.2 Part-of-speech (POS)
tagging using sequential labeling

action for reserving something ("I need to book a flight"). Downstream NLP tasks, such as parsing and classification, benefit greatly by knowing what each appearance of "book" actually means to process the input sentence. If you were to build a speech synthesis system, you must know the POS of certain words to pronounce them correctly—"lead" as a noun (a kind of metal) rhymes with "bed," whereas "lead" as a verb (to direct, guide) rhymes with "bead." POS tagging is an important first step toward solving this ambiguity.

Another scenario is when you want to extract some pieces of information from a sentence. For example, if you want to extract subsequences (phrases) such as noun phrases and verb phrases, this is also a sequential-labeling task. How can you achieve extraction using labeling? The idea is to mark the beginning and the end (or the beginning and the continuation, depending on how you represent it) of the desired piece of information using labeling. An example of this is *named entity recognition* (NER), which is a task to identify mentions to real-world entities, such as proper nouns and numerical expressions, from a sentence (illustrated in figure 5.3.).

Named entity recognition (NER)

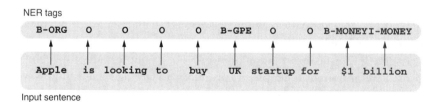

Figure 5.3 Named entity recognition (NER) using sequential labeling

Notice that all the words that are not part of any named entities are tagged as O (for "Outside"). For now, you can ignore some cryptic labels in figure 5.3 such as B-GPE and I-MONEY. I'll talk more about how to formulate NER as a sequential-labeling problem in section 5.4.

5.1.2 Using RNNs to encode sequences

In sentence classification, we used recurrent neural networks (RNNs) to convert an input of variable length into a fixed-length vector. The fixed-length vector, which is converted to a set of "scores" by a linear layer, captures the information about the input sentence that is necessary for deriving the sentence label. As a reminder, what this RNN does can be represented by the following pseudocode and the diagram shown in figure 5.4:

```
def rnn_vec(words):
    state = init_state()
    for word in words:
        state = update(state, word)
    return state
```

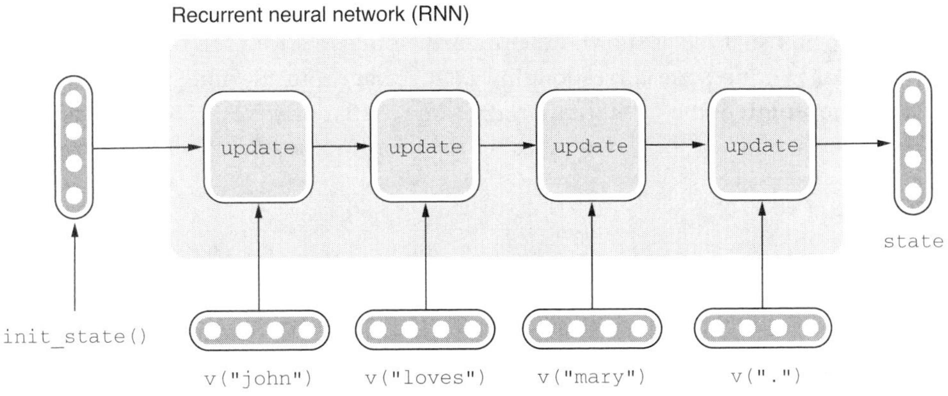

Figure 5.4 Recurrent neural network (RNN) for sentence classification

What kind of neural network could be used for sequential tagging? We seem to need some information for every input word in the sentence, not just at the end. If you look at the pseudocode for rnn_vec() carefully, you can notice that we already have information for every word in the input, which is captured by state. The function just happens to return only the final value of state, but there is no reason we can't store intermediate values of state and return them as a list instead, as in the following function:

```
def rnn_seq(words):
    state = init_state()
    states = []
    for word in words:
        state = update(state, word)
        states.append(state)
    return states
```

If you apply this function to the "time flies" example shown in figure 5.2 and unroll it—that is, write it without using a loop—it will look like the following:

```
state = init_state()
states = []
state = update(state, v("time"))
states.append(state)
state = update(state, v("flies"))
states.append(state)
state = update(state, v("like"))
states.append(state)
state = update(state, v("an"))
states.append(state)
state = update(state, v("arrow"))
states.append(state)
state = update(state, v("."))
states.append(state)
```

Note that v() here is a function that returns the embedding for the given word. This can be visualized as shown in figure 5.5. Notice that for each input word word, the network produces the corresponding state that captures some information about word. The length of the list states is the same as that of words. The final value of states, that is, states[-1], is identical to the return value of rnn_vec() from earlier.

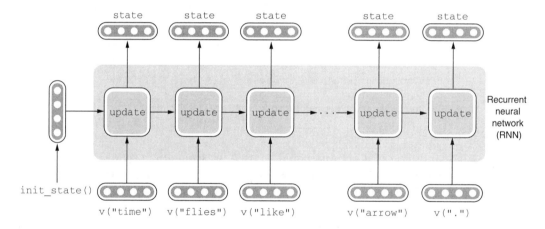

Figure 5.5   Recurrent neural network (RNN) for sequential labeling

If you think of this RNN as a black box, it takes a sequence of something (e.g., word embeddings) and converts it to a sequence of vectors that encode some information about individual words in the input, so this architecture is called a *Seq2Seq* (for "sequence-to-sequence") encoder in AllenNLP.

The final step is to apply a linear layer to each state of this RNN to derive a set of scores that correspond to how likely each label is. If this is a part-of-speech tagger, we need one score for the label NOUN, another for VERB, and so on for each and every word. This conversion is illustrated in figure 5.6. Note that the same linear layer (with the same set of parameters) is applied to every `state`.

To sum up, we can use almost the same structure for sequential labeling as the one we used for sentence classification. The only difference is the former produces a hidden state per each word, not just per sentence. To derive scores used for determining labels, a linear layer is applied to every hidden state.

5.1.3 *Implementing a Seq2Seq encoder in AllenNLP*

AllenNLP implements an abstract class called `Seq2SeqEncoder` for abstracting all Seq2Seq encoders that take in a sequence of vectors and return another sequence of modified vectors. In theory, you can inherit the

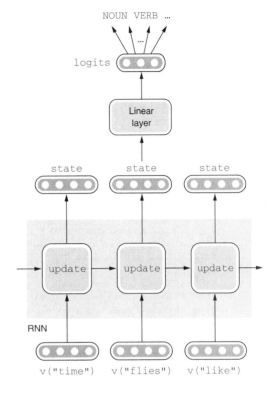

Figure 5.6   Applying a linear layer to RNN

class and implement your own Seq2Seq encoder. In practice, however, you most likely will use one of the off-the-shelf implementations that PyTorch/AllenNLP provide, such as LSTM and GRU. Remember, when we built the encoder for the sentiment analyzer, we used PyTorch's built-in `torch.nn.LSTM` and wrapped it with `PytorchSeq2Vec-Wrapper`, as shown next, which makes it compatible with AllenNLP's abstraction:

```
encoder = PytorchSeq2VecWrapper(
    torch.nn.LSTM(EMBEDDING_DIM, HIDDEN_DIM, batch_first=True))
```

AllenNLP also implements `PytorchSeq2SeqWrapper`, which takes one of PyTorch's built-in RNN implementations and makes it compliant with AllenNLP's `Seq2Seq-Encoder`, so there's very little change you need to initialize a Seq2Seq encoder, as shown here:

```
encoder = PytorchSeq2SeqWrapper(
    torch.nn.LSTM(EMBEDDING_DIM, HIDDEN_DIM, batch_first=True))
```

That's it! There are a couple more things to note, but there's surprisingly few changes you need to make to the sentence classification code to make it work for sequential labeling. This is thanks to the powerful abstraction of AllenNLP—most of the time you need to worry only about how individual components interact with each other, not about how these components work internally.

5.2   *Building a part-of-speech tagger*

In this section, we are going to build our first sequential-labeling application—a part-of-speech (POS) tagger. You can see the entire code for this section on the Google Colab notebook (http://realworldnlpbook.com/ch5.html#pos-nb). We assume that you have already imported all necessary dependencies as follows:

```
from itertools import chain
from typing import Dict

import numpy as np
import torch
import torch.optim as optim

from allennlp.data.data_loaders import MultiProcessDataLoader
from allennlp.data.samplers import BucketBatchSampler
from allennlp.data.vocabulary import Vocabulary
from allennlp.models import Model
from allennlp.modules.seq2seq_encoders import Seq2SeqEncoder,
    PytorchSeq2SeqWrapper
from allennlp.modules.text_field_embedders import TextFieldEmbedder,
    BasicTextFieldEmbedder
from allennlp.modules.token_embedders import Embedding
from allennlp.nn.util import get_text_field_mask,
    sequence_cross_entropy_with_logits
from allennlp.training.metrics import CategoricalAccuracy
from allennlp.training import GradientDescentTrainer
from
    allennlp_models.structured_prediction.dataset_readers.universal_dependen
    cies import UniversalDependenciesDatasetReader

from realworldnlp.predictors import UniversalPOSPredictor
```

5.2.1   *Reading a dataset*

As we saw in chapter 1, a *part of speech* (POS) is a category of words that share similar grammatical properties. Part-of-speech tagging is the process of tagging each word in a sentence with a corresponding part-of-speech tag. A training set for POS tagging follows a tagset, which is a set of predefined POS tags for the language.

To train a POS tagger, we need a dataset where every word in every sentence is tagged with its corresponding POS tag. In this experiment, we are going to use the English Universal Dependencies (UD) dataset. Universal Dependencies is a language-independent dependency grammar framework developed by a group of researchers. UD also defines a tagset called the *Universal part-of-speech tagset* (http://realworldnlp-book.com/ch1.html#universal-pos). The use of UD and the Universal POS tagset has been very popular in the NLP community, especially for language-independent tasks and models such as POS tagging and parsing.

We are going to use one subcorpus of UD called *A Gold Standard Universal Dependencies Corpus for English*, which is built on top of the English Web Treebank (EWT) (http://realworldnlpbook.com/ch5.html#ewt) and can be used under a Creative Commons license. You can download the entire dataset from the dataset page (http://realworldnlpbook.com/ch5.html#ewt-data), if needed.

Universal Dependencies datasets are distributed in a format called the *CoNLL-U format* (http://universaldependencies.org/docs/format.html). The AllenNLP models package already implements a dataset reader called `UniversalDependencies-DatasetReader` that reads datasets in this format and returns a collection of instances that include information like word forms, POS tags, and dependency relationship, so all you need to do is initialize and use it as follows:

```
reader = UniversalDependenciesDatasetReader()
train_path = ('https://s3.amazonaws.com/realworldnlpbook/data/'
              'ud-treebanks-v2.3/UD_English-EWT/en_ewt-ud-train.conllu')
dev_path = ('https://s3.amazonaws.com/realworldnlpbook/'
            'data/ud-treebanks-v2.3/UD_English-EWT/en_ewt-ud-dev.conllu')
```

Also, don't forget to initialize data loaders and a `Vocabulary` instance, too, as shown next:

```
sampler = BucketBatchSampler(batch_size=32, sorting_keys=["words"])
train_data_loader = MultiProcessDataLoader(
    reader, train_path, batch_sampler=sampler)
dev_data_loader = MultiProcessDataLoader(
    reader, dev_path, batch_sampler=sampler)

vocab = Vocabulary.from_instances(chain(train_data_loader.iter_instances(),
                                        dev_data_loader.iter_instances()))
train_data_loader.index_with(vocab)
dev_data_loader.index_with(vocab)
```

5.2.2 Defining the model and the loss

The next step for building a POS tagger is to define the model. In the previous section, we already saw that you can initialize a Seq2Seq encoder with very little modification using AllenNLP's built-in `PytorchSeq2VecWrapper`. Let's define other components (word embeddings and LSTM) and some variables necessary for the model as follows:

```
EMBEDDING_SIZE = 128
HIDDEN_SIZE = 128

token_embedding = Embedding(num_embeddings=vocab.get_vocab_size('tokens'),
                            embedding_dim=EMBEDDING_SIZE)
word_embeddings = BasicTextFieldEmbedder({"tokens": token_embedding})

lstm = PytorchSeq2SeqWrapper(
    torch.nn.LSTM(EMBEDDING_SIZE, HIDDEN_SIZE, batch_first=True))
```

Now we are ready to define the body of the POS tagger model, as shown here.

Listing 5.1   POS tagger model

```python
class LstmTagger(Model):
    def __init__(self,
                 embedder: TextFieldEmbedder,
                 encoder: Seq2SeqEncoder,
                 vocab: Vocabulary) -> None:
        super().__init__(vocab)
        self.embedder = embedder
        self.encoder = encoder

        self.linear = torch.nn.Linear(
            in_features=encoder.get_output_dim(),
            out_features=vocab.get_vocab_size('pos'))

        self.accuracy = CategoricalAccuracy()

    def forward(self,
                words: Dict[str, torch.Tensor],
                pos_tags: torch.Tensor = None,
                **args) -> Dict[str, torch.Tensor]:
        mask = get_text_field_mask(words)

        embeddings = self.embedder(words)
        encoder_out = self.encoder(embeddings, mask)
        tag_logits = self.linear(encoder_out)

        output = {"tag_logits": tag_logits}
        if pos_tags is not None:
            self.accuracy(tag_logits, pos_tags, mask)
            output["loss"] = sequence_cross_entropy_with_logits(
                tag_logits, pos_tags, mask)

        return output

    def get_metrics(self, reset: bool = False) -> Dict[str, float]:
        return {"accuracy": self.accuracy.get_metric(reset)}
```

We use accuracy to evaluate the POS tagger.

We need **args to capture unnecessary instance fields that AllenNLP automatically destructures.

The Seq2Seq encoder is trained using a sequence cross-entropy loss.

Notice that the code shown in listing 5.1 is very similar to the code for `LstmClassifier` (listing 4.1), which we used for building a sentiment analyzer. In fact, except for some naming differences, only one fundamental difference exists—the type of loss function.

Recall that we used a loss function called *cross entropy* for sentence classification tasks, which basically measures how far apart two distributions are. If the model produces a high probability for the true label, the loss will be low. Otherwise, it will be high. But this assumed that there is only one label per sentence. How can we measure how far the prediction is from the true label when there is one label per word?

The answer is: still use the cross entropy, but average it over all the elements in the input sequence. For POS tagging, you compute the cross entropy per word as if it were an individual classification task, sum it over all the words in the input sentence, and divide by the length of the sentence. This will give you a number reflecting how well your model is predicting the POS tags for the input sentence on average. See figure 5.7 for an illustration.

As for the evaluation metric, POS taggers are usually evaluated using accuracy, which we are going to use here. Average human performance on POS tagging is around 97%, whereas the state-of-the-art POS taggers slightly outperform this (http://realworldnlp book.com/ch5.html#pos-sota). You need to note that accuracy

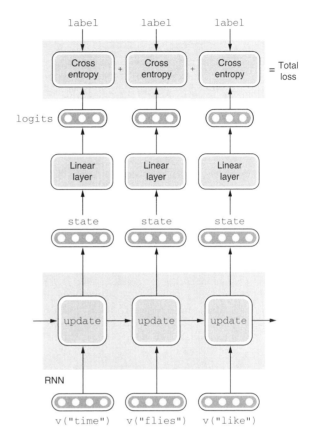

Figure 5.7 Computing loss for sequence

is not without a problem, however—assume there is a relatively rare POS tag (e.g., SCONJ, which means subordinating conjugation), which accounts for only 2% of total tokens, and a POS tagger messes it up every time it appears. If the tagger gets the rest of the tokens all correct, it still achieves 98% accuracy.

5.2.3 Building the training pipeline

Now we are ready to move on to building the training pipeline. As with the previous tasks, training pipelines in AllenNLP look very similar to each other. See the next listing for the training code.

Listing 5.2 Training pipeline for POS tagger

```
model = LstmTagger(word_embeddings, encoder, vocab)

optimizer = optim.Adam(model.parameters())
```

```
trainer = GradientDescentTrainer(
    model=model,
    optimizer=optimizer,
    data_loader=train_data_loader,
    validation_data_loader=dev_data_loader,
    patience=10,
    num_epochs=10,
    cuda_device=-1)

trainer.train()
```

When you run this code, AllenNLP alternates between two phases: 1) training the model using the train set, and 2) evaluating it using the validation set for each epoch, while monitoring the loss and accuracy on both sets. Validation set accuracy plateaus around 88% after several epochs. After the training is over, you can run the model for an unseen instance as shown next:

```
predictor = UniversalPOSPredictor(model, reader)
tokens = ['The', 'dog', 'ate', 'the', 'apple', '.']
logits = predictor.predict(tokens)['tag_logits']
tag_ids = np.argmax(logits, axis=-1)

print([vocab.get_token_from_index(tag_id, 'pos') for tag_id in tag_ids])
```

This code uses `UniversalPOSPredictor`, a predictor that I wrote for this particular POS tagger. Although its details are not important, you can look at its code if you are interested (http://realworldnlpbook.com/ch5#upos-predictor). If successful, this will show a list of POS tags: [`'DET'`, `'NOUN'`, `'VERB'`, `'DET'`, `'NOUN'`, `'PUNCT'`], which is indeed a correct POS tag sequence for the input sentence.

5.3   *Multilayer and bidirectional RNNs*

As we've seen so far, RNNs are a powerful tool for building NLP applications. In this section, I talk about their structural variants—multilayer and bidirectional RNNs—which are even more powerful components for building highly accurate NLP applications.

5.3.1   *Multilayer RNNs*

If you look at an RNN as a black box, it is a neural network structure that converts a sequence of vectors (word embeddings) into another sequence of vectors (hidden states). The input and output sequences are of the same length, usually the number of input tokens. This means that you can repeat this "encoding" process multiple times by stacking RNNs on top of each other. The output (hidden states) of one RNN becomes the input of another RNN that is just above the previous one. A substructure (such as a single RNN) of a bigger neural network is called a *layer*, because you can stack them together like layers. The structure of a two-layered RNN is shown in figure 5.8.

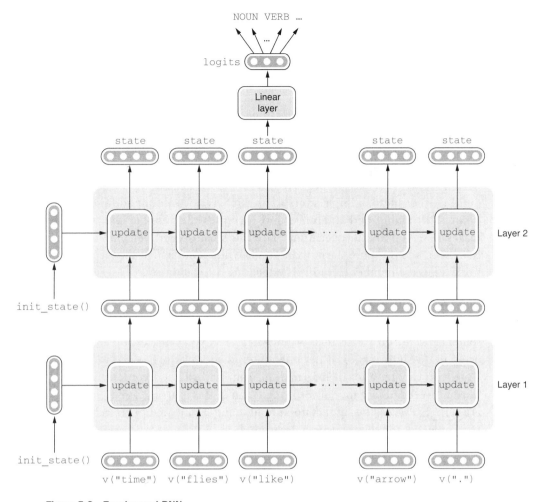

Figure 5.8 Two-layered RNN

Why is this a good idea? If you think of a layer of RNN as a machine that takes in something concrete (e.g., word embeddings) and extracts some abstract concepts (e.g., scores for POS tags), you can expect that, by repeating this process, RNNs are able to extract increasingly more abstract concepts as the number of layers increases. Although not fully theoretically proven, many real-world NLP applications use multi-layer RNNs. For example, Google's Neural Machine Translation (NMT) system uses a stacked RNN consisting of eight layers for both the encoder and the decoder (http://realworldnlpbook.com/ch5.html#nmt-paper).

To use multilayer RNNs in your NLP application, all you need to do is change how the encoder is initialized. Specifically, you need to specify only the number of layers using the num_layers parameter, as shown in the next code snippet, and AllenNLP makes sure that the rest of the training pipeline works as-is:

```
encoder = PytorchSeq2SeqWrapper(
    torch.nn.LSTM(
        EMBEDDING_SIZE, HIDDEN_SIZE, num_layers=2, batch_first=True))
```

If you change this line and rerun the POS tagger training pipeline, you will notice that accuracy on the validation set is almost unchanged or slightly lower than the previous model with a single-layer RNN. This is not surprising—information required for POS tagging is mostly superficial, such as the identity of the word being tagged and neighboring words. Very rarely does it require deep understanding of the input sentence. On the other hand, adding layers to an RNN is not without additional cost. It slows down the training and inference and increases the number of parameters, which makes it susceptible to overfitting. For this small experiment, adding layers to the RNN seems to do more harm than good. When you change the structure of the network, always remember to verify its effect on a validation set.

5.3.2   *Bidirectional RNNs*

So far, we've been feeding words to RNNs as they come in—from the beginning of the sentence to the end. This means that when an RNN is processing a word, it can leverage only the information it has encountered so far, which is the word's left context. True, you can get a lot of information from a word's left context. For example, if a word is preceded by a modal verb (e.g., "can"), it is a strong signal that the next word is a verb. However, the right context holds a lot of information as well. For example, if you know that the next word is a determiner (e.g., "a"), it is a strong signal that "book" on its left is a verb, not a noun.

Bidirectional RNNs (or simply biRNNs) solve this problem by combining two RNNs with opposite directions. A forward RNN is a forward-facing RNN that we've been using so far in this book—it scans the input sentence left to right and uses the input word and all the information on its left to update the state. A backward RNN, on the other hand, scans the input sentence right to left. It uses the input word and all the information on its right to update the state. This is equivalent to flipping the order of the input sentence and feeding it to a forward RNN. The final hidden states produced by biRNNs are concatenations of hidden states from the forward and backward RNNs. See figure 5.9 for an illustration.

Let's use a concrete example to illustrate this. Assume the input sentence is "time flies like an arrow" and you'd like to know the POS tag for the word "like" in the middle of this sentence. The forward RNN processes "time" and "flies," and by the time it reaches "like," its internal state (A in figure 5.9) encodes all the information about "time flies like." Similarly, the backward RNN processes "arrow" and "an," and by the time it reaches "like," the internal state (B in figure 5.9) has encoded all the information about "like an arrow." The internal state from the biRNN for "like" is the

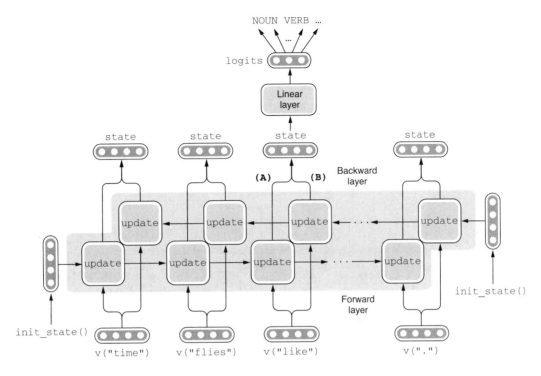

Figure 5.9 Bidirectional RNN

concatenation of these two states (A + B). You literally stitch together two vectors—no mathematical operations involved. As a result, the internal state for "like" encodes all the information from the entire sentence. This is a great improvement over just knowing half the sentence!

Implementing a biRNN is similarly easy—you just need to add the `bidirectional=True` flag when initializing the RNN as follows:

```
encoder = PytorchSeq2SeqWrapper(
    torch.nn.LSTM(
        EMBEDDING_SIZE, HIDDEN_SIZE, bidirectional=True, batch_first=True))
```

If you train the POS tagger with this change, the validation set accuracy will jump from ~88% to 91%. This implies that incorporating the information on both sides of the word is effective for POS tagging.

Note that you can combine the two techniques introduced in this section by stacking bidirectional RNNs. The output from one layer of biRNN (concatenation of a forward and a backward layer) becomes the input to another layer of biRNN (see figure 5.10). You can implement this by specifying both flags—`num_layers` and `bidirectional`—when initializing the RNN in PyTorch/AllenNLP.

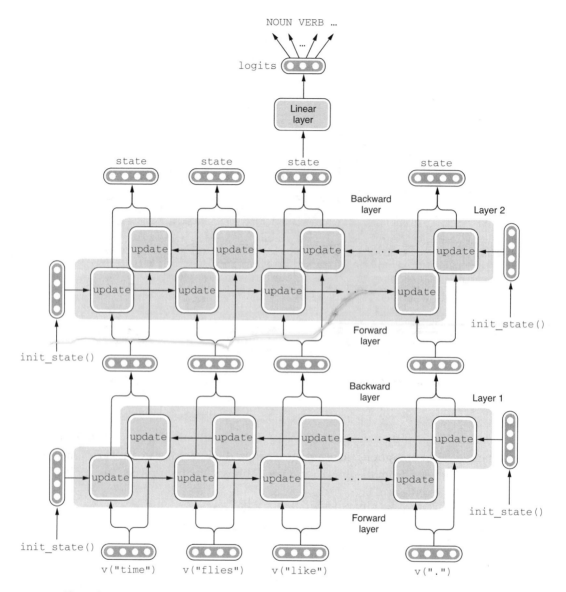

Figure 5.10 Two-layered bidirectional RNN

5.4   *Named entity recognition*

Sequential labeling can be applied to many information extraction tasks, not just to part-of-speech tagging. In this section, I'll introduce the task of named entity recognition (NER) and demonstrate how to build an NER tagger using sequential labeling. The code for this section can be viewed and executed via the Google Colab platform (http://realworldnlpbook.com/ch5#ner-nb).

5.4.1 *What is named entity recognition?*

As mentioned earlier, named entities are mentions of real-world entities such as proper nouns. Common named entities that are usually covered by NER systems include the following:

- Personal name (PER): Alan Turing, Lady Gaga, Elon Musk
- Organization (ORG): Google, United Nations, Giants
- Location (LOC): Mount Rainer, Bali Island, Nile
- Geopolitical entity (GPE): UK, San Francisco, Southeast Asia

However, different NER systems deal with different sets of named entities. The concept of named entities is a bit overloaded in NLP to mean any mentions that are of interest to the application's user. For example, in the medical domain, you may want to extract mentions to names of drugs and chemical compounds. In the financial domain, companies, products, and stock symbols may be of interest. In many domains, numerical and temporal expressions are also considered.

Identifying named entities is in itself important, because named entities (who, what, where, when, and so on) are often what most people are interested in. But NER is also an important first step for many other NLP applications. One such task is *relation extraction*: extracting all relations between named entities from the given document. For example, given a press release document, you may want to extract an event described in the release, such as which company purchased which other company for what price. This often assumes that all the parties are already identified via NER. Another task that is closely related to NER is *entity linking*, where mentions of named entities are linked to some knowledge base, such as Wikipedia. When Wikipedia is used as a knowledge base, entity linking is also called *Wikification*.

But you may be wondering, what's so difficult about simply extracting named entities? If they are just proper nouns, can you simply compile a dictionary of, say, all the celebrities (or all the countries, or whatever you are interested in) and use it? The idea is, whenever the system encounters a noun, it would run the name through this dictionary and tag the mention if it appears in it. Such dictionaries are called *gazetteers*, and many NER systems do use them as a component.

However, relying solely on such dictionaries has one major issue—*ambiguity*. Earlier we saw that a single word type could have multiple parts of speech (e.g., "book" as a noun and a verb), and named entities are no exception. For example, "Georgia" can be the name of a country, a US state, towns and communities across the United States (Georgia, Indiana; Georgia, Nebraska), a film, a number of songs, ships, and a personal name. Simple words like "book" could also be named entities, including: Book (a community in Louisiana), Book/Books (a surname), The Books (an American band), and so on. Simply matching mentions against dictionaries would tell you nothing about their identities if they are ambiguous.

Fortunately, sentences often offer clues that can be used to *disambiguate* the mentions. For example, if the sentence reads "I live in Georgia," it's usually a strong signal that "Georgia" is a name of a place, not a film or a person's name. NER systems use a combination of signals about the mentions themselves (e.g., whether they are in a pre-defined dictionary) and about their context (whether they are preceded or followed by certain words) to determine their tags.

5.4.2   Tagging spans

Unlike POS tagging, where each word is assigned a POS tag, mentions to named entities can span over more than one word, for example, "the United States" and "World Trade Organization." A *span* in NLP is simply a range over one or more contiguous words. How can we use the same sequential tagging framework to model spans?

A common practice in NLP is to use some form of encoding to convert spans into per-word tags. The most common encoding scheme used in NER is called *IOB2 tagging*. It represents spans by a combination of the positional tag and the category tag. Three types of positional tags follow:

- B (Beginning): assigned to the first (or the only) token of a span
- I (Inside): assigned to all but the first token of a span
- O (Outside): assigned to all words outside of any spans

Now, let's take a look at the NER example we saw earlier and is shown in figure 5.11. The token "Apple" is the first (and the only) token of ORG (for "organization"), and it is assigned a B-ORG tag. Similarly, "UK", the first and the only token of GPE (for "geo-political entity"), is assigned B-GPE. For "$1" and "billion," the first and the second tokens of a monetary expression (MONEY), B-MONEY and I-MONEY are assigned, respectively. All the other tokens are given O.

Named entity recognition (NER)

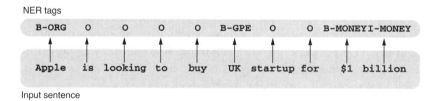

Figure 5.11   Named entity recognition (NER) using sequential labeling

The rest of the pipeline for solving NER is very similar to that of part-of-speech tagging: both are concerned with assigning an appropriate tag for each word and can be solved by RNNs. In the next section, we are going to build a simple NER system using neural networks.

5.4.3   Implementing a named entity recognizer

To build an NER system, we use the Annotated Corpus for Named Entity Recognition prepared by Abhinav Walia published on Kaggle (http://realworldnlpbook.com/

ch5.html#ner-data). In what follows, I'm going to assume that you downloaded and expanded the dataset under data/entity-annotated-corpus. Alternatively, you can use the copy of the dataset I uploaded to S3 (http://realworldnlpbook.com/ch5.html#ner-data-s3), which is what the following code does. I wrote a dataset reader for this dataset (http://realworldnlpbook.com/ch5.html#ner-reader), so you can simply import (or copy and paste) it and use it:

```
reader = NERDatasetReader('https://s3.amazonaws.com/realworldnlpbook/'
                          'data/entity-annotated-corpus/ner_dataset.csv')
```

Because the dataset is not separated into train, validation, and test sets, the dataset reader will separate it into train and validation splits for you. All you need to do is specify which split you want when you initialize data loaders, as shown here:

```
sampler = BucketBatchSampler(batch_size=16, sorting_keys=["tokens"])
train_data_loader = MultiProcessDataLoader(
    reader, 'train', batch_sampler=sampler)
dev_data_loader = MultiProcessDataLoader(
    reader, 'dev', batch_sampler=sampler)
```

The RNN-based sequential tagging model and the rest of the training pipeline look almost the same as the previous example (POS tagger). The only difference is how we evaluate our NER model. Because most of the tags for a typical NER dataset are simply "O," using tag accuracy is misleading—a stupid system that tags everything "O" would achieve very high accuracy. Instead, NER is usually evaluated as an information extraction task, where the goal is to extract named entities from texts, not just to tag them. We'd like to evaluate NER systems based on the "cleanness" of retrieved named entities (how many of them are actual entities) and their "completeness" (how many of actual entities the system was able to retrieve). Does any of this sound familiar to you? Yes, these are the definition of recall and precision we talked about in section 4.3. Because there are usually multiple types of named entities, these metrics (precision, recall, and F1-measure) are computed per entity type.

> **NOTE** If these metrics are computed while ignoring entity types, it's called a *micro average*. For example, the micro-averaged precision is the total number of true positives of all types divided by the total number of retrieved named entities regardless of the type. On the other hand, if these metrics are computed per entity type and are then averaged, it's called a *macro average*. For example, if the precision for PER and GPE is 80% and 90%, respectively, its macro average is 85%. What AllenNLP computes in the following is the micro average.

AllenNLP implements SpanBasedF1Measure, which computes per-type metrics (precision, recall, and F1-measure) as well as the average. You can define the metric in __init__() of your model as follows:

```
self.f1 = SpanBasedF1Measure(vocab, tag_namespace='labels')
```

And use it to get metrics during training and validation, as shown next:

```
def get_metrics(self, reset: bool = False) -> Dict[str, float]:
    f1_metrics = self.f1.get_metric(reset)
    return {'accuracy': self.accuracy.get_metric(reset),
            'prec': f1_metrics['precision-overall'],
            'rec': f1_metrics['recall-overall'],
            'f1': f1_metrics['f1-measure-overall']}
```

If you run this training pipeline, you get an accuracy around 0.97, and precision, recall, F1-measure will all hover around 0.83. You can also use the `predict()` method to obtain named entity tags for an unseen sentence as

```
tokens = ['Apple', 'is', 'looking', 'to', 'buy', 'UK', 'startup',
          'for', '$1', 'billion', '.']
labels = predict(tokens, model)
print(' '.join('{}/{}'.format(token, label)
               for token, label in zip(tokens, labels)))
```

which produces the following:

```
Apple/B-org is/O looking/O to/O buy/O UK/O startup/O for/O $1/O billion/O ./O
```

This is not perfect—the NER tagger got the first named entity ("Apple") correct but missed two others ("UK" and "$1 billion"). If you look at the training data, the mention "UK" never appears, and no monetary values are tagged. It is not surprising that the system is struggling to tag entities that it has never seen before. In NLP (and also machine learning in general), the characteristic of the test instances needs to match that of the train data for the model to be fully effective.

5.5 Modeling a language

In this section, I'll switch gears a little bit and introduce *language models,* which is one of the most important concepts in NLP. We'll discuss what they are, why they are important, and how to train them using the neural network components we've introduced so far.

5.5.1 What is a language model?

Imagine you are asked to predict what word comes next given a partial sentence: "My trip to the beach was ruined by bad ___." What words could come next? Many things could ruin a trip to a beach, but most likely it's bad weather. Maybe it's bad-mannered people at the beach, or maybe it's bad food that the person had eaten before the trip, but most would agree that "weather" is a likely word that comes after this partial sentence. Few other nouns (*people, food, dogs*) and words of other parts of speech (*be, the, run, green*) are as appropriate as "weather" in this context.

What you just did is to assign some belief (or probability) to an English sentence. You just compared several alternatives and judged how likely they are as English sentences. Most people would agree that the probability of "My trip to the beach was ruined by bad weather" is a lot higher than "My trip to the beach was ruined by bad dogs."

Formally, a *language model* is a statistical model that gives a probability to a piece of text. An English language model would assign higher probabilities to sentences that look like English. For example, an English language model would give a higher probability to "My trip to the beach was ruined by bad weather" than it does to "My trip to the beach was ruined by bad dogs" or even "by weather was trip my bad beach the ruined to." The more grammatical and the more "sense" the sentence makes, the higher the probability is.

5.5.2 *Why are language models useful?*

You may be wondering what use such a statistical model has. Although predicting the next word might come in handy when you are answering fill-in-the-blank questions for an exam, what particular roles do language models play in NLP?

The answer is, it is essential for any systems that generate natural language. For example, machine translation systems, which generate a sentence in a language given a sentence in another language, would benefit greatly from high-quality language models. Why? Let's say we'd like to translate a Spanish sentence "Está lloviendo fuerte" into English ("It is raining hard"). The last word "fuerte" has several English equivalents— *strong, sharp, loud, heavy,* and so on. How would you determine which English equivalent is the most appropriate in this context? There could be many approaches to solve this problem, but one of the simplest is to use an English language model and rerank several different translation candidates. Assuming you've finished translating up to "It is raining," you would simply replace the word "fuerte" with all the equivalents you can find in a Spanish–English dictionary, which generates "It is raining strong," "It is raining sharp," "It is raining loud," "It is raining hard." Then all you need to do is ask the language model which one of these candidates has the highest probability.

> **NOTE** In fact, neural machine translation models can be thought of as a variation of a language model that generates sentences in the target language conditioned on its input (sentences in the source language). Such a language model is a called a *conditional language model* as opposed to an *unconditional language model,* which we discuss here. We'll discuss machine translation models in chapter 6.

A similar situation arises in speech recognition, too, which is another task that generates text given spoken audio input. For example, if somebody uttered "You're right," how would a speech recognition system know it's actually "you're right?" Because "you're" and "your" can have the same pronunciation, and so can "right" and "write" and even "Wright" and "rite," the system output could be any one of "You're write," "You're Wright," "You're rite," "Your right," "Your write," "Your Wright," and so on. Again, the simplest approach to resolving this ambiguity is to use a language model. An English language model would properly rerank these candidates and determine "you're right" is the most likely transcription.

In fact, humans do this type of disambiguation all the time, though unconsciously. When you are having a conversation with somebody else at a large party, the actual audio signal you receive is often very noisy. Most people can still understand each other without any issues because people's language models help them "correct" what you hear and interpolate any missing parts. You'll notice this most if you try to converse in a less proficient, second language—you'd have a lot harder time understanding the other person in a noisy environment, because your language model is not as good as your first language's.

5.5.3   *Training an RNN language model*

At this point, you may be wondering what the connection is between predicting the next word and assigning a probability to a sentence. These two are actually equivalent. Instead of explaining the theory behind it, which requires you to understand some math (especially probability theory), I'll attempt an intuitive example next without going into mathematical details.

Imagine you want to estimate the chance of tomorrow's weather being rainy and the ground wet. Let's simplify this and assume there are only two types of weather, sunny and rainy. There are only two outcomes for the ground: dry or wet. This is equivalent to estimating the probably of a sequence: [rain, wet].

Further assume that there's a 50-50 chance of rain on a given day. After raining, the ground is wet with a 90% chance. Then, what is the probability of the rain and the ground being wet? It's simply 50% times 90%, which is 45%, or 0.45. If we know the probability of one event happening after another, you can simply multiply two probabilities to get the total probability for the sequence. This is called the *chain rule* in probability theory.

Similarly, if you can correctly estimate the probability of one word occurring after a partial sentence, you can simply multiply it with the probability of the partial sentence. Starting from the first word, you can keep doing this until you reach the end of the sentence. For example, if you'd like to compute the probability for "The trip to the beach was . . . ," you can multiply the following:

- The probability of "The" occurring at the beginning of a sentence
- The probability of "trip" occurring after "The"
- The probability of "to" occurring after "The trip"
- The probability of "the" occurring after "The trip to"
- And so on

This means that to build a language model, you need a model that predicts the probability (or, more precisely, the probability distribution) of the next word given the context. You may have noticed that this sounds a little familiar. Indeed, what's done here is very similar to the sequential-labeling models that we've been talking about in this chapter. For example, a part-of-speech (POS) tagging model predicts the probability distribution over the possible POS tags given the context. A named entity recognition (NER) model does it for the possible named entity tags. The difference is that a language model does it for the possible next words, given what the model has encountered so far. Hopefully it's starting to make some sense why I talk about language models in this chapter!

In summary, to build a language model, you tweak an RNN-based sequence-labeling model a little bit so that it gives the estimates for the next word, instead of POS or NER tags. In chapter 3, I talked about the Skip-gram model, which predicts the words in a context given the target word. Notice the similarity here—both models predict the probability over possible words. The input to the Skip-gram model is just a single word, whereas the input to the language model is the partial sequence. You can use a similar mechanism for converting one vector to another using a linear layer, then converting it to a probability distribution using softmax, as we discussed in chapter 3. The architecture is shown in figure 5.12.

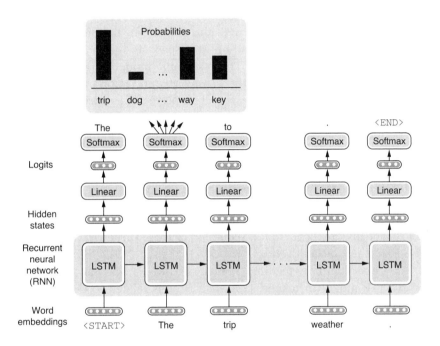

Figure 5.12   Architecture of RNN-based language model

The way RNN-based language models are trained is similar to other sequential-labeling models. The loss function we use is the sequential cross-entropy loss, which measures how "off" the predicted words are from actual words. The cross-entropy loss is computed per word and averaged over all words in the sentence.

5.6   *Text generation using RNNs*

We saw that language models give probabilities to natural language sentences. But the more fun part is you can generate natural language sentences from scratch using a language model! In the final section of this chapter, we are going to build a language model. You can use the trained model to evaluate and generate English sentences.

You can find the entire script for this subsection on a Google Colab notebook (http://realworldnlpbook.com/ch5.html#lm-nb).

5.6.1   *Feeding characters to an RNN*

In the first half of this section, we are going to build an English language model and train it using a generic English corpus. Before we start, we note that the RNN language model we build in this chapter operates on *characters*, not on words or tokens. All the RNN models we've seen so far operate on words, which means the input to the RNN was always sequences of words. On the other hand, the RNN we are going to use in this section takes sequences of characters as the input.

In theory, RNNs can operate on sequences of anything, be it tokens or characters or something completely different (e.g., waveform for speech recognition), as long as they are something that can be turned into vectors. In building language models, we often feed characters, even including whitespace and punctuations as the input, treating them as words of length 1. The rest of the model works exactly the same—individual characters are first embedded (converted to vectors) and then fed into the RNN, which is in turn trained so that it can best predict the distribution over the characters that are likely to come next.

You have a couple of considerations when you are deciding whether you should feed words or characters to an RNN. Using characters will definitely make the RNN less efficient, meaning that it would need more computation to "figure out" the same concept. For example, a word-based RNN can receive the word "dog" at a timestep and update its internal states, whereas a character-based RNN would not able to do it until it receives three elements *d*, *o*, and *g*, and probably "_" (whitespace). A character-based RNN needs to "learn" that a sequence of these three characters means something special (the concept of "dog").

On the other hand, by feeding characters to RNNs, you can bypass many issues arising from dealing with tokens. One such issue is related to out-of-vocabulary (or OOV) words. When training a word-based RNN, you usually fix the entire set of vocabulary, often by enumerating all words that appeared in the train set. But whenever it encounters an OOV word in the test set, it doesn't know what to do with it. Oftentimes, it assigns a special token <UNK> to all OOV words and treats them in the same way, which is not ideal. A character-based RNN, on the contrary, can still operate on individual characters, so it may be able to figure out what "doggy" means, for example, based on the rules it has learned by observing "dog" in the train set, even though it has never seen the exact word "doggy" before.

5.6.2   *Evaluating text using a language model*

Let's start building a character-based language model. The first step is to read a plain text dataset file and generate instances for training the model. I'm going to show how to construct an instance without using a dataset reader for a demonstration purpose. Suppose you have a Python string object `text` that you'd like to turn into an instance for training a language model. First you need to segment it into characters using `CharacterTokenizer` as follows:

```
from allennlp.data.tokenizers import CharacterTokenizer

tokenizer = CharacterTokenizer()
tokens = tokenizer.tokenize(text)
```

Note that `tokens` here is a list of `Token` objects. Each `Token` object contains a single character, instead of a single word. Then you insert the `<START>` and `<END>` symbols at the beginning and at the end of the list as shown next:

```
from allennlp.common.util import START_SYMBOL, END_SYMBOL

tokens.insert(0, Token(START_SYMBOL))
tokens.append(Token(END_SYMBOL))
```

Inserting special symbols like these at the beginning and end of each sentence is a common practice in NLP. With these symbols, models can distinguish between occurrences of a token in the middle of a sentence versus at the beginning/end of a sentence. For example, a period is a lot more likely to occur at the end of a sentence (". <END>") than the beginning ("<START> ."), to which a language model can give two very different probabilities, which is impossible to do without the use of these symbols.

Finally, you can construct an instance by specifying individual text fields. Notice that the "output" of a language model is identical to the input, simply shifted by one token, as shown here:

```
from allennlp.data.fields import TextField
from allennlp.data.instance import Instance

input_field = TextField(tokens[:-1], token_indexers)
output_field = TextField(tokens[1:], token_indexers)
instance = Instance({'input_tokens': input_field,
                     'output_tokens': output_field})
```

Here `token_indexers` specifies how individual tokens are mapped into IDs. We simply use `SingleIdTokenIndexer` we've been using so far as follows:

```
from allennlp.data.token_indexers import TokenIndexer

token_indexers = {'tokens': SingleIdTokenIndexer()}
```

Figure 5.13 shows an instance created from this process.

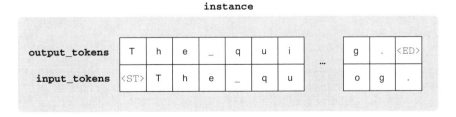

Figure 5.13 Instance for training a language model

The rest of the training pipeline, as well as the model, is very similar to that for sequential labeling mentioned earlier in this chapter. See the Colab notebook for more details. As shown in the next code snippet, after the model is fully trained, you can construct instances from new texts, turn them into instances, and compute the loss, which basically measures how successful the model was in predicting what comes next:

```
predict('The trip to the beach was ruined by bad weather.', model)
{'loss': 1.3882852}

predict('The trip to the beach was ruined by bad dogs.', model)
{'loss': 1.5099115}

predict('by weather was trip my bad beach the ruined to.', model)
{'loss': 1.8084583}
```

The loss here is the cross-entropy loss between the predicted and the expected characters. The more "unexpected" the characters there are, the higher the values will be, so you can use these values to measure how natural the input is as English text. As expected, natural sentences (such as the first one) are given scores that are lower than unnatural sentences (such as the last one).

> **NOTE** If you calculate 2 to the power of the cross entropy, the value is called *perplexity*. Given a fixed natural language text, perplexity becomes lower because the language model is better at predicting what comes next, so it is commonly used for evaluating the quality of language models in the literature.

5.6.3 *Generating text using a language model*

The most interesting aspect of (fully trained) language models is that they can predict possible characters that may appear next given some context. Specifically, they can give you a probability distribution over possible characters that may come next, from which you choose to determine the next character. For example, if the model has generated "t" and "h," and the LM is trained on generic English text, it would probably assign a high probability on the letter "e," generating common English words including *the, they, them*, and so on. If you start this process from the <START> token and keep doing this until you reach the end of the sentence (i.e., by generating <END>), you can generate an English sentence from scratch. By the way, this is another reason why tokens such as <START> and <END> are useful—you need something to feed to the RNN to kick off the generation, and you also need to know when the sentence stops.

Let's look at this process in a Python-like pseudocode next:

```
def generate():
    state = init_state()
    token = <START>
    tokens = [<START>]
    while token != <END>:
        state = update(state, token)
        probs = softmax(linear(state))
        token = sample(probs)
```

```
        tokens.append(token)
    return tokens
```

This loop looks very similar to the one for updating RNNs with one key difference: here, we are not receiving any input but instead are generating characters and feeding them as the input. In other words, the RNN operates on the sequence of characters that the RNN itself generated so far. Such models that operate on past sequences they produced are called *autoregressive models*. See figure 5.14 for an illustration of this.

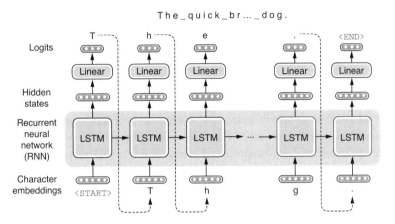

Figure 5.14   Generating text using an RNN

In the previous code snippet, `init_state()` and `update()` functions are the ones that initialize and update the hidden states of the RNN, as we've seen earlier. In generating text, we assume that the model and its parameters are already trained on a large amount of natural language text. `softmax()` is a function to run Softmax on the given vector, and `linear()` is the linear layer to expand/shrink the size of the vector. The function `sample()` returns a character according to the given probability distribution. For example, if the distribution is "a": 0.6, "b": 0.3, "c": 0.1, it will choose "a" 60% of the time, "b" 30% of the time, and "c" 10% of the time. This ensures that the generated string is different every time while every string is likely to look like a real English sentence.

> **NOTE** You can use PyTorch's `torch.multinomial()` for sampling an element from a probability distribution.

If you train this language model using the English sentences from Tatoeba and generate sentences according to this algorithm, the system will produce something similar to the following cherry-picked examples:

```
You can say that you don't know it, and why decided of yourself.
Pike of your value is to talk of hubies.
```

```
The meeting despoit from a police?
That's a problem, but us?
The sky as going to send nire into better.
We'll be look of the best ever studented.
There's you seen anything every's redusention day.
How a fail is to go there.
It sad not distaples with money.
What you see him go as famous to eat!
```

This is not a bad start! If you look at these sentences, there are many words and phrases that make sense as valid English (*You can say that, That's a problem, to go there, see him go*, etc.). Even when the system generates peculiar words (*despoit, studented, redusention, distaples*), they look almost like real English words because they all basically follow morphological and phonological rules of English. This means that the language model was successful in learning the basic building blocks of English, such as how to arrange letters (orthography), how to form words (morphology), and how to form basic sentence structures (syntax).

However, if you look at sentences as a whole, few of them make any sense (e.g., *What you see him go as famous to eat!*). This means the language model we trained falls short of modeling semantic consistency of sentences. This is potentially because our model is not powerful enough (our LSTM-RNN needs to compress everything about the sentence into a 256-dimensional vector) or the training dataset is too small (just 10,000 sentences), or both. But you can easily imagine that if we keep increasing the model capacity as well as the size of the train set, the model gets incredibly good at producing realistic natural language text. In February 2019, OpenAI announced that it developed a huge language model based on the Transformer model (which we'll cover in chapter 8) trained on 40 GB of internet text. The model shows that it can produce realistic-looking text that shows near-perfect grammar and long-term topical consistency given a prompt. In fact, the model was so good that OpenAI decided not to release the large model they had trained due to their concerns about malicious use of the technology. But it is important to keep in mind that, no matter how intelligent the output looks, their model is trained on the same principle as our toy example in this chapter—just trying to predict the next character!

Summary

- Sequential-labeling models tag each word in the input with a label, which can be achieved by recurrent neural networks (RNNs).
- Part-of-speech (POS) tagging and named entity recognition (NER) are two instances of sequential-labeling tasks.
- Multilayer RNNs stack multiple layers of RNNs, whereas bidirectional RNNs combine forward and backward RNNs to encode the entire sentence.
- Language models assign probabilities to natural language text, which is achieved by predicting the next word.
- You can use a trained language model to assess how "natural" a natural language sentence is or even to generate realistic-looking text from scratch.

Part 2

Advanced models

The field of NLP has seen rapid progress in the past few years. Specifically, the advent of the Transformer and pretrained language models such as BERT have completely changed the landscape of the field and how practitioners build NLP applications. This part of the book will help you catch up with these latest developments.

Chapter 6 introduces sequence-to-sequence models, an important class of models that will enable you to build more complex applications such as machine translation systems and chatbots. Chapter 7 discusses another type of popular neural network architecture, *convolutional neural networks* (CNNs).

Chapters 8 and 9 are arguably the most important and exciting chapters of this book. They cover the Transformer and transfer learning methods (such as BERT) respectively. We'll demonstrate how to build advanced NLP applications such as high-quality machine translation and spell-checkers, using those technologies.

By the time you finish reading this part, you'll feel confident that you can now solve a wide range of NLP tasks with what you have learned so far.

Sequence-to-sequence models

In this chapter, we are going to discuss sequence-to-sequence (Seq2Seq) models, which are some of the most important complex NLP models and are used for a wide range of applications, including machine translation. Seq2Seq models and their variations are already used as the fundamental building blocks in many real-world applications, including Google Translate and speech recognition. We are going to build a simple neural machine translation system using a powerful framework to learn how the models work and how to generate the output using greedy and beam search algorithms. At the end of this chapter, we will build a chatbot—an NLP application with which you can have a conversation. We'll also discuss the challenges and limitations of simple Seq2Seq models.

6.1   *Introducing sequence-to-sequence models*

In the previous chapter, we discussed two types of powerful NLP models, namely, sequential labeling and language models. To recap, a sequence-labeling model takes a sequence of some units (e.g., words) and assigns a label (e.g., a part-of-speech (POS) tag) to each unit, whereas a language model takes a sequence of some units (e.g., words) and estimates how probable the given sequence is in the domain in which the model is trained. You can also use a language model to generate realistic-looking text from scratch. See figure 6.1 for the overview of these two models.

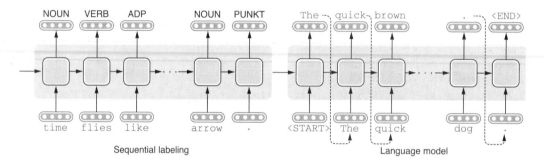

Figure 6.1   Sequential labeling and language models

Although these two models are useful for a number of NLP tasks, for some, you may want the best of both worlds—you may want your model to take some input (e.g., a sentence) and generate something else (e.g., another sentence) in response. For example, if you wish to translate some text written in one language into another, you need your model to take a sentence and produce another. Can you do this with sequential-labeling models? No, because they can produce only the same number of output labels as there are tokens in the input sentence. This is obviously too limiting for translation—one expression in a language (say, "Enchanté" in French) can have an arbitrarily large or small number of words in another (say, "Nice to meet you" in English). Can you do this with language models? Again, not really. Although you can generate realistic-looking text using language models, you have almost no control over the text they generate. In fact, language models do not take any input.

But if you look at figure 6.1 more carefully, you might notice something. The model on the left (the sequential-labeling model) takes a sentence as its input and produces some form of representations, whereas the model on the right produces a sentence with variable length that looks like natural language text. We already have the components needed to build what we want, that is, a model that takes a sentence and transforms it into another. The only missing part is a way to connect these two so that we can control what the language model generates.

In fact, by the time the model on the left finishes processing the input sentence, the RNN has already produced its abstract representation, which is encoded in the RNN's hidden states. If you can simply connect these two so that the sentence representation is passed from left to right and the language model can generate another sentence based on the representation, it seems like you can achieve what you wanted to do in the first place!

Sequence-to-sequence models—or *Seq2Seq* models, in short—are built on this insight. A Seq2Seq model consists of two subcomponents—an encoder and a decoder. See figure 6.2 for an illustration. An encoder takes a sequence of some units (e.g., a sentence) and converts it into some internal representation. A decoder, on the other hand, generates a sequence of some units (e.g., a sentence) from the internal representation. As a whole, a Seq2Seq model takes a sequence and generates another sequence. As with the language model, the generation stops when the decoder produces a special token, <END>, which enables a Seq2Seq model to generate an output that can be longer or shorter than the input sequence.

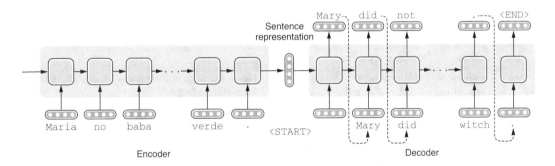

Figure 6.2 Sequence-to-sequence model

Many variants of Seq2Seq models exist, depending on what architecture you use for the encoder, what architecture you use for the decoder, and how information flows between the two. This chapter covers the most basic type of Seq2Seq model—simply connecting two RNNs via the sentence representation. We'll discuss more advanced variants in chapter 8.

Machine translation is the first, and by far the most popular, application of Seq2Seq models. However, the Seq2Seq architecture is a generic model applicable to numerous NLP tasks. In one such task, summarization, an NLP system takes a long text (e.g., a news article) and produces its summary (e.g., a news headline). A Seq2Seq model can be used to "translate" the longer text into the shorter one. Another task is a dialogue system, or a *chatbot*. If you think of a user's utterance as the input and the system's response as the output, the dialogue system's job is to "translate" the former into the latter. Later in this chapter, we will discuss a case study where we actually build a chatbot using a Seq2Seq model. Yet another (somewhat surprising) application is parsing—if you think of the input text as one language and its syntax representation as another, you can parse natural language texts with a Seq2Seq model.[1]

6.2   *Machine translation 101*

We briefly touched upon machine translation in section 1.2.1. To recap, machine translation (MT) systems are NLP systems that translate a given text from one language to another. The language the input text is written in is called the *source language*, whereas the one for the output is called the *target language*. The combination of the source and target languages is called the *language pair*.

First, let's look at a couple of examples to see what it's like and why it's difficult to translate a foreign language to English (or any other language you understand). In the first example, let's translate a Spanish sentence, "Maria no daba una bofetada a la bruja verde." to the English counterpart, "Mary did not slap the green witch." A common practice in illustrating the process of translation is to draw how words or phrases of the same meaning map between the two sentences. Correspondence of linguistic units between two instances is called *alignment*. Figure 6.3 shows the alignment between the Spanish and English sentences.

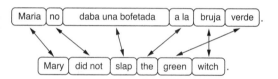

Figure 6.3   Translation and word alignment between Spanish and English

Some words (e.g., "Maria" and "Mary," "bruja" and "witch," and "verde" and "green") match exactly one to one. However, some expressions (e.g., "daba una bofetada" and "slap") differ in such a significant way that you can only align phrases between Spanish and English. Finally, even where there's one-to-one correspondence between words, the way words are arranged, or *word order*, may differ between the two languages. For example, adjectives are added after nouns in Spanish ("la bruja verde") whereas in English, they come before nouns ("the green witch"). Spanish and English are linguistically similar in terms of grammar and vocabulary, especially when compared to, say, Chinese and English, although this single example shows translating between the two may be a challenging task.

---

[1] See Oriol Vinyals et al., "Grammar as a Foreign Language," (2015; https://arxiv.org/abs/1412.7449) for more details.

Things start to look more complicated between Mandarin Chinese and English. Figure 6.4 illustrates the alignment between a Chinese sentence ("Bushi yu Shalong juxing le huitan.") and its English translation ("Bush held a talk with Shalon."). Although Chinese uses ideographic characters of its own, we use romanized sentences here for simplicity.

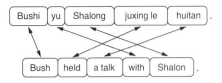

Figure 6.4 Translation and word alignment between Mandarin Chinese and English

You can now see more crossing arrows in the figure. Unlike English, Chinese prepositional phrases such as "with Shalon" are usually attached to verbs from the left. Also, the Chinese language doesn't explicitly mark tense, and MT systems (and human translators alike) need to "guess" the correct tense to use for the English translation. Finally, Chinese-to-English MT systems also need to infer the correct number (singular or plural) of each noun, because Chinese nouns are not explicitly marked according to their number (e.g., "huitan" just means "talk" with no explicit mention of number). This is a good example showing how the difficulty of translation depends on the language pair. Development of MT systems between linguistically different languages (such as Chinese and English) is usually more challenging than those between linguistically similar ones (such as Spanish and Portuguese).

Let's take a look at one more example—translating from Japanese to English, illustrated in figure 6.5. All the arrows in the figure are crossed, meaning that the word order is almost exactly opposite in these two sentences. In addition to the fact that Japanese prepositional phrases ("to music") and relative clauses attach from the left like Chinese, objects (such as "listening" in "I love listening" in the example) come before the

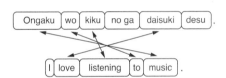

Figure 6.5 Translation and word alignment between Japanese and English

verb. In other words, Japanese is an SOV (subject-object-verb) language, whereas all the other languages we mentioned so far (English, Spanish, and Chinese) are SVO (subject-verb-object) languages. Structural differences are a reason why direct, word-to-word translation doesn't work very well.

NOTE This word-order classification system of language (such as SOV and SVO) is often used in linguistic typology. The vast majority of world languages are either SOV (most common) or SVO (slightly less common), although a small number of languages follow other word-order systems, such as VSO (verb-subject-object), used by Arabic and Irish, for example. Very few languages (less than 3% of all languages) follow other types (VOS, OVS, and OSV).

Besides the structural differences shown in the previous figures, many other factors can make MT a difficult task. One such factor is lexical difference. If you are translating, for example, the Japanese word "ongaku" to the English "music," there's little ambiguity. "Ongaku" is almost always "music." However, if you are translating, say, the English word "brother" to Chinese, you face ambiguity, because Chinese uses distinct words for "elder brother" and "younger brother." In an even more extreme case, if you are translating "cousin" to Chinese, you have eight different choices, because in the Chinese family system, you need to use distinct words depending on whether your cousin is maternal or paternal, female or male, and older or younger than you.

Another factor that makes MT challenging is omission. You can see that in figure 6.5, there's no Japanese word for "I." In languages such as Chinese, Japanese, Spanish, and many others, you can omit the subject pronoun when it's clear from the context and/or the verb form. This is called *zero pronoun*, and it can become a problem when translating from a pronoun-dropping language to a language where it happens less often (e.g., English).

One of the earliest MT systems, developed during the Georgetown-IBM experiment, was built to translate Russian sentences into English during the Cold War. But all it did was not much different from looking up each word in a bilingual dictionary and replacing it with its translation. The three examples shown above should be enough to convince you that simply replacing word by word is too limiting. Later systems incorporated a larger set of lexicons and grammar rules, but these rules are written manually by linguists and are not enough to capture the complexities of language (again, remember the poor software engineer from chapter 1).

The main paradigm for MT that remained dominant both in academia and industry before the advent of neural machine translation (NMT) is called *statistical machine translation* (SMT). The idea behind it is simple: learn how to translate from data, not by manually crafting rules. Specifically, SMT systems learn how to translate from datasets that contain a collection of texts in the source language and their translation in the target language. Such datasets are called *parallel corpora* (or *parallel texts*, or *bitexts*). By looking at a collection of paired sentences in both languages, the algorithm seeks patterns of how words in one language should be translated to another. The resulting statistical model is called a *translation model*. At the same time, by looking at a collection of target sentences, the algorithm can learn what valid sentences in the target languages should look like. Sounds familiar? This is exactly what a *language model* is all about (see the previous chapter). The final SMT model combines these two models and produces output that is a plausible translation of the input and is a valid, fluent sentence in the target language on its own.

Around 2015, the advent of powerful neural machine translation (NMT) models subverted the dominance of SMT. SMT and NMT have two key differences. First, by definition, NMT is based on neural networks, which are well known for their power to model language accurately. As a result, target sentences generated by NMT tend to be more fluent and natural than those generated by SMT. Second, NMT models are trained end-to-end, as I briefly touched on in chapter 1. This means that NMT models consist of a single neural network that takes an input and directly produces an output, instead of a patchwork of submodels and submodules that you need to train independently. As a result, NMT models are simpler to train and smaller in code size than SMT models.

MT is already used in many different industries and aspects of our lives. Translating foreign text into a language that you understand to grasp its meaning quickly is called *gisting*. If the text is deemed important enough after gisting, it may be sent to formal, manual translation. Professional translators also use MT for their work. Oftentimes, the source text is first translated to the target language using an MT system, then the produced text is edited by human translators. Such editing is called *postediting*. The use of automated systems (called *computer-aided translation*, or CAT) can accelerate the translation process and reduce the cost.

6.3   *Building your first translator*

In this section, we are going to build a working MT system. Instead of writing any Python code to do that, we'll make the most of existing MT frameworks. A number of open source frameworks make it easier to build MT systems, including Moses (http://www.statmt.org/moses/) for SMT and OpenNMT (http://opennmt.net/) for NMT. In this section, we will use Fairseq (https://github.com/pytorch/fairseq), an NMT toolkit developed by Facebook that is becoming more and more popular among NLP practitioners these days. The following aspects make Fairseq a good choice for developing an NMT system quickly: 1) it is a modern framework that comes with a number of predefined state-of-the-art NMT models that you can use out of the box; 2) it is very extensible, meaning you can quickly implement your own model by following their API; and 3) it is very fast, supporting multi-GPU and distributed training by default. Thanks to its powerful models, you can build a decent quality NMT system within a couple of hours.

Before you start, install Fairseq by running `pip install fairseq` in the root of your project directory. Also, run the following commands in your shell to download and expand the dataset (you may need to install `unzip` if you are using Ubuntu by running `sudo apt-get install unzip`):[2]

```
$ mkdir -p data/mt
$ wget https://realworldnlpbook.s3.amazonaws.com/data/mt/tatoeba.eng_spa.zip
$ unzip tatoeba.eng_spa.zip -d data/mt
```

We are going to use Spanish and English parallel sentences from the Tatoeba project, which we used previously in chapter 4, to train a Spanish-to-English MT system. The corpus consists of approximately 200,000 English sentences and their Spanish translations. I went ahead and already formatted the dataset so that you can use it without

---

[2]   Note that $ at the beginning of every line is rendered by the shell, and you don't need to type it.

worrying about obtaining the data, tokenizing the text, and so on. The dataset is already split into train, validate, and test subsets.

6.3.1 Preparing the datasets

As mentioned previously, MT systems (both SMT and NMT) are machine learning models and thus are trained from data. The development process of MT systems looks similar to any other modern NLP systems, as shown in figure 6.6. First, the training portion of the parallel corpus is preprocessed and used to train a set of NMT model candidates. Next, the validation portion is used to choose the best-performing model out of all the candidates. This process is called *model selection* (see chapter 2 for a review). Finally, the best model is tested on the test portion of the dataset to obtain evaluation metrics, which reflect how good the model is.

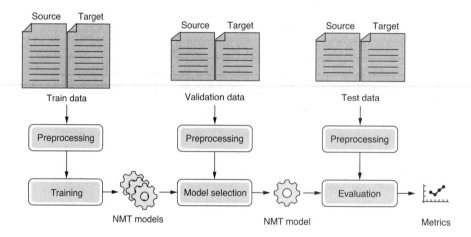

Figure 6.6   Pipeline for building an NMT system

The first step in MT development is preprocessing the dataset. But before preprocessing, you need to convert the dataset into an easy-to-use format, which is usually plain text in NLP. In practice, the raw data for training MT systems come in many different formats, for example, plain text files (if you are lucky), XML formats of proprietary software, PDF files, and database records. Your first job is to format the raw files so that source sentences and their target translations are aligned sentence by sentence. The resulting file is often a TSV file where each line is a tab-separated *sentence pair*, which looks like the following:

```
Let's try something.                 Permíteme intentarlo.
Muiriel is 20 now.                   Ahora, Muiriel tiene 20 años.
I just don't know what to say.       No sé qué decir.
You are in my way.                   Estás en mi camino.
Sometimes he can be a strange guy.   A veces él puede ser un chico raro.
...
```

After the translations are aligned, the parallel corpus is fed into the preprocessing pipeline. Specific operations applied in this process differ from application to application, and from language to language, but the following steps are most common:

1 Filtering
2 Cleaning
3 Tokenization

In the filtering step, any sentence pairs that are not suitable for training an MT system are removed from the dataset. What makes a sentence pair not suitable depends on many factors, but, for example, any sentence pair where either text is too long (say, more than 1,000 words) is not useful, because most MT models are not capable of modeling such a long sentence. Also, any sentence pairs where one sentence is too long but the other is too short are probably noise caused by a data processing or alignment error. For example, if a Spanish sentence is 10 words long, the length of its English translation should fall within a 5- to 15-word range. Finally, if, for any reason, the parallel corpus contains any languages other than the source and target languages, you should remove such sentence pairs. This happens a lot more often than you'd imagine—many documents are multilingual due to, for example, quotes, explanation, or code switching (mixing more than one language in a sentence). Language detection (see chapter 4) can help detect such anomalies.

After filtering, sentences in the dataset can be cleaned further. This process may include such things as removal of HTML tags and any special characters and normalization of characters (e.g., traditional and simplified Chinese) and spelling (e.g., American and British English).

If the target language uses scripts such as the Latin (a, b, c, …) or Cyrillic (а, б, в, …) alphabets, which distinguish upper- and lowercases, you may want to normalize case. By doing so, your MT system will group "NLP" with "nlp" and "Nlp." This step is usually a good thing, because by having three different representations of a single concept, the MT model needs to learn that they are in fact a single concept purely from the data. Normalizing cases also reduces the number of distinct words, which makes training and prediction faster. However, this also groups "US" and "Us" and "us," which might not be a desirable behavior, depending on the type of data and the domain you are working with. In practice, such decisions, including whether to normalize cases, are carefully made by observing their effect on the validation data performance.

Data cleaning for machine translation and NLP

Note that the cleaning techniques mentioned here are not specific to MT. Any NLP applications and tasks can benefit from a carefully crafted pipeline of filtering and cleaning operations. However, cleaning of the training data is particularly important for MT, because the consistency of translation goes a long way in building a robust MT model. If your training data uses "NLP" in some cases and "nlp" in others, the model will have a difficulty figuring out the proper way to translate the word, whereas humans would easily understand that the two words represent a single concept.

At this point, the dataset is still a bunch of strings of characters. Most MT systems operate on words, so you need to tokenize the input (section 3.3) to identify words. Depending on the language, you may need to run a different pipeline (e.g., word segmentation is needed for Chinese and Japanese).

The Tatoeba dataset you downloaded and expanded earlier has already gone through all this preprocessing pipeline. Now you are ready to hand the dataset over to Fairseq. The first step is to tell Fairseq to convert the input files to the binary format so that the training script can read them easily, as follows:

```
$ fairseq-preprocess \
      --source-lang es \
      --target-lang en \
      --trainpref data/mt/tatoeba.eng_spa.train.tok \
      --validpref data/mt/tatoeba.eng_spa.valid.tok \
      --testpref data/mt/tatoeba.eng_spa.test.tok \
      --destdir data/mt-bin \
      --thresholdsrc 3 \
      --thresholdtgt 3
```

When this succeeds, you should see a message `Wrote preprocessed data to data/mt-bin` on your terminal. You should also find the following group of files under the `data/mt-bin` directory:

```
dict.en.txt dict.es.txt  test.es-en.en.bin  test.es-en.en.idx  test.es-
    en.es.bin  test.es-en.es.idx  train.es-en.en.bin  train.es-en.en.idx
    train.es-en.es.bin  train.es-en.es.idx  valid.es-en.en.bin  valid.es-
    en.en.idx  valid.es-en.es.bin  valid.es-en.es.idx
```

One of the key functionalities of this preprocessing step is to build the vocabulary (called the *dictionary* in Fairseq), which is a mapping from vocabulary items (usually words) to their IDs. Notice the two dictionary files in the directory, `dict.en.txt` and `dict.es.txt`. MT deals with two languages, so the system needs to maintain two mappings, one for each language.

6.3.2 *Training the model*

Now that the train data is converted into the binary format, you are ready to train the MT model. Invoke the `fairseq-train` command with the directory where the binary files are located, along with several hyperparameters, as shown next:

```
$ fairseq-train \
    data/mt-bin \
    --arch lstm \
    --share-decoder-input-output-embed \
    --optimizer adam \
    --lr 1.0e-3 \
    --max-tokens 4096 \
    --save-dir data/mt-ckpt
```

You don't have to worry about understanding what most of the parameters here mean (just yet). At this point, you need to know only that you are training a model using the data stored in the directory specified by the first parameter (`data/mt-bin`) using an LSTM architecture (`--arch lstm`) with a bunch of other hyperparameters, and saving the results in `data/mt-ckpt` (short for "checkpoint").

When you run this command, your terminal will show two types of progress bars alternatively—one for training and another for validating, as shown here:

```
| epoch 001:  16%|???|                    | 61/389 [00:13<01:23,  3.91it/s,
    loss=8.347, ppl=325.58, wps=17473, ups=4, wpb=3740.967, bsz=417.180,
    num_updates=61, lr=0.001, gnorm=2.099, clip=0.000, oom=0.000, wall=17,
    train_wall=12]

| epoch 001 | valid on 'valid' subset | loss 4.208 | ppl 18.48 | num_updates
    389
```

The lines corresponding to validation results are easily distinguishable by their contents—they say "valid" subset. For each epoch, the training process alternates two stages: training and validation. An *epoch*, a concept used in machine learning, means one pass through the entire train data. In the training stage, the loss is calculated using the training data, then the model parameters are adjusted in such a way that the new set of parameters lowers the loss. In the validation stage, the model parameters are fixed, and a separate dataset (validation set) is used to measure how well the model is performing against the dataset.

I mentioned in chapter 1 that validation sets are used for model selection, a process where the best machine learning model is chosen among all the possible models trained from a single training set. Here, by alternating between training and validation stages, we use the validation set to check the performance of all the intermediary models (i.e., the model after the first epoch, the one after two epochs, and so on). In other words, we use the validation stage to monitor the progress of the training.

Why is this a good idea? We gain many benefits by inserting the validation stage after every epoch, but the most important one is to avoid overfitting—the very reason why a validation data is important in the first place. To illustrate this further, let's look at how the loss changes over the course of the training of our Spanish-to-English MT model, for both the train and the validation sets, as shown in figure 6.7.

As the training continues, the train loss becomes smaller and smaller and gradually approaches zero, because this is exactly what we told the optimizer to do: decrease the loss as much as possible. Checking whether the train loss is decreasing steadily epoch after epoch is a good "sanity check" that your model and the training pipeline are working as expected.

On the other hand, if you look at the validation loss, it goes down at first for several epochs, but after a certain point, it gradually goes back up, forming a U-shaped curve—a typical sign of overfitting. After several epochs of training, your model fits the train set so well that it begins to lose its generalizability on the validation set.

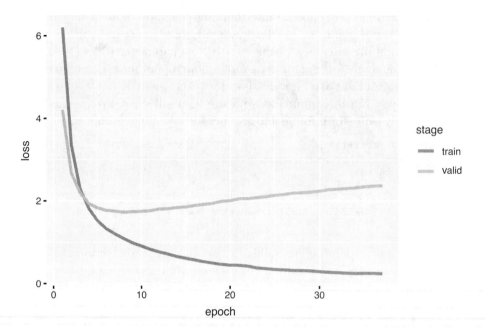

Figure 6.7   Train and validation loss

Let's use a concrete example in MT to illustrate what's really going on when a model is overfitted. For example, if your training data contains the English sentence "It is raining hard" and its Spanish translation "Esta lloviendo fuerte," with no other sentences having the word "hard" in them, the overfitted model may believe that "fuerte" is the only possible translation of "hard." A properly fitted model might leave some wiggle room for other Spanish words to appear as a translation for "hard," but an overfitted MT system would always translate "hard" to "fuerte," which is the "correct" thing to do according to the train set but obviously not ideal if you'd like to build a robust MT system. For example, the best way to translate "hard" in "She is trying hard" is not "fuerte."

If you see your validation loss starting to creep up, there's little point keeping the training process running, because chances are, your model has already overfitted to the data to some extent. A common practice in such a situation, called *early stopping*, is to terminate the training. Specifically, if your validation loss is not improving for a certain number of epochs, you stop the training and use the model at the point when the validation loss was the lowest. The number of epochs you wait until the training is terminated is called *patience*. In practice, the metric you care about the most (such as BLEU; see section 6.5.2) is used for early stopping instead of the validation loss.

OK, that was enough about training and validating for now. The graph in figure 6.7 indicates that the validation loss is lowest around epoch 8, so you can stop (by pressing Ctrl + C) the `fairseq-train` command after around 10 epochs; otherwise, the command would keep running indefinitely. Fairseq will automatically save the best model parameters (in terms of the validation loss) to the checkpoint_best.pt file.

> **WARNING** Note that the training may take a long time if you are just using a CPU. Chapter 11 explains how to use GPUs to accelerate the training.

6.3.3 Running the translator

After the model is trained, you can invoke the fairseq-interactive command to run your MT model on any input in an interactive way. You can run the command by specifying the binary file location and the model parameter file as follows:

```
$ fairseq-interactive \
    data/mt-bin \
    --path data/mt-ckpt/checkpoint_best.pt \
    --beam 5 \
    --source-lang es \
    --target-lang en
```

After you see the prompt Type the input sentence and press return, try typing (or copying and pasting) the following Spanish sentences one by one:

```
¡ Buenos días !
¡ Hola !
¿ Dónde está el baño ?
¿ Hay habitaciones libres ?
¿ Acepta tarjeta de crédito ?
La cuenta , por favor .
```

Note the punctuation and the whitespace in these sentences—Fairseq assumes that the input is already tokenized. Your results may vary slightly, depending on many factors (the training of deep learning models usually involves some randomness), but you get something along the line of the following (I added boldface for emphasis):

```
¡ Buenos días !
S-0      ¡ Buenos días !
H-0      -0.20546913146972656      Good morning !
P-0      -0.3342 -0.3968 -0.0901 -0.0007
¡ Hola !
S-1      ¡ Hola !
H-1      -0.12050756067037582      Hi !
P-1      -0.3437 -0.0119 -0.0059
¿ Dónde está el baño ?
S-2      ¿ Dónde está el baño ?
H-2      -0.24064254760742188      Where &apos;s the restroom ?
P-2      -0.0036 -0.4080 -0.0012 -1.0285 -0.0024 -0.0002
¿ Hay habitaciones libres ?
S-3      ¿ Hay habitaciones libres ?
H-3      -0.25766071677207947      Is there free rooms ?
P-3      -0.8187 -0.0018 -0.5702 -0.1484 -0.0064 -0.0004
¿ Acepta tarjeta de crédito ?
S-4      ¿ Acepta tarjeta de crédito ?
H-4      -0.10596384853124619      Do you accept credit card ?
```

```
P-4      -0.1347 -0.0297 -0.3110 -0.1826 -0.0675 -0.0161 -0.0001
La cuenta , por favor .
S-5      La cuenta , por favor .
H-5      -0.4411449432373047      Check , please .
P-5      -1.9730 -0.1928 -0.0071 -0.0328 -0.0001
```

Most of the output sentences here are almost perfect, except the fourth one (I would translate to "Are there free rooms?"). Even considering the fact that these sentences are all simple examples you can find in any travel Spanish phrasebook, this is not a bad start for a system built within an hour!

6.4   How Seq2Seq models work

In this section, we will dive deep into the individual components that constitute a Seq2Seq model, which include the encoder and the decoder. We'll also cover the algorithms used for decoding the target sentence—greedy decoding and beam search decoding.

6.4.1   Encoder

As we saw in the beginning of this chapter, the encoder of a Seq2Seq model is not much different from the sequential-labeling models we covered in chapter 5. Its main job is to take the input sequence (usually a sentence) and convert it into a vector representation of a fixed length. You can use an LSTM-RNN as shown in figure 6.8.

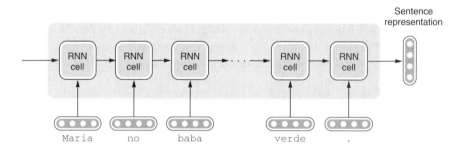

Figure 6.8   Encoder of a Seq2Seq model

Unlike sequential-labeling models, we need only the final hidden state of an RNN, which is then passed to the decoder to generate the target sentence. You can also use a multilayer RNN as an encoder, in which case the sentence representation is the concatenation of the output of each layer, as illustrated in figure 6.9.

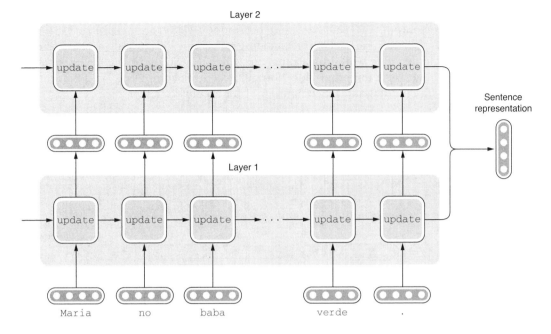

Figure 6.9   Using a multilayer RNN as an encoder

Similarly, you can use a bidirectional (or even a bidirectional multilayer) RNN as an encoder. The final sentence representation is a concatenation of the output of the forward and the backward layers, as shown in figure 6.10.

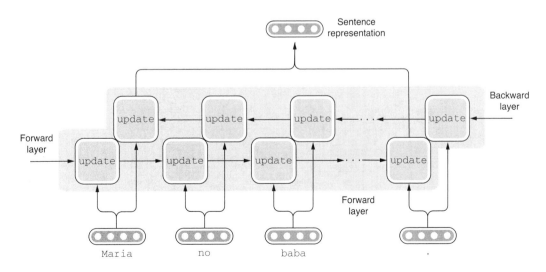

Figure 6.10   Using a bidirectional RNN as an encoder

NOTE   This is a small detail, but remember that an LSTM cell produces two types of output: the cell state and the hidden state (see section 4.2.2 for review). When using LSTM for encoding a sequence, we usually just use the final hidden state while discarding the cell state. Think of the cell state as something like a temporary loop variable used for computing the final outcome (the hidden state). See figure 6.11 for an illustration.

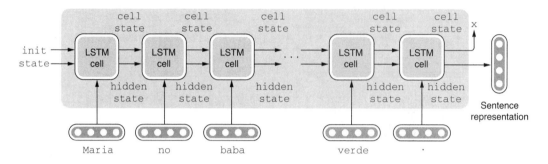

Figure 6.11   An encoder using LSTM cells

6.4.2   Decoder

Likewise, the decoder of a Seq2Seq model is similar to the language model we covered in chapter 5. In fact, they are identical except for one crucial difference—a decoder takes an input from the encoder. The language models we covered in chapter 5 are called *unconditional language models* because they generate language without any input or precondition. On the other hand, language models that generate language based on some input (condition) are called *conditional language models*. A Seq2Seq decoder is one type of conditional language model, where the condition is the sentence representation produced by the encoder. See figure 6.12 for an illustration of how a Seq2Seq decoder works.

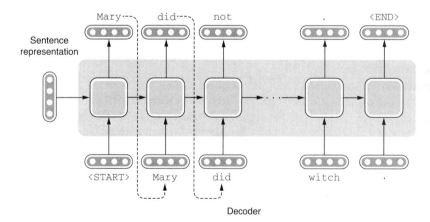

Figure 6.12   A decoder of a Seq2Seq model

Just as with language models, Seq2Seq decoders generate text from left to right. Like the encoder, you can use an RNN to do this. A decoder can also be a multilayer RNN. However, a decoder cannot be bidirectional—you cannot generate a sentence from both sides. As was mentioned in chapter 5, models that operate on the past sequence they produced are called *autoregressive models*.

Non-autoregressive models

If you think simply generating text from left to right is too limiting, you have a good point. Humans also do not always write language linearly—we often revise, add, and delete words and phrases afterward. Also, generating text in a linear fashion is not very efficient. The latter half of a sentence needs to wait until its first half is completed, which makes it very difficult to parallelize the generation process. As of this writing, researchers are putting a lot of effort into developing non-autoregressive MT models that do not generate the target sentence in a linear fashion (see, for example, this paper from Salesforce Research: https://arxiv.org/abs/1711.02281). However, they haven't exceeded autoregressive models in terms of translation quality, and most research and production MT systems still adopt autoregressive models.

How the decoder behaves is a bit different between the training and the prediction stages. Let's see how it is trained first. At the training stage, we know exactly how the source sentence should be translated into the target sentence. In other words, we know exactly what the decoder should produce, word by word. Because of this, decoders are trained in a similar way to how sequential-labeling models are trained (see chapter 5).

First, the decoder is fed the sentence representation produced by the encoder and a special token <START>, which indicates the start of a sentence. The first RNN cell processes these two inputs and produces the first hidden state. The hidden state vector is fed to a linear layer that shrinks or expands this vector to match the size of the vocabulary. The resulting vector then goes through softmax, which converts it to a probability distribution. This distribution dictates how likely each word in the vocabulary is to come next.

Then, this is where the training happens. If the input is "Maria no daba una bofetada a la bruja verde," then we would like the decoder to produce its English equivalent: "Mary did not slap the green witch." This means that we would like to maximize the probability that the first RNN cell generates "Mary" given the input sentence. This is a multiclass classification problem we have seen many times so far in this book—word embeddings (chapter 3), sentence classification (chapter 4), and sequential labeling (chapter 5). You use the cross-entropy loss to measure how far apart the desired outcome is from the actual output of your network. If the probability for "Mary" is large, then good—the network incurs a small loss. On the other hand, if the probability for "Mary" is small, then the network incurs a large loss, which encourages the optimization algorithm to change the parameters (magic constants) by a large amount.

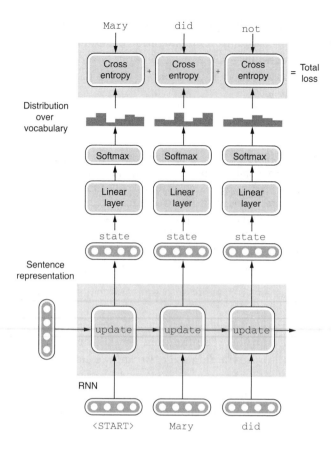

Distribution over vocabulary

Sentence representation

RNN

<START>   Mary   did

Figure 6.13   Training a Seq2Seq decoder

Then, we move on to the next cell. The next cell receives the hidden state computed by the first cell and the word "Mary," *regardless of what the first cell generated.* Instead of feeding the token generated by the previous cell, as we did when generating text using a language model, we constrain the input to the decoder so that it won't "go astray." The second cell produces the hidden state based on these two inputs, which is then used to compute the probability distribution for the second word. We compute the cross-entropy loss by comparing the distribution against the desired output "did" and move on to the next cell. We keep doing this until we reach the final token, which is <END>. The total loss for the sentence is the average of all the losses incurred for all the words in the sentence, as shown in figure 6.13.

Finally, the loss computed this way is used to adjust the model parameters of the decoder, so that it can generate the desired output the next time around. Note that the parameters of the encoder are also adjusted in this process, because the loss propagates all the way back to the encoder through the sentence representation. If the sentence representation produced by the encoder is not good, the decoder won't be able to produce high-quality target sentences no matter how hard it tries.

6.4.3   *Greedy decoding*

Now let's look at how the decoder behaves at the prediction stage, where a source sentence is given to the network, but we don't know what the correct translation should be. At this stage, a decoder behaves a lot like the language models we discussed in chapter 5. It is fed the sentence representation produced by the encoder, as well as a special token <START>, which indicates the start of a sentence. The first RNN cell processes these two inputs and produces the first hidden state, which is then fed to the linear layer and the softmax layer to produce the probability distribution over the target vocabulary. Here comes the key part—unlike the training phase, you don't know the correct word to come next, so you have multiple options. You can choose any random word that has a reasonably high probability (say, "dog"), but probably the best you can do is pick the word whose probability is the highest (you are lucky if it's "Mary"). The MT system produces the word that was just picked and then feeds it to the next RNN cell. This is repeated until the special token <END> is encountered. Figure 6.14 illustrates this process.

OK, so are we all good, then? Can we move on to evaluating our MT system, because it is doing everything it can to produce the best possible translation? Not so fast—many things could go wrong by decoding the target sentence in this manner.

First of all, the goal of MT decoding is to maximize the

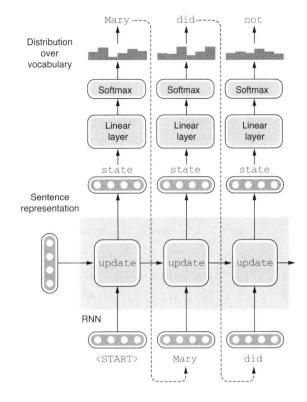

Figure 6.14   A prediction using a Seq2Seq decoder

probability of the target sentence as a whole, not just individual words. This is exactly what you trained the network to do—to produce the largest probability for correct sentences. However, the way words are picked at each step described earlier is to maximize the probability of that word only. In other words, this decoding process guarantees only the locally maximum probability. This type of myopic, locally optimal algorithm is called *greedy* in computer science, and the decoding algorithm I just explained is called *greedy decoding*. However, just because you are maximizing the probability of individual words at each step doesn't mean you are maximizing the probability of the whole sentence. Greedy algorithms, in general, are not guaranteed to produce the globally optimal solution, and using greedy decoding can leave you stuck with suboptimal translations. This is not very intuitive to understand, so let me use a simple example to illustrate this.

When you are picking words at each timestep, you have multiple words to pick from. You pick one of them and move on to the next RNN cell, which produces another set of possible words to pick from, depending on the word you picked previously. This can be represented using a tree structure like the one shown in figure 6.15. The diagram shows how the word you pick at one timestep (e.g., "did") branches out to another set of possible words ("you" and "not") to pick from at the next timestep.

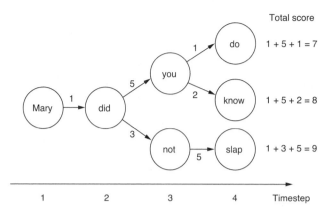

Figure 6.15   A decoding decision tree

Each transition from word to word is labeled with a score, which corresponds to how large the probability of choosing that transition is. Your goal here is to maximize the total sum of the scores when you traverse one path from timestep 1 to 4. Mathematically, probabilities are real numbers between 0 to 1, and you should multiply (instead of add) each probability to get the total, but I'm simplifying things here. For example, if you go from "Mary" to "did," then on to "you" and "do," you just generated a sentence "Mary did you do" and the total score is $1 + 5 + 1 = 7$.

The greedy decoder we saw earlier will face two choices after it generates "did" at timestep 2: either generate "you" with a score of 5 or "not" with a score of 3. Because all it does is pick the one with the highest score, it will pick "you" and move on. Then it will face another branch after timestep 3—generating "do" with a score of 1 or generating "know" with a score of 2. Again, it will pick the largest score, and you will end up with the translation "Mary did you know" whose score is $1+ 5 + 1 = 8$.

This is not a bad result. At least, it is not as bad as the first path, which sums up to a score of 7. By picking the maximum score at each branch, you are making sure that your final result is at least decent. However, what if you picked "not" at timestep 3? At first glance, this doesn't seem like a good idea, because the score you get is only 3, which is smaller than you'd get by taking the other path, 5. But at the next timestep, by generating "slap," you get a score of 5. In retrospect, this was the right thing to do—in total, you get $1 + 3 + 5 = 9$, which is larger than any scores you'd get by taking the other "you" path. By sacrificing short-term rewards, you are able to gain even larger rewards in the long run. But due to the myopic nature of the greedy decoder, it will never choose this path—it can't backtrack and change its mind once it's taken one branch over another.

Choosing which way to go to maximize the total score seems easy if you look at the toy example in figure 6.15, but in reality, you can't "foresee" the future—if you are at timestep t, you can't predict what will happen at timestep t + 1 and onward, until you actually choose one word and feed it to the RNN. But the path that maximizes the individual probability is not necessarily the optimal solution. You just can't try every possible path and see what score you'd get, either, because the vocabulary usually contains tens of thousands of unique words, meaning the number of possible paths is exponentially large.

The sad truth is that you can't realistically expect to find the optimal path that maximizes the probability for the entire sentence within a reasonable amount of time. But you can avoid being stuck (or at least, make it less likely to be stuck) with a suboptimal solution, which is what the beam search decoder does.

6.4.4 *Beam search decoding*

Let's think what you would do if you were in the same situation. Let's use an analogy and say you are a college sophomore and need to decide which major to pursue by the end of the school year. Your goal is to maximize the total amount of income (or happiness or whatever thing you care about) over the course of your lifetime, but you don't know which major is the best for this. You can't simply try every possible major and see what happens after a couple of years—there are too many majors and you can't go back in time. Also, just because some particular majors look appealing in the short run (e.g., choosing an economics major may lead to some good internship opportunities at large investment banks) doesn't mean that path is the best in the long run (see what happened in 2008).

In such a situation, one thing you could do is to hedge your bet by pursuing more than one major (as a double major or a minor) at the same time instead of committing 100% to one particular major. After a couple of years, if the situation is more different than you had imagined, you can still change your mind and pursue another option, which is not possible if you choose your major greedily (i.e., based only on the short-term prospects).

The main idea of beam search decoding is similar to this—instead of committing to one path, it purses multiple paths (called *hypotheses*) at the same time. In this way, you leave some room for "dark horses," that is, hypotheses that had low scores at first but may prove promising later. Let's see this in action using the example in figure 6.16, a slightly modified version of figure 6.15.

The key idea of beam search decoding is to use a *beam* (figure 6.16 bottom), which you can think of as some sort of buffer that can retain multiple hypotheses at the same time. The size of the beam, that is, the number of hypotheses it can retain, is called the *beam width*. Let's use a beam of size 2 and see what happens. Initially, your first hypothesis consists of only one word, "Mary," and a score of 0. When you move on to the next word, the word you chose is appended to the hypothesis, and the score is incremented by the score of the path you have just taken. For example, when you move on to "did," it will make a new hypothesis consisting of "Mary did" and a score of 1.

If you have multiple words to choose from at any particular timestep, a hypothesis can spawn multiple child hypotheses. At timestep 2, you have three different

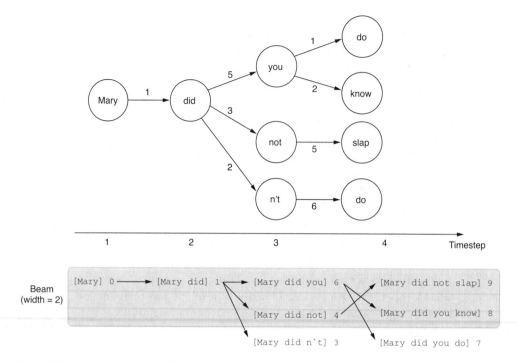

Figure 6.16   Beam search decoding

choices—"you," "not," and "n't"—which generate three new child hypotheses: [Mary did you] (6), [Mary did not] (4), and [Mary did n't] (3). And here's the key part of beam search decoding: because there's only so much room in the beam, any hypotheses that are not good enough fall off of the beam after sorting them by their scores. Because the beam can hold up to only two hypotheses in this example, anything except the top two gets kicked out of the beam, which leaves [Mary did you] (6) and [Mary did not] (4).

At timestep 3, each remaining hypothesis can spawn up to two child hypotheses. The first one ([Mary did you] (6)) will generate [Mary did you know] (8) and [Mary did you do] (7), whereas the second one ([Mary did not] (4)) turns into [Mary did not slap] (9). These three hypotheses are sorted by their scores, and the best two will be returned as the result of the beam search decoding.

Congratulations—now your algorithm was able to find the path that maximizes the total sum of the scores. By considering multiple hypotheses at the same time, beam search decoding can increase the chance that you will find better solutions. However, it is never perfect—notice that an equally good path [Mary did n't do] with a score of 9 fell out of the beam as early as timestep 3. To "rescue" it, you'd need to increase the beam width to 3 or larger. In general, the larger the beam width, the higher the expected quality of the translation results will be. However, there's a tradeoff: because the computer needs to consider multiple hypotheses, it will be linearly slower as the beam width increases.

In Fairseq, you can use the `--beam` option to change the beam size. In the example in section 6.3.3, I used `--beam 5` to use a beam width of 5. You were already using beam search without noticing. If you invoke the same command with `--beam 1`, which means you are using greedy decoding instead of a beam search, you may get slightly different results. When I tried this, I got almost the same results except the last one: "counts, please," which is not a great translation for "La cuenta, por favor." This means using a beam search indeed helps improve the translation quality!

6.5 *Evaluating translation systems*

In this section, I'd like to briefly touch on the topic of evaluating machine translation systems. Accurately evaluating MT systems is an important topic, both in theory and practice.

6.5.1 *Human evaluation*

The simplest and the most accurate way to evaluate MT systems' output is to use human evaluation. After all, language is translated for humans. Translations that are deemed good by humans should be good.

As mentioned previously, we have a few considerations for what makes a translation good. There are two most important and commonly used concepts for this—*adequacy* (also called *fidelity*) and *fluency* (also closely related to intelligibility). Adequacy is the degree to which the information in the source sentence is reflected in the translation. If you can reconstruct a lot of information expressed by the source sentence by reading its translation, then the translation has high adequacy. Fluency is, on the other hand, how natural the translation is in the target language. If you are translating into English, for example, "Mary did not slap the green witch" is a fluent translation, whereas "Mary no had a hit with witch, green" is not, although both translations are almost equally adequate. Note that these two aspects are somewhat independent—you can think of a translation that is fluent but not adequate (e.g., "Mary saw a witch in the forest" is a perfectly fluent but inadequate translation) and vice versa, like the earlier example. MT systems that produce output that is both adequate and fluent are desirable.

An MT system is usually evaluated by presenting its translations to human annotators and having them judge its output on a 5- or 7-point scale for each aspect. Fluency is easier to judge because it requires only monolingual speakers of the target sentence, whereas adequacy requires bilingual speakers of both the source and target languages.

6.5.2 *Automatic evaluation*

Although human evaluation gives the most accurate assessment to MT systems' quality, it's not always feasible. In most cases, you cannot afford to hire human evaluators to assess an MT system's output every time you need it. If you are dealing with language pairs that are not common, you might not be able to find bilingual speakers for evaluating adequacy at all.

But more importantly, you need to constantly evaluate and monitor an MT system's quality when you are developing one. For example, if you use a Seq2Seq model to train an NMT system, you need to reevaluate its performance every time you adjust one of the hyperparameters. Otherwise, you wouldn't know whether your change has a good or bad effect on its final performance. Even worse, if you were to do something like early stopping (see section 6.3.2) to determine when to stop the training process, you would need to evaluate its performance *after every epoch.* You can't possibly hire somebody and have them evaluate your intermediate models at each epoch—that would be a terribly slow way to develop an MT system. It's also a huge waste of time, because the output of initial models is largely garbage and does not warrant human evaluation. A large amount of correlation exists between the outputs of intermediate models, and human evaluators would be spending a lot of time evaluating very similar, if not identical, sentences.

For this reason, it'd be desirable if we could use some automatic way to assess translation quality. The way this works is similar to some automatic metrics for other NLP tasks that we saw earlier, such as accuracy, precision, recall, and F1-measure for classification. The idea is to create the desirable output for each input instance in advance and compare a system's output against it. This is usually done by preparing a set of human-created translations called *reference* for each source sentence and calculating some sort of similarity between the reference and a system's output. Once you create the reference and define the metric, you can automatically evaluate translation quality as many times as you want.

One of the simplest ways to compute the similarity between the reference and a system output is to use the *word error rate* (WER). WER reflects how many errors the system made compared to the reference, measured by the relative number of insertions, deletions, and substitutions. The concept is similar to the edit distance, except that WER is counted for words, not characters. For example, when the reference sentence is "Mary did not slap the green witch" and a system translation is "Mary did hit the green wicked witch," you need three "edits" to match the latter to the former—insert "not," replace "hit" with "slap," and delete "wicked." If you divide three by the length of the reference (= 7), it's your WER (= 3/7, or 0.43). The lower the WER, the better the quality of your translation.

Although WER is simple and easy to compute, it is not widely used for evaluating MT systems nowadays. One reason is related to multiple references. There may be multiple, equally valid translations for a single source sentence, but it is not clear how to apply WER when there are multiple references. A slightly more advanced and by far the most commonly used metric for automatic evaluation in MT is BLEU (bilingual evaluation understudy). BLEU solves the problem of multiple references by using *modified precision.* I'll illustrate this next using a simple example.

In the following table, we are evaluating a candidate (a system's output) "the the the the the the the" (which is, by the way, a terrible translation) against two references: "the cat is on the mat" and "there is a cat on the mat." The basic idea of BLEU is to calculate the precision of all unique words in the candidate. Because there's only one unique word in the candidate, "the," if you calculate its precision, it will automatically become the candidate's score, which is 1, or 100%. But there seems to be something wrong about this.

Candidate	the	the	the	the	the	the	the
Reference 1	the	cat	is	on	the	mat	
Reference 2	there	is	a	cat	on	the	mat

Because only two "thes" exist in the references, the spurious "thes" generated by the system shouldn't count toward the precision. In other words, we should treat them as false positives. We can do this by capping the denominator of precision by the maximum number of occurrences of that word in any of the references. Because it's 2 in this case (in reference 1), its modified precision will be 2/7, or about 29%. In practice, BLEU uses not only unique words (i.e., unigrams) but also all unique sequences of words (n-grams) up to a length of 4 in the candidate and the references.

However, we can game this metric in another way—because it's based on precision, not on recall, an MT system can easily obtain high scores by producing very few words that the system is confident about. In the previous example, you can simply produce "cat" (or even more simply, "the"), and the BLEU score will be 100%, which is obviously not a good translation. BLEU solves this issue by introducing the brevity penalty, which discounts the score if the candidate is shorter than the references.

Development of accurate automatic metrics has been an active research area. Many new metrics are proposed and used to address the shortcomings of BLEU. We barely scratched the surface in this section. Although new metrics show higher correlations with human evaluations and are claimed to be better, BLEU is still by far the most widely used metric, mainly due to its simplicity and long tradition.

6.6 Case study: Building a chatbot

In this section, I'm going to go over another application of a Seq2Seq model—a chatbot, which is an NLP application with which you can have a conversation. We are going to build a very simple yet functional chatbot using a Seq2Seq model and discuss techniques and challenges in building intelligent agents.

6.6.1 Introducing dialogue systems

I briefly touched upon dialogue systems in section 1.2.1. To recap, two main types of dialogue systems exist: task-oriented and chatbots. Although task-oriented dialogue systems are used to achieve some specific goals, such as making a reservation at a restaurant and obtaining some information, chatbots are used to have conversations with humans. Conversational technologies are currently a hot topic among NLP practitioners, due to the success and proliferation of commercial conversational AI systems such as Amazon Alexa, Apple Siri, and Google Assistant.

You may not have a clue as to how we can get started with building an NLP application that can have conversations. How can we build something "intelligent" that "thinks" so that it can generate meaningful responses to human input? This seems far-fetched and difficult. But if you step back and look at a typical conversation we have with other people, how much of it is actually "intelligent?" If you are like most of us, a large fraction of the conversation you are having is autopilot: "How are you?" "I'm doing good, thanks" "Have a good day" "You, too!" and so on. You may also have a set of "template" responses to a lot of everyday questions such as "What do you do?" and "Where are you from?" These questions can be answered just by looking at the input. Even more complex questions like "What's your favorite restaurant in X?" (where X is the name of a neighborhood in your city) and "Did you see any Y movies lately?" (where Y is a genre) can be answered just by "pattern matching" and retrieving relevant information from your memory.

If you think of a conversation as a set of "turns" where the response is generated by pattern matching against the previous utterance, this starts to look a lot like a typical NLP problem. In particular, if you regard dialogues as a problem where an NLP system is simply converting your question to its response, this is exactly where we can apply the Seq2Seq models we covered in this chapter so far. We can treat the previous (human's) utterance as a foreign sentence and have the chatbot "translate" it into another language. Even though these two languages are both English in this case, it is a common practice in NLP to treat the input and the output as two different languages and apply a Seq2Seq model to them, including summarization (longer text to a shorter one) and grammatical error correction (text with errors to one without).

6.6.2   *Preparing a dataset*

In this case study, we are going to use The Self-dialogue Corpus (https://github.com/jfainberg/self_dialogue_corpus), a collection of 24,165 conversations. What's special about this dataset is that these conversations are not actual ones between two people, but fictitious ones written by one person who plays both sides. You could use several conversation datasets for text-based chatbots (e.g., the OpenSubtitles dataset, http://opus.nlpl.eu/OpenSubtitles-v2018.php), but these datasets are often noisy and often contain obscenities. By collecting made-up conversations instead, the Self-dialogue Corpus improves the quality for half the original cost (because you need only one person versus two people!).

The same as earlier, I tokenized and converted the corpus into a format that is interpretable by Fairseq. You can obtain the converted dataset as follows:

```
$ mkdir -p data/chatbot
$ wget https://realworldnlpbook.s3.amazonaws.com/data/chatbot/selfdialog.zip
$ unzip selfdialog.zip -d data/chatbot
```

You can use the following combination of the `paste` command (to stitch files horizontally) and the `head` command to peek at the beginning of the training portion.

Note that we are using `fr` (for "foreign," not "French") to denote the "language" we are translating from:

```
$ paste data/chatbot/selfdialog.train.tok.fr data/chatbot/
    selfdialog.train.tok.en | head
...
Have you played in a band ?    What type of band ?
What type of band ?    A rock and roll band .
A rock and roll band .    Sure , I played in one for years .
Sure , I played in one for years .    No kidding ?
No kidding ?    I played in rock love love .
I played in rock love love .    You played local ?
You played local ?    Yes
Yes    Would you play again ?
Would you play again ?    Why ?
...
```

As you can see, each line consists of an utterance (on the left) and a response to it (on the right). Notice that this dataset has the same structure as the Spanish-English parallel corpus we used in section 6.3.1. The next step is to run the `fairseq-preprocess` command to convert it to a binary format as follows:

```
$ fairseq-preprocess \
    --source-lang fr \
    --target-lang en \
    --trainpref data/chatbot/selfdialog.train.tok \
    --validpref data/chatbot/selfdialog.valid.tok \
    --destdir data/chatbot-bin \
    --thresholdsrc 3 \
    --thresholdtgt 3
```

Again, this is similar to what we ran for the Spanish translator example. Just pay attention to what you specify as the source language—we are using `fr` instead of `es` here.

6.6.3 *Training and running a chatbot*

Now that the training data for the chatbot is ready, let's train a Seq2Seq model from this data. You can invoke the `fairseq-train` command with almost identical parameters to the last time, as shown next:

```
$ fairseq-train \
    data/chatbot-bin \
    --arch lstm \
    --share-decoder-input-output-embed \
    --optimizer adam \
    --lr 1.0e-3 \
    --max-tokens 4096 \
    --save-dir data/chatbot-ckpt
```

As previously, pay attention to how the validation loss changes every epoch. When I tried this, the validation loss decreased for about five epochs but then started to slowly creep back up. Feel free to stop the training command by pressing Ctrl + C after you observe the validation loss leveling out. Fairseq will automatically save the best model (measured by the validation loss) to checkpoint_best.pt.

Finally, you can run the chatbot model by invoking the fairseq-interactive command, as shown here:

```
$ fairseq-interactive \
    data/chatbot-bin \
    --path data/chatbot-ckpt/checkpoint_best.pt \
    --beam 5 \
    --source-lang fr \
    --target-lang en
```

As with the previous example, you can type your source sentences and have a conversion with your chatbot by having them "translate" to another language! Here's part of a conversation that I had with the model that I trained (I added boldface for clarity). Again, your results might be different:

```
Hi !
S-0      Hi !
H-0      -1.011711835861206      Hey .
P-0      -0.6860 -2.1352 -0.2140
How are you ?
S-1      How are you ?
H-1      -0.6552960276603699     Doing good , you ?
P-1      -0.6472 -0.8651 -1.0960 -0.9257 -0.3337 -0.0640
Good .
S-2      Good .
H-2      -0.8540937900543213     Do you have a favorite team ?
P-2      -2.3027 -0.0550 -1.7088 -0.4403 -0.1763 -2.0262 -0.1150 -0.0085
Yeah I like the Seahawks .
S-3      Yeah I like the Seahawks .
H-3      -0.6036218404769897     Do you have a favorite team ?
P-3      -2.7614 -0.0525 -1.0905 -0.3178 -0.3213 -0.1049 -0.1701 -0.0106
How about you ?
S-4      How about you ?
H-4      -1.2329542636871338     I 'm a big fan of them .
P-4      -0.7648 -1.8435 -1.6808 -1.2868 -0.2102 -0.1362 -3.5273 -1.0031 -0.6438
What 's your favorite movie ?
S-5      What 's your favorite movie ?
H-5      -0.8238655924797058     Oh , that 's a tough one . I 'd have to say
    Ghost Busters .
P-5      -3.2622 -0.3213 -1.4815 -0.1012 -0.3417 -0.3069 -0.2432 -0.6954 -
    1.0858 -2.3246 -0.4296 -0.0039 -0.0905 -2.6429 -0.1676 -0.3853 -0.1221
Oh yeah , I like that movie too .
S-6      Oh yeah , I like that movie too .
H-6      -1.0659444332122803     Yeah , that 's a good one .
P-6      -2.0782 -0.1724 -2.5089 -0.9560 -1.5034 -0.9040 -0.4471 -0.5435 -0.4801
```

In this example, the conversation looks natural. Because the Self-dialogue Corpus is built by restricting the set of possible conversation topics, the conversation is more likely to go smoothly if you stay on such topics (movie, sports, music, and so on).

However, as soon as you start talking about unfamiliar topics, the chatbot loses its confidence in its answers, as shown next:

```
What 's your name ?
S-0      What 's your name ?
H-0      -0.9807574152946472      I do n't know , but I do n't think I 've
                                   heard of them .
P-0      -1.4680 -2.2938 -0.0635 -1.0242 -1.2039 -0.5201 -0.3381 -2.2612 -
         0.1665 -1.6033 -0.6112 -1.5515 -0.8739 -0.8453 -1.0143 -0.4702 -0.3637
What do you do ?
S-1      What do you do ?
H-1      -1.170507788658142       I do n't know .
P-1      -0.9807 -2.1846 -0.3276 -0.9733 -1.3650 -1.1919
Are you a student ?
S-2      Are you a student ?
H-2      -0.9505285024642944      I 'm not sure .
P-2      -1.5676 -1.5270 -0.6944 -0.2493 -0.8445 -0.8204
```

This is a well-known phenomenon—a simple Seq2Seq-based chatbot quickly regresses to producing cookie-cutter answers such as "I don't know" and "I'm not sure" whenever asked about something it's not familiar with. This has to do with the way we trained this chatbot. Because we trained the model so that it minimizes the loss in the training data, the best strategy it can take to reduce the loss is to produce something applicable to as many input sentences as possible. Very generic phrases such as "I don't know" can be an answer for many questions, so it's a great way to play it safe and reduce the loss!

6.6.4 Next steps

Although our chatbot can produce realistic-looking responses for many inputs, it's far from perfect. One issue that it's not great at dealing with is proper nouns. You can see this when you ask questions that solicit specific answers, like the following:

```
What 's your favorite show ?
S-0      What 's your favorite show ?
H-0      -0.9829921722412109      I would have to say <unk> .
P-0      -0.8807 -2.2181 -0.4752 -0.0093 -0.0673 -2.9091 -0.9338 -0.3705
```

Here <unk> is the catch-all special symbol for unknown words. The chatbot is trying to answer something, but that something occurs too infrequently in the training data to be treated as an independent word. This is an issue seen in simple NMT systems in general. Because the models need to cram everything about a word in a 200-something-dimensional vector of numbers, many details and distinctions between similar words are sacrificed. Imagine compressing all the information about all the restaurants in your city into a 200-dimensional vector!

Also, the chatbot we trained doesn't have any "memory" or any notion of context whatsoever. You can test this by asking a series of related questions as follows:

```
Do you like Mexican food ?
S-0      Do you like Mexican food ?
```

```
H-0     -0.805641770362854        Yes I do .
P-0     -1.0476 -1.1101 -0.6642 -0.6651 -0.5411
Why do you like it ?
S-1     Why do you like it ?
H-1     -1.2453081607818604        I think it 's a great movie .
P-1     -0.7999 -2.1023 -0.7766 -0.7130 -1.4816 -2.2745 -1.5750 -1.0524 -0.4324
```

In the second question, the chatbot is having difficulties understanding the context and produces a completely irrelevant response. To answer such questions correctly, the model needs to understand that the pronoun "it" refers to a previous noun, namely, "Mexican food" in this case. The task where NLP systems resolve which mentions refer to which entities in the real world is called *coreference resolution*. The system also needs to maintain some type of memory to keep track of what was discussed so far in the dialogue.

Finally, the simple Seq2Seq models we discussed in this chapter are not great at dealing with long sentences. If you look back at figure 6.2, you'll understand why—the model reads the input sentence using an RNN and represents everything about the sentence using a fixed-length sentence representation vector and then generates the target sentence from that vector. It doesn't matter whether the input is "Hi!" or "The quick brown fox jumped over the lazy dog." The sentence representation becomes a bottleneck, especially for longer input. Because of this, neural MT models couldn't beat traditional phrase-based statistical MT models until around 2015, when a mechanism called *attention* was invented to tackle this very problem. We'll discuss attention in detail in chapter 8.

Summary

- Sequence-to-sequence (Seq2Seq) models transform one sequence into another using an encoder and a decoder.
- You can use the `fairseq` framework to build a working MT system within an hour.
- A Seq2Seq model uses a decoding algorithm to generate the target sequence. Greedy decoding maximizes the probability at each step, whereas beam search tries to find better solutions by considering multiple hypotheses at once.
- A metric called BLEU is commonly used for automatically evaluating MT systems.
- A simple chatbot can be built by using a Seq2Seq model and a conversation dataset.

Convolutional neural networks

This chapter covers

- Solving text classification by detecting patterns
- Using convolutional layers to detect patterns and produce scores
- Using pooling layers to aggregate the scores produced by convolution
- Building a convolutional neural network (CNN) by combining convolution and pooling
- Building a CNN-based text classifier using AllenNLP

In previous chapters, we covered linear layers and RNNs, two main neural network architectures commonly used in NLP. In this chapter, we introduce another important class of neural networks called *convolutional neural networks* (CNNs). CNNs have different characteristics than RNNs that make them suitable for NLP tasks where detecting linguistic patterns is important, such as text classification.

7.1 *Introducing convolutional neural networks (CNNs)*

This section introduces convolutional neural networks (CNNs), another type of neural network architecture that operates in a different way from how RNNs work. CNNs are particularly good at pattern-matching tasks and are increasingly popular in the NLP community.

7.1.1 *RNNs and their shortcomings*

In chapter 4, we covered sentence classification, which is an NLP task that receives some text as the input and produces a label for it. We also discussed how to use recurrent neural networks (RNNs) for that task. As a refresher, an RNN is a type of neural network that has a "loop" in it, which processes the input sequence one element at a time from the beginning until the end. The internal loop variable, which is updated at every step, is called the *hidden state*. When the RNN finishes processing the entire sequence, the hidden state at the final timestep represents the compressed content of the input sequence, which can be used for NLP tasks including sentence classification. Alternatively, you can take out the hidden state after every step and use it to assign labels (such as PoS and named entity tags) to individual words. The structure that is applied repeatedly in the loop is called a *cell*. An RNN with a simple multiplication and nonlinearity is called a *vanilla* or an *Elman* RNN. On the other hand, LSTM and GRU-based RNNs use more complicated cells that employ memory and gating.

RNNs are a powerful tool in modern NLP with a wide range of applications; however, they are not without shortcomings. First, RNNs are slow—they need to scan the input sequence element by element no matter what. Their computational complexity is proportional to the length of the input sequences. Second, due to their sequential nature, RNNs are hard to parallelize. Think of a multilayer RNN where multiple RNN layers are stacked on top of each other (as shown in figure 7.1). In a naive implementation, each layer needs to wait until all the layers below it finish processing the input.

Third, the RNN structure is simply overkill and inefficient for some tasks. For example, recall the task of detecting grammatical English sentences that we covered in chapter 4. In its simplest form, the task is to recognize valid and invalid subject-verb agreement in a two-word sentence. If a sentence contains phrases such as "I am" and "you are," it's grammatical. If it contains "I are" or "you am," it's not. In chapter 4, we built a simple LSTM-RNN with a nonlinearity to recognize the grammaticality of two-word sentences with a vocabulary of four words. But what if you need to classify whether an arbitrary long sentence with a very large vocabulary is grammatical? Suddenly, this process starts to sound very complex. Your LSTM needs to learn to pick up the signal (subject-verb agreement) from a large amount of noise (all other words and phrases that have nothing to do with agreement), while learning to do all this using the update operation that gets repeated for every single element of the input.

But if you think about it, no matter how long the sentence is or how large the vocabulary is, your network's job should still be quite simple—if the sentence contains valid collocations (such as "I am" and "you are"), it's grammatical. Otherwise, it's not.

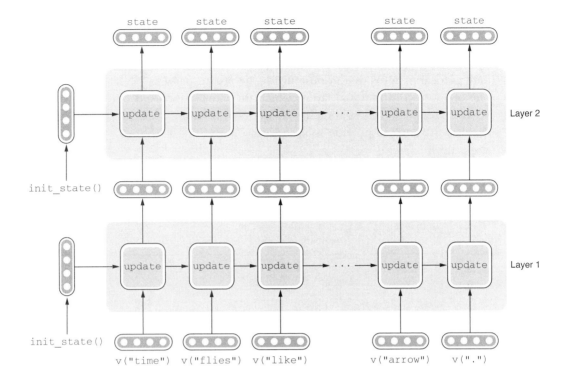

Figure 7.1 Multilayer RNN

The task is actually not very far from the "if-then" sentiment analyzer that we saw in chapter 1. It is obvious that the structure of LSTM RNNs is overkill for this task, where simple pattern matching over words and phrases would suffice.

7.1.2 Pattern matching for sentence classification

If you look at text classification in general, many tasks can be effectively solved by this "pattern matching." Take spam filtering, for example—if you want to detect spam emails, simply look for words and phrases such as "v1agra" and "business opportunity" without even reading the entire email; it doesn't matter where these patterns appear. If you want to detect sentiment from movie reviews, detecting positive and negative words such as "amazing" and "awful" would go a long way. In other words, learning and detecting such local linguistic patterns, regardless of their location, is an effective and efficient strategy for text-classification tasks, and possibly for other NLP tasks as well.

In chapter 3, we learned the concept of n-grams—contiguous sequences of one or more words. They are often used in NLP as proxies for more formally defined linguistic units such as phrases and clauses. If there's some tool that can wade through a large amount of noise in text and detect n-grams that serve as signals, it would be a great fit for text classification.

7.1.3   *Convolutional neural networks (CNNs)*

Convolutional neural networks, or CNNs, do exactly this. A CNN is a type of neural network that involves a mathematical operation called *convolution*, which, put simply, detects local patterns that are useful for the task at hand. A CNN usually consists of one or more convolutional layers, which do convolution, and pooling layers, which are responsible for aggregating the result of convolution. See figure 7.2 for a diagram. Sections 7.2 and 7.3 provide some detail of convolutional layers and pooling layers, respectively.

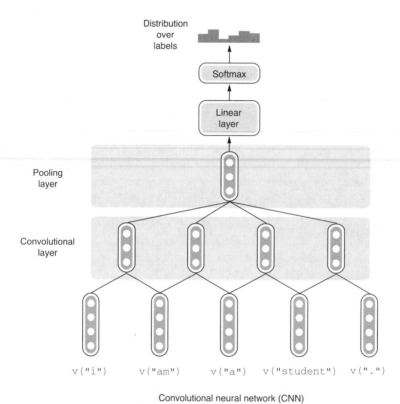

Convolutional neural network (CNN)

**Figure 7.2
Convolutional
neural network**

CNNs, which are inspired by the visual system in the human brain, have been widely used for computer vision tasks such as image classification and object detection. In recent years, the use of CNNs has been increasingly popular in NLP, especially for tasks such as text classification, sequential labeling, and machine translation.

7.2   *Convolutional layers*

In this section, we'll discuss convolutional layers, the essential part of the CNN architecture. The term *convolution* may sound a bit scary, but at its essence, it's just pattern matching. We'll use diagrams and intuitive examples to illustrate how it really works.

7.2.1 Pattern matching using filters

Convolutional layers are the most important component in CNNs. As mentioned earlier, convolutional layers apply a mathematical operation called convolution to input vectors and produce output. But what is convolution? Understanding the strict definition of convolution requires knowing linear algebra, so we'll use some analogy and concrete examples to understand it. Imagine holding a rectangular-shaped patch of colored glass with complex patterns (like the stained glass you see in a church) and sliding it over the input sequence while looking through it. If the input pattern matches that of the patch, more light goes through the glass and you get larger output values. If the input pattern does not look like that of the patch or looks the opposite, you get smaller output values. In other words, you are looking for particular patterns in the input sequence using a patch of colored glass.

This analogy is a little bit too vague, so let's revisit the grammaticality-detection example we used in chapter 4 and see how we'd apply a convolutional layer to the task. To recap, our neural network receives a two-word sentence as an input and needs to distinguish grammatical sequences from ungrammatical ones. There are only four words in the vocabulary—"I," "you," "am," and "are," which are represented by word embeddings. Similarly, there are only four possibilities for the input sentence—"I am," "I are," "you am," and "you are." You want the network to produce 1s for the first and the last cases and 0s for others. See figure 7.3 for an illustration.

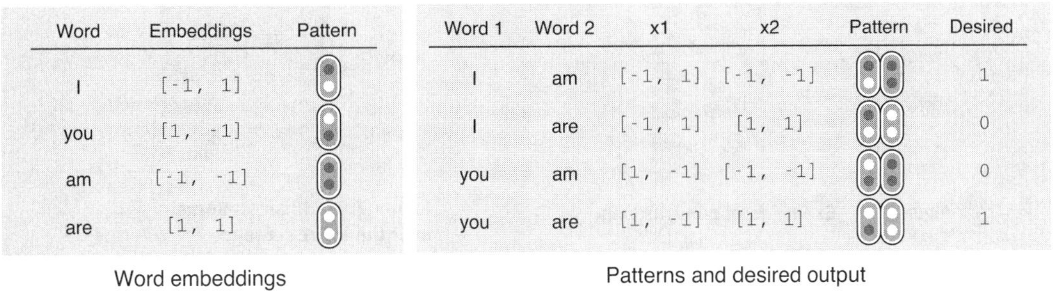

Word	Embeddings	Pattern
I	[-1, 1]	
you	[1, -1]	
am	[-1, -1]	
are	[1, 1]	

Word embeddings

Word 1	Word 2	x1	x2	Pattern	Desired
I	am	[-1, 1]	[-1, -1]		1
I	are	[-1, 1]	[1, 1]		0
you	am	[1, -1]	[-1, -1]		0
you	are	[1, -1]	[1, 1]		1

Patterns and desired output

Figure 7.3 Recognizing grammatical English sentences

Now, let's represent word embeddings as patterns. We'll draw a black circle for value −1 and a white one for 1. Then you can represent each word vector as a pair of two circles (see the table on the left in figure 7.3). Similarly, you can represent each two-word sentence as a small "patch" of two vectors, or four circles (see the table on the right in figure 7.3). Our task is beginning to look more like a pattern-recognition task, where the network needs to learn black-and-white patterns that correspond to grammatical sentences.

Then, let's think of a "filter" of the same size (two circles × two circles) that acts as the colored glass we talked about earlier. Each circle of this filter is also either black or white, corresponding to values −1 and 1. You are going to look at a pattern through this filter and determine whether the pattern is the one you are looking for. You do this by putting the filter over a pattern and counting the number of color matches between the two. For each one of four positions, you get a score of +1 if the colors match (black-black or white-white) and a score of –1 if they don't (black-white or white-black). Your final score is the sum of four scores, which varies from –4 (no matches) to +4 (four matches). See figure 7.4 for some examples.

The score you get varies depending on the pattern and the filter, but as you can see in the figure, the score becomes larger when the filter looks similar to the pattern and becomes smaller when the two are not similar. You get the largest score (4) when the two match exactly and the smallest score (–4) when the two are exactly opposite. The filter acts as a pattern detector against the input. Although this is a very simplified example, it basically shows what a convolutional layer is doing. In convolutional neural networks, such filters are called *kernels*.

In a more general setting, you have an input sentence of arbitrary length, and you slide a kernel over the sentence from left to right. See figure 7.5 for an illustration of this. The kernel is repeatedly applied to two consecutive words to produce a sequence of scores. Because the kernel we are using here covers two words, it is said to have a *size* of 2. Also, because there are two dimensions in the input embeddings (which are called *channels*), the number of the kernel's input channels is 2.

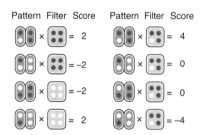

Figure 7.4   Examples of convolutional filters

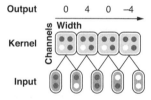

Figure 7.5   Sliding a kernel over the input sentence

NOTE The reason embedding dimensions are called channels is because CNNs are most commonly applied to computer vision tasks where the input is often a 2-D image of different channels that correspond to intensities of different colors (such as red, green, and blue). In computer vision, kernels are two dimensional and move over the input 2-D images, which is also called *2-D convolution*. In NLP, however, kernels are usually one-dimensional (1-D convolution) and have only one size.

7.2.2   *Rectified linear unit (ReLU)*

As the next step, let's think about how we can get the desired output (the Desired column in figure 7.3) using kernels. How about if we use the filter shown in the second column of figure 7.4? The kernel, which we'll call kernel 1 from now on, matches the first pattern exactly and gives it a high score, while giving zero or negative scores to others. Figure 7.6 shows the score (called score 1) when kernel 1 is applied to each pattern.

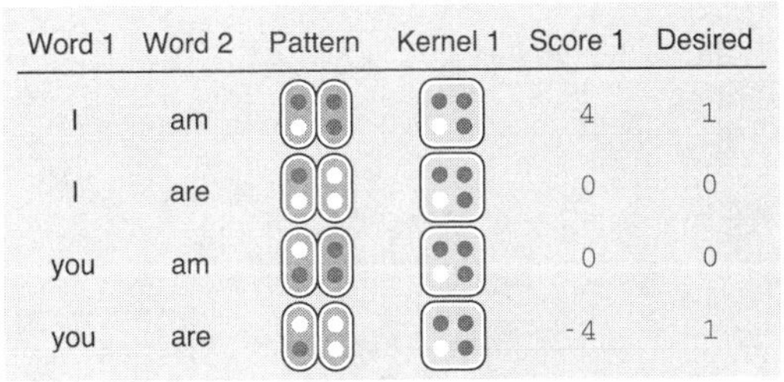

Word 1	Word 2	Pattern	Kernel 1	Score 1	Desired
I	am			4	1
I	are			0	0
you	am			0	0
you	are			-4	1

Figure 7.6 **Applying kernel 1 to patterns**

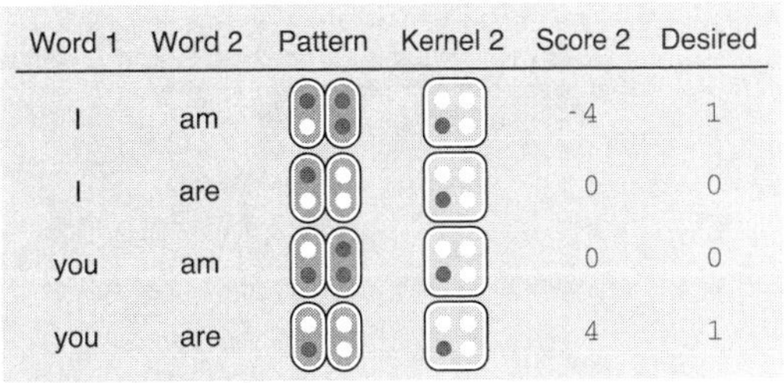

Word 1	Word 2	Pattern	Kernel 2	Score 2	Desired
I	am			-4	1
I	are			0	0
you	am			0	0
you	are			4	1

Figure 7.7 **Applying kernel 2 to patterns**

Let's forget the magnitude of the scores for now and focus on their signs (positive and negative). The signs for the first three patterns match between Score 1 and Desired, but not for the last pattern. To score it correctly—that is, to give it a positive score—you need to use another filter that matches the last pattern exactly. Let's call this kernel 2. Figure 7.7 shows the score (called score 2) when kernel 2 is applied to each pattern.

Kernel 2 can give correct scores that match the signs of the desired ones for the last three patterns, but not for the first one. But if you observe figures 7.6 and 7.7 carefully, it looks like you could get closer to the desired scores if there was a way to somehow disregard the output when a kernel gives negative scores and then combine the scores from multiple kernels.

Let's think of a function that clamps any negative input to zero while passing any positive values through unchanged. In Python, this function can be written as follows:

```
def f(x):
    if x >= 0:
        return x
    else:
        return 0
```

or even simpler

```
def f(x):
    return max(0, x)
```

You can disregard negative values by applying this function to score 1 and score 2, as shown in figures 7.8 and 7.9.

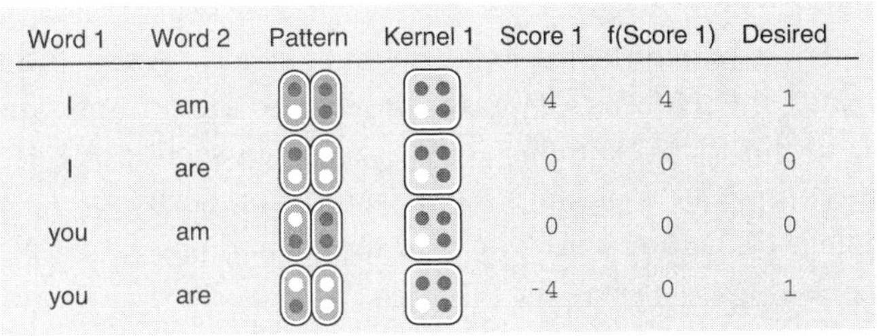

Word 1	Word 2	Pattern	Kernel 1	Score 1	f(Score 1)	Desired
I	am			4	4	1
I	are			0	0	0
you	am			0	0	0
you	are			-4	0	1

Figure 7.8 **Applying ReLU to score 1**

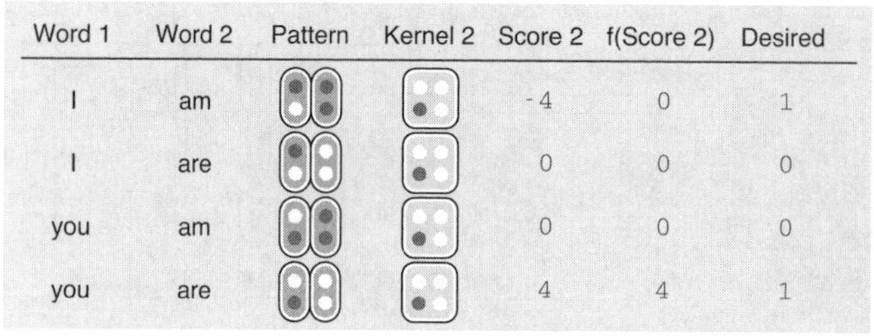

Word 1	Word 2	Pattern	Kernel 2	Score 2	f(Score 2)	Desired
I	am			-4	0	1
I	are			0	0	0
you	am			0	0	0
you	are			4	4	1

Figure 7.9 Applying ReLU to score 2

This function, which is called a *rectified linear unit*, or ReLU (pronounced "rel-you"), is one of the simplest yet most commonly used activation functions in deep learning. It is often used with a convolutional layer, and although it is very simple (all it does is just clamp negative values to zero), it is still an activation function that enables neural networks to learn complex nonlinear functions (see chapter 4 for why nonlinear activation functions are important). It also has favorable mathematical properties that make it easier to optimize the network, although the theoretical details are beyond the scope of this book.

7.2.3 Combining scores

If you look at both figures 7.8 and 7.9, the "clamped" scores—shown in the f(Score 1) and f(Score 2) columns—capture the desired scores at least partially. All you need to do is combine them together (by summing) and adjust the range (by dividing by 4). Figure 7.10 shows the result of this.

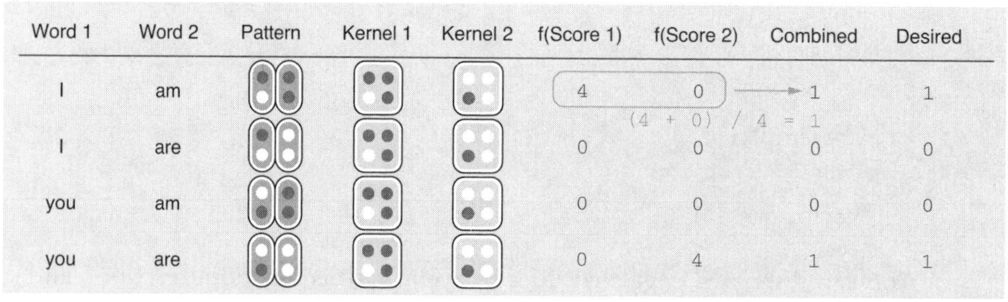

Word 1	Word 2	Pattern	Kernel 1	Kernel 2	f(Score 1)	f(Score 2)	Combined	Desired
I	am				4	0	1	1
						(4 + 0) / 4 = 1		
I	are				0	0	0	0
you	am				0	0	0	0
you	are				0	4	1	1

Figure 7.10 Combining the results from two kernels

After combining, the scores match the desired outcomes exactly. All we did so far was design kernels that match the patterns we want to detect and then simply combine the scores. Compare this to the RNN example we worked on in section 4.1.3, where we needed to use some complicated numeric computation to derive the parameters. Hopefully this example is enough to show you how simple and powerful CNNs can be for text classification!

The example we worked on in this section is simply for introducing the basic concepts of CNNs, so we cut many corners. First, in practice, patterns and kernels are not just black and white but contain real-valued numbers. The score after applying a kernel to a pattern is obtained not by counting color matches but through a mathematical operation called *inner product*, which captures the similarity between the two. Second, the scores produced by kernels aren't combined by some arbitrary operation (like we did in this section) but usually by a linear layer (see section 3.4.3), which can learn a linear transformation against the input to produce the output. Finally, kernels and the weights (magic constants w and b) in the final linear layer are all trainable parameters of a CNN, meaning that their values are adjusted so that the CNN can produce the desired scores.

7.3 Pooling layers

In the previous section, we assumed that the input is just a combination of two words—subjects and verbs—although in practice, the input to a CNN can be of arbitrary length. Your CNN needs to not only detect patterns but also find them in a potentially large amount of noise in the input. As we saw in section 7.2, you slide a kernel over the sentence from left to right, and the kernel is repeatedly applied to two consecutive words to produce a sequence of scores. The remaining question is what to do with these produced scores. Specifically, what operation should we use in the "?" position in figure 7.11 to derive the desired score? This operation needs to have some properties—it must be something that can be applied to an arbitrarily large number of scores, because the sentence can be very long. It also needs to aggregate the scores in a way that is agnostic to where the target pattern (word embeddings for "I am") is in the input sentence. Can you figure out the answer?

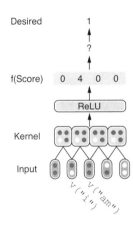

Figure 7.11 Aggregating scores to derive the desired score

The simplest thing you can do to aggregate the scores is to take their maximum. Because the largest score in figure 7.11 is 4, it will become the output of this layer. This aggregation operation is called *pooling*, and the neural network substructure that does pooling is called a *pooling layer*. You can also do other types of mathematical operations that do aggregation, such as taking the average, although taking the maximum (called *max pooling*) is most commonly used.

The pooled score will be fed to a linear layer, optionally combined with scores from other kernels, and used as a predicted score. This entire process is illustrated in figure 7.12. Now we have a fully functional CNN!

As with other neural networks we've seen so far, the output from the linear layer is fed to softmax to produce a probability distribution over labels. These predicted values are then compared with the true labels to produce the loss and used for optimizing the network.

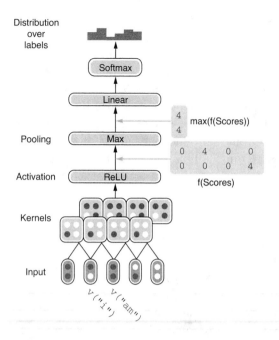

Figure 7.12   A full CNN with multiple kernels

Before we wrap up, a few more words on CNNs: notice that the CNN in figure 7.12 produces the same prediction value no matter where the search pattern ("I am") is in the input sentence. This is due to the kernel locality as well as the property of the max pooling layer we just added. In general, CNNs produce the same prediction, even if the input sentence is modified by shifting by a few words. In a technical term, the CNN is called *transformation invariant*, which is an important property of CNNs. This property is perhaps more intuitive if you use an image recognition example. An image of a cat is still an image of a cat, no matter where the cat is in the image. Similarly, a grammatical English sentence (e.g., "I am a student") is still grammatical, even if the sentence is transformed by adding a few words (e.g., "that's right") to the beginning, making it "That's right, I am a student."

Because the kernels in a CNN do not depend on each other (unlike RNNs, where one cell needs to wait until all the preceding cells finish processing the input), CNNs are computationally efficient. GPUs can process these kernels in parallel without waiting on other kernels' output. Due to this property, CNNs are usually faster than RNNs of similar size.

7.4   *Case study: Text classification*

Now that we know the basics of CNNs, in this section we are going to build an NLP application using a CNN and see how it works in practice. As mentioned previously, one of the most popular and straightforward applications of CNNs in NLP is text classification. CNNs are good at detecting patterns (such as salient words and phrases in text), which is also the key to accurate text classification.

7.4.1   *Review: Text classification*

We already covered text classification in chapters 2 and 4, but to recap, text classification is a task where an NLP system assigns a label to a given piece of text. If the text is an email and the label is whether the email is spam, it's spam filtering. If the text is a document (such as a news article) and the label is its topic (such as politics, business, technology, or sports), it's called *document classification*. Many other variants of text classification exist, depending on what the input and the output are. But the task we'll be working on in this section is again sentiment analysis, where the input is some text in which the writer's subjective opinions are expressed (such as movie and product reviews) and the output is the label for the opinion (such as positive or negative, or even the number of stars), also called *polarity*.

In chapters 2 and 4, we built an NLP system that detected the polarity given a movie review using the Stanford Sentiment Treebank, a dataset containing movie reviews and their polarity (strongly positive, positive, neutral, negative, or strongly negative). In this section, we will build the same text classifier but with a CNN instead of an RNN. The good news is that we can reuse most of the code we wrote in chapter 2 in this section—in fact, we need to modify only a few lines of code to swap the RNN with a CNN. This is largely thanks to AllenNLP's powerful, well-designed abstractions, which let you work with many modules with different architectures through the common interfaces. Let's see this in action next.

7.4.2 Using CnnEncoder

Remember that back in section 4.4, we defined our `LstmClassifier` for text classification as follows:

```
class LstmClassifier(Model):
    def __init__(self,
                 embedder: TextFieldEmbedder,
                 encoder: Seq2VecEncoder,
                 vocab: Vocabulary,
                 positive_label: str = '4') -> None:
        ...
```

We hadn't put much thought into what this definition meant, but from this constructor we can see that the model is built on top of two subcomponents: a `TextField-Embedder` called `embedder` and a `Seq2VecEncoder` called `encoder`, in addition to the vocabulary and the string for the positive label, which are not relevant to our discussion here. We discussed word embeddings in chapter 3 at length, although we only briefly touched on the encoder. What does this `Seq2VecEncoder` actually mean?

In AllenNLP, `Seq2VecEncoder` is a class of neural network architectures that take a sequence of vectors (or tensors in general) and return a single vector. An RNN, one example of this, takes a variable-length input consisting of multiple vectors and converts it into a single vector at the last cell. We created an instance of `Seq2VecEncoder` based on an LSTM-RNN using the following code:

```
encoder = PytorchSeq2VecWrapper(
    torch.nn.LSTM(EMBEDDING_DIM, HIDDEN_DIM, batch_first=True))
```

But as long as your component has the same input and output specifications, you can use any neural network architecture as a `Seq2VecEncoder`. In programming language, `Seq2VecEncoder` is analogous to an interface in Java (and in many other languages)—interfaces define what your class looks like and what it does, but they do not care about *how* your class does it. In fact, your model can do something as simple as just summing up all the input vectors to produce the output, without any complex transformations such as nonlinearities. This is, in fact, what `BagOfEmbeddings-Encoder`—one of the `Seq2VecEncoders` implemented in AllenNLP—does.

Next, we use a CNN to "squash" a sequence of vectors into a single vector. A CNN-based `Seq2VecEncoder` is implemented as `CnnEncoder` in AllenNLP, which can be instantiated as follows:

```
encoder = CnnEncoder(
    embedding_dim=EMBEDDING_DIM,
    num_filters=8,
    ngram_filter_sizes=(2, 3, 4, 5))
```

In this example, `embedding_dim` specifies the dimensionality of the input embeddings. The second argument, `num_filters`, tells how many filters (or kernels, as explained in section 7.2.1) will be used per n-gram. The final argument, `ngram_filter_sizes`, specifies the list of n-gram sizes, which are the sizes of these kernels. Here, we are using n-gram sizes of 2, 3, 4, and 5, meaning there are 8 kernels for bigrams, 8 kernels for trigrams, and so on, up to 5-grams. In total, this CNN can learn 32 different kernels to detect patterns. `CnnEncoder` runs these results from the kernels through a max pooling layer and comes up with a single vector that summarizes the input.

The rest of the training pipeline looks almost identical to the LSTM version we saw in chapter 2. The entire code is available on Google Colab (http://www.realworld nlpbook.com/ch7.html#cnn-nb). There is one caveat: because some n-gram filters have a wide shape (e.g., 4- and 5-grams), you need to make sure that each text field is at least that long, even when the original text is short (e.g., just one or two words). You need to know how batching and padding work in AllenNLP (which we'll cover in chapter 10) to fully understand how to deal with this, but in a nutshell, you need to specify the `token_min_padding_length` parameter when initializing the token indexer as follows:

```
token_indexer = SingleIdTokenIndexer(token_min_padding_length=5)
reader = StanfordSentimentTreeBankDatasetReader(
    token_indexers={'tokens': token_indexer})
```

7.4.3   *Training and running the classifier*

When you run the script, you'll see something like the following log output at the end of the training:

```
{'best_epoch': 1,
 'best_validation_accuracy': 0.40236148955495005,
 'best_validation_f1_measure': 0.37362638115882874,
 'best_validation_loss': 1.346440097263881,
 'best_validation_precision': 0.4722222089767456,
 'best_validation_recall': 0.30909091234207153,
 'epoch': 10,
 'peak_cpu_memory_MB': 601.656,
 'training_accuracy': 0.993562734082397,
```

```
'training_cpu_memory_MB': 601.656,
'training_duration': '0:01:10.138277',
'training_epochs': 10,
'training_f1_measure': 0.994552493095398,
'training_loss': 0.03471498479299275,
'training_precision': 0.9968798756599426,
'training_recall': 0.9922360181808472,
'training_start_epoch': 0,
'validation_accuracy': 0.35149863760217986,
'validation_f1_measure': 0.376996785402298,
'validation_loss': 3.045241366113935,
'validation_precision': 0.3986486494541168,
'validation_recall': 0.35757574439048767}
```

This means that the training accuracy reaches ~99%, whereas the validation accuracy tops around 40%. Again, this is a typical symptom of overfitting, where your model is so powerful that it fits the training data well, but it doesn't generalize to the validation and test datasets as well. Our CNN has many filters that can remember salient patterns in the training data, but these patterns are not necessarily the ones that help predict the labels for the validation instances. We are not worried too much about overfitting in this chapter. See chapter 10 for common techniques for avoiding overfitting.

If you want to make predictions for new instances, you can use the same `Predictor` as we did in chapter 2. Predictors in AllenNLP are a thin wrapper around your trained model, which take care of formatting the input and output in a JSON format and feeding the instance to the model. You can use the following snippet to make predictions using your trained CNN model:

```
predictor = SentenceClassifierPredictor(model, dataset_reader=reader)
logits = predictor.predict('This is the best movie ever!')['logits']
label_id = np.argmax(logits)

print(model.vocab.get_token_from_index(label_id, 'labels'))
```

Summary

- CNNs use filters called kernels and an operation called convolution to detect local linguistic patterns in the input.
- An activation function called ReLU, which clamps negative values to zero, is used with convolution layers.
- CNNs then use pooling layers to aggregate the result from the convolutional layer.
- CNN prediction is transformation invariant, meaning it remains unchanged even after linear modification of the input.
- You can use a CNN-based encoder as a `Seq2VecEncoder` in AllenNLP by modifying a few lines of code of your text classifier.

Attention and Transformer

This chapter covers

- Using attention to produce summaries of the input and improve the quality of Seq2Seq models
- Replacing RNN-style loops with self-attention, a mechanism for the input to summarize itself
- Improving machine translation systems with the Transformer model
- Building a high-quality spell-checker using the Transformer model and publicly available datasets

Our focus so far in this book has been recurrent neural networks (RNNs), which are a powerful model that can be applied to various NLP tasks such as sentiment analysis, named entity recognition, and machine translation. In this chapter, we will introduce an even more powerful model—the *Transformer*[1]—a new type of encoder-decoder neural network architecture based on the concept of self-attention. It is without a doubt the most important NLP model since it appeared in 2017. Not only

---

[1] Vaswani et al., "Attention Is All You Need," (2017). https://arxiv.org/abs/1706.03762.

is it a powerful model itself (for machine translation and various Seq2Seq tasks, for example), but it is also used as the underlying architecture that powers numerous modern NLP pretrained models, including GPT-2 (section 8.4.3) and BERT (section 9.2). The developments in modern NLP since 2017 can be best summarized as "the era of the Transformer."

In this chapter, we start with attention, a mechanism that made a breakthrough in machine translation, then move on to introducing self-attention, the concept that forms the foundation of the Transformer model. We will build two NLP applications—a Spanish-to-English machine translator and a high-quality spell-checker—and learn how to apply the Transformer model to your everyday applications. As we'll see later, the Transformer models can improve the quality of NLP systems over RNNs by a large margin and achieve almost human-level performance in some tasks, such as translation and generation.

8.1 What is attention?

In chapter 6, we covered Seq2Seq models—NLP models that transform one sequence to another using an encoder and a decoder. Seq2Seq is a versatile and powerful paradigm with many applications, although the "vanilla" Seq2Seq models are not without limitation. In this section, we discuss the Seq2Seq models' bottleneck and motivate the use of an attention mechanism.

8.1.1 Limitation of vanilla Seq2Seq models

Let's remind ourselves how Seq2Seq models work. Seq2Seq models consist of an encoder and a decoder. The decoder takes a sequence of tokens in the source language and runs it through an RNN, which produces a fixed-length vector at the end. This fixed-length vector is a representation of the input sentence. The decoder, which is another RNN, takes this vector and produces a sequence in the target language, token by token. Figure 8.1 illustrates how Spanish sentences are translated into English with a vanilla Seq2Seq model.

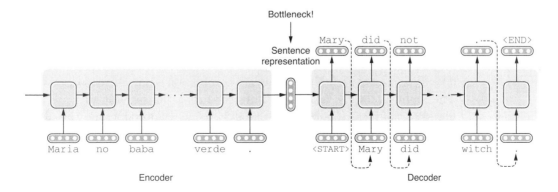

Figure 8.1 A bottleneck in a vanilla Seq2Seq model

This Seq2Seq architecture is quite simple and powerful, but it is known that its vanilla version (shown in figure 8.1) does not translate sentences as well as other traditional machine translation algorithms (such as phrase-based statistical machine translation models). You may be able to guess why this is the case if you look at its structure carefully—its encoder is trying to "compress" all the information in the source sentence into the sentence representation, which is a vector of some fixed length (e.g., 256 floating-point numbers), and the decoder is trying to restore the entire target sentence just from that vector. The size of the vector is fixed no matter how long (or how short) the source sentence is. The intermediate vector is a huge bottleneck. If you think of how humans actually translate between languages, this sounds quite difficult and somewhat unusual. Professional translators do not just read the source sentence and write down its translation in one breath. They refer to the source sentences as many times as necessary to translate the relevant parts in the target sentence.

Compressing all the information into one vector may (and does) work for short sentences, as we'll see later in section 8.2.2, but it becomes increasingly difficult as the sentences get longer and longer. Studies have shown that the translation quality of a vanilla Seq2Seq model gets worse as the sentence gets longer.[2]

8.1.2   *Attention mechanism*

Instead of relying on a single, fixed-length vector to represent all the information in a sentence, the decoder would have a much easier time if there was a mechanism where it can refer to some specific part of the encoder as it generates the target tokens. This is similar to how human translators (the decoder) reference the source sentence (the encoder) as needed.

This can be achieved by using *attention*, which is a mechanism in neural networks that focuses on a specific part of the input and computes its context-dependent summary. It is like having some sort of key-value store that contains all of the input's information and then looking it up with a query (the current context). The stored values are not just a single vector but usually a list of vectors, one for each token, associated with corresponding keys. This effectively increases the size of the "memory" the decoder can refer to when it's making a prediction.

Before we discuss how the attention mechanism works for Seq2Seq models, let's see it in action in a general form. Figure 8.2 illustrates a generic attention mechanism with the following features:

1   The inputs to an attention mechanism are the values and their associated keys. The input values can take many different forms, but in NLP, they are almost always lists of vectors. For Seq2Seq models, the keys and values here are the hidden states of the encoder, which represent token-by-token encoding of the input sentence.

---

[2] Bahdanau et al., "Neural Machine Translation by Jointly Learning to Align and Translate," (2014). https://arxiv.org/abs/1409.0473.

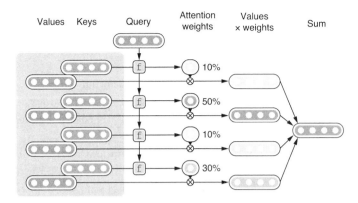

Figure 8.2 Using an attention mechanism to summarize the input

2 Each key associated with a value is compared against the query using an attention function f. By applying f to the query and each one of the keys, you get a set of scores, one per key-value pair, which are then normalized to obtain a set of attention weights. The specific function f depends on the architecture (more on this later). For Seq2Seq models, this gives you a distribution over the input tokens. The more relevant an input token is, the larger the weight it gets.

3 The input values are weighted by their corresponding weights obtained in step 2 and summed up to compute the final summary vector. For Seq2Seq models, this summary vector is appended to the decoder hidden states to aid the translation process.

Because of step 3, the output of an attention mechanism is always a weighted sum of the input vectors, but how they are weighted is determined by the attention weights, which are in turn are calculated from the keys and the query. In other words, what an attention mechanism computes is *a context (query)-dependent summary of the input.* Downstream components of a neural network (e.g., the decoder of an RNN-based Seq2Seq model, or the upper layers of a Transformer model) use this summary to further process the input.

In the following sections, we will learn the two most commonly used types of attention mechanisms in NLP—encoder-decoder attention (also called *cross-attention*; used in both RNN-based Seq2Seq models and the Transformer) and self-attention (used in the Transformer).

8.2 *Sequence-to-sequence with attention*

In this section, we'll learn how the attention mechanism is applied to an RNN-based Seq2Seq model for which the attention mechanism was first invented. We'll study how it works with specific examples, and then we'll experiment with Seq2Seq models with and without the attention mechanism using `fairseq` to observe how it affects the translation quality.

8.2.1   *Encoder-decoder attention*

As we saw earlier, attention is a mechanism for creating a summary of the input under a specific context. We used a key-value store and a query as an analogy for how it works. Let's see how an attention mechanism is used with RNN-based Seq2Seq models using the concrete examples that follow.

Figure 8.3 illustrates a Seq2Seq model with attention. It looks complex at first, but it is just an RNN-based Seq2Seq model with some extra "things" added on top of the encoder (the lightly shaded box in top left corner of the figure). If you ignore what's inside and see it as a black box, all it does is simply take a query and return some sort of summary created from the input. The way it computes this summary is just a variant of the generic form of attention we covered in section 8.1.2. It proceeds as follows:

1   The input to the attention mechanism is the list of hidden states computed by the encoder. These hidden states are used as both keys and values (i.e., the keys and the values are identical). The encoder hidden state at a certain token (e.g., at token "no") reflects the information about that token and all the tokens leading up to it (if the RNN is unidirectional) or the entire sentence (if the RNN is bidirectional).

2   Let's say you finished decoding up to "Mary did." The hidden states of the decoder at that point are used as the query, which is compared against every key using function f. This produces a list of attention scores, one per each key-value

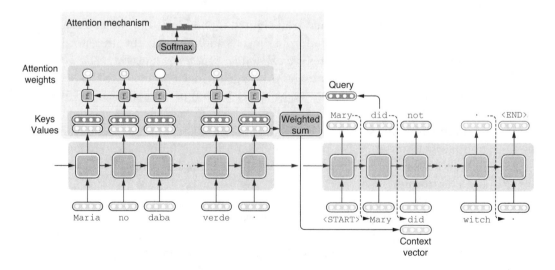

Figure 8.3   Adding an attention mechanism to an RNN-based Seq2Seq model (the lightly shaded box)

pair. These scores determine which part of the input the decoder should attend to when it's trying to generate a word that follows "Mary did."

3   These scores are converted to a probability distribution (a set of positive values that sum to one), which is used to determine which vectors should get the most attention. The return value from this attention mechanism is the sum of all values, weighted by the attention scores after normalizing with softmax.

You may be wondering what the attention function f looks like. A couple of variants of f are possible, depending on how it computes the attention scores between the key and the query, but these details do not matter much here. One thing to note is that in the original paper proposing the attention mechanism,[3] the authors used a "mini" neural network to calculate attention scores from the key and the query.

This "mini" network-based attention function is not something you just plug in to an RNN model post hoc and expect it to work. It is optimized as part of the entire network—that is, as the entire network gets optimized by minimizing the loss function, the attention mechanism also gets better at generating summaries because doing so well also helps the decoder generate better translation and lower the loss function. In other words, the entire network, including the attention mechanism, is trained end to end. This usually means that, as the network is optimized, the attention mechanism starts to learn to focus only on the relevant part of the input, which is usually where the target tokens are aligned with the source tokens. In other words, attention is calculating some sort of "soft" word alignment between the source and the target tokens.

8.2.2   *Building a Seq2Seq machine translation with attention*

In section 6.3, we built our first machine translation (MT) system using fairseq, an NMT toolkit developed by Facebook. Using the parallel dataset from Tatoeba, we built an LSTM-based Seq2Seq model to translate Spanish sentences into English.

In this section, we are going to experiment with a Seq2Seq machine translation system and see how attention affects the translation quality. We assume that you've already gone through the steps we took when we built the MT system by downloading the dataset and running the fairseq-preprocess and fairseq-train commands (section 6.3). After that, you ran the fairseq-interactive command to interactively translate Spanish sentences into English. You might have noticed that the translation you get from this MT system that took you just 30 minutes to build was actually decent. In fact, the model architecture we used (--arch lstm) has an attention mechanism built in by default. Notice when you ran the following fairseq-train command

```
$ fairseq-train \
    data/mt-bin \
    --arch lstm \
    --share-decoder-input-output-embed \
    --optimizer adam \
```

---

3   Bahdanau et al., "Neural Machine Translation by Jointly Learning to Align and Translate," (2014). https://arxiv.org/abs/1409.0473.

```
    --lr 1.0e-3 \
    --max-tokens 4096 \
    --save-dir data/mt-ckpt
```

you should have seen the dump of what your model looks like in your terminal as
follows:

```
...
LSTMModel(
  (encoder): LSTMEncoder(
    (embed_tokens): Embedding(16832, 512, padding_idx=1)
    (lstm): LSTM(512, 512)
  )
  (decoder): LSTMDecoder(
    (embed_tokens): Embedding(11416, 512, padding_idx=1)
    (layers): ModuleList(
      (0): LSTMCell(1024, 512)
    )
    (attention): AttentionLayer(
      (input_proj): Linear(in_features=512, out_features=512, bias=False)
      (output_proj): Linear(in_features=1024, out_features=512, bias=False)
    )
  )
)
...
```

This tells you that your model has an encoder and a decoder, but the decoder also has
a component called `attention` (which is of type `AttentionLayer`), shown in bold in
the code snippet. This is exactly the "mini-network" that we covered in section 8.2.1.

Now let's train the same model, but without attention. You can add `--decoder-
attention 0` to `fairseq-train` to disable the attention mechanism, while keeping
everything else the same, as shown here:

```
$ fairseq-train \
    data/mt-bin \
    --arch lstm \
    --decoder-attention 0 \
    --share-decoder-input-output-embed \
    --optimizer adam \
    --lr 1.0e-3 \
    --max-tokens 4096 \
    --save-dir data/mt-ckpt-no-attn
```

When you run this, you'll see a similar dump, shown next, that shows the architecture
of the model but without attention:

```
LSTMModel(
  (encoder): LSTMEncoder(
    (embed_tokens): Embedding(16832, 512, padding_idx=1)
    (lstm): LSTM(512, 512)
  )
  (decoder): LSTMDecoder(
    (embed_tokens): Embedding(11416, 512, padding_idx=1)
```

```
    (layers): ModuleList(
      (0): LSTMCell(1024, 512)
    )
  )
)
```

As we saw in section 6.3.2, the training process alternates between training and valida-tion. In the training phase, the parameters of the neural network are optimized by the optimizer. In the validation phase, these parameters are fixed, and the model is run on a held-out portion of the dataset called the *validation set*. In addition to making sure the training loss decreases, you should be looking at the validation loss during training, because it better represents how well the model generalizes outside the training data.

During this experiment, you should observe that the lowest validation loss achieved by the attention model is around 1.727, whereas that for the attention-less model is around 2.243. Lower loss values mean the model is fitting the dataset better, so this indicates the attention is helping improve the translation. Let's see if this is actually the case. As we've done in section 6.3.2, you can generate translations interac-tively by running the following fairseq-interactive command:

```
$ fairseq-interactive \
    data/mt-bin \
    --path data/mt-ckpt/checkpoint_best.pt \
    --beam 5 \
    --source-lang es \
    --target-lang en
```

In table 8.1, we compare the translations generated by the model with and without attention. The translations you get from the attention-based model are the same as the ones we saw in section 6.3.3. Notice that the translations you get from the attention-less model are a lot worse than those from the attention model. If you look at the translations for "¿Hay habitaciones libres?" and "Maria no daba una bofetada a la bruja verde," you see unfamiliar tokens "<unk>" (for "unknown") in them. What's happening here?

Table 8.1   Translation generated by the model with and without attention

Spanish (input)	With attention	Without attention
¡Buenos días!	Good morning!	Good morning!
¡Hola!	Hi!	Hi!
¿Dónde está el baño?	Where's the restroom?	Where's the toilet?
¿Hay habitaciones libres?	Is there free rooms?	Are there <unk> rooms?
¿Acepta tarjeta de crédito?	Do you accept credit card?	Do you accept credit card?
La cuenta, por favor.	The bill, please.	Check, please.
Maria no daba una bofetada a la bruja verde.	Maria didn't give the green witch.	Mary wasn't a <unk> of the pants.

These are special tokens that are assigned to out-of-vocabulary (OOV) words. We touched upon OOV words in section 3.6.1 (when we introduced the concept of subwords used for FastText). Most NLP applications operate within a fixed vocabulary, and whenever they encounter or try to produce words that are outside that predefined set, the words are replaced with a special token, <unk>. This is akin to a special value (such as None in Python) returned when a method doesn't know what to do with the input. Because these sentences contain certain words (I suspect they are "libres" and "bofetada"), the Seq2Seq model without attention, whose memory is limited, didn't know what to do with them and simply fell back on a safest thing to do, which is to produce a generic, catch-all symbol, <unk>. On the other hand, you can see that attention prevents the system from producing these symbols and helps improve the overall quality of the produced translations.

8.3 *Transformer and self-attention*

In this section, we are going to learn how the Transformer model works and, specifically, how it generates high-quality translations by using a new mechanism called *self-attention*. Self-attention creates a summary of the entire input, but it does this for each token using the token as the context.

8.3.1 *Self-attention*

As we've seen before, attention is a mechanism that creates a context-dependent summary of the input. For RNN-based Seq2Seq models, the input is the encoder hidden states, whereas the context is the decoder hidden states. The core idea of the Transformer, self-attention, also creates a summary of the input, except for one key difference—the context in which the summary is created is also the input itself. See figure 8.4 for a simplified illustration of a self-attention mechanism.

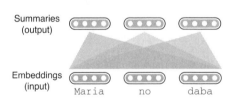

Summaries (output)

Embeddings (input)

Maria   no   daba

Figure 8.4 Self-attention transforms the input into summaries.

Why is this a good thing? Why does it even work? As we discussed in chapter 4, RNNs can also create a summary of the input by looping over the input tokens while updating an internal variable (hidden states). This works—we previously saw that RNNs can generate good translations when combined with attention, but they have one critical issue: because RNNs process the input sequentially, it becomes progressively more difficult to deal with long-range dependencies between tokens as the sentence gets longer.

Let's look at a concrete example. If the input sentence is "The Law will never be perfect, but its application should be just," understanding what the pronoun "its" refers to ("The Law") is important for understanding what the sentence means and for any subsequent tasks (such as translating the sentence accurately). However, if you use an RNN to encode this sentence, to learn this coreference relationship, the RNN needs to learn to remember the noun "The Law" in the hidden states first, then wait until the loop encounters the target pronoun ("its") while learning to ignore everything unrelated in between. This sounds like a complicated trick for a neural network to learn.

But things shouldn't be that complicated. Singular possessive pronouns like "its" usually refer to their nearest singular nouns that appear before them, regardless of the words in between, so simple rules like "replace it with the nearest noun that appeared before" will suffice. In other words, such "random access" is better suited in this situation than "sequential access" is. Self-attention is better at learning such long-range dependencies, as we'll see later.

Let's walk through how self-attention works with an example. Let's assume we are translating Spanish into English and would like to encode the first few words, "Maria no daba," in the input sentence. Let's also focus on one specific token, "no," and how its embeddings are computed from the entire input. The first step is to compare the target token against all tokens in the input. Self-attention does this by converting the target into a query by using projection W_Q as well as converting all the tokens into keys using projection W_K and computing attention weights using function f. The attention weights computed by f are normalized and converted to a probability distribution by the softmax function. Figure 8.5 illustrates these steps where attention weights are computed. As with the encoder-decoder attention mechanism we covered in section 8.2.1, these weights determine how to "mix" values we obtained from the input tokens. For words like "its," we expect that the weight will be higher for related words such as "Law" in the example shown earlier.

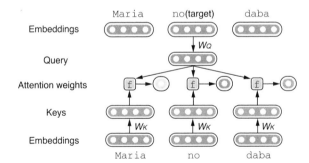

Figure 8.5 Computing attention weights from keys and queries

In the next step, the vector corresponding to each input token is converted to a value vector by projection W_V. Each projected value is weighted by the corresponding attention weight and is summed up to produce a summary vector. See figure 8.6 for an illustration.

This would be it if this were the "regular" encoder-decoder attention mechanism. You need only one summary vector per each token during decoding. However, one key difference between encoder-decoder attention and self-attention is the latter repeats

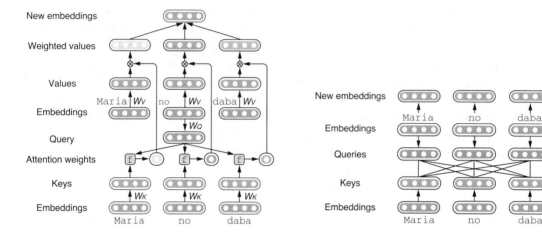

Figure 8.6   Calculating the sum of all values weighted by attention weights

Figure 8.7   Producing summaries for the entire input sequence (details are omitted)

this process for every single token in the input. As shown in figure 8.7, this produces a new set of embeddings for the input, one for each token.

Each summary produced by self-attention takes all the tokens in the input sequence into consideration, but with different weights. It is, therefore, straightforward for words like "its" to incorporate some information from related words, such as "The Law," no matter how far apart these two words are. Using an analogy, self-attention produces summaries through random access over the input. This is in contrast to RNNs, which allow only sequential access over the input, and is one of the key reasons why the Transformer is such a powerful model for encoding and decoding natural language text.

We need to cover one final piece of detail to fully understand self-attention. As it is, the self-attention mechanism illustrated previously can use only one aspect of the input sequence to generate summaries. For example, if you want self-attention to learn which word each pronoun refers to, it can do that—but you may also want to "mix in" information from other words based on some other linguistic aspects. For example, you may want to refer to some other words that the pronoun modifies ("applications," in this case). The solution is to have multiple sets of keys, values, and queries per token and compute multiple sets of attention weights to "mix" values that focus on different aspects of the input. The final embeddings are a combination of summaries generated this way. This mechanism is called *multihead self-attention* (figure 8.8).

You would need to learn some additional details if you were to fully understand how a Transformer layer works, but this section has covered the most important concepts. If you are interested in more details, check out *The Illustrated Transformer* (http://jalammar.github.io/illustrated-transformer/), a well-written guide for understanding

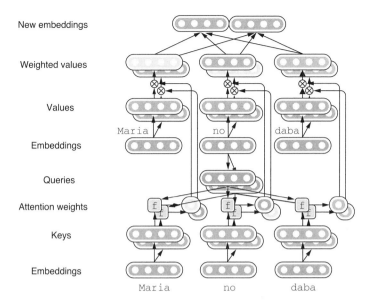

Figure 8.8 Multihead self-attention produces summaries with multiple keys, values, and queries.

the Transformer model with easy-to-understand illustrations. Also, if you are interested in implementing the Transformer model from scratch in Python, check out "The Annotated Transformer" (http://nlp.seas.harvard.edu/2018/04/03/attention.html).

8.3.2 Transformer

The Transformer model doesn't just use a single step of self-attention to encode or decode natural language text. It applies self-attention repeatedly to the inputs to gradually transform them. As with multilayer RNNs, the Transformer also groups a series of transformation operations into a layer and applies it repeatedly. Figure 8.9 shows one layer of the Transformer encoder.

A lot is going on within each layer, and it's not our goal to explain every bit of its detail—you need to understand only that the multihead self-attention is at its core, followed by transformation by a feed-forward neural network ("FF" in figure 8.9). Residual connections and normalization layers are introduced

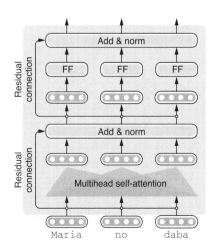

Figure 8.9 A Transformer encoder layer with self-attention and a feed-forward layer

to make it easier to train the model, although the details of these operations are outside the scope of this book. The Transformer model applies this layer repeatedly to transform the input from something literal (raw word embeddings) to something more abstract (the "meaning" of the sentence). In the original Transformer paper, Vaswani et al. used six layers for machine translation, although it is not uncommon for larger models to use 10–20 layers these days.

At this point, you may have noticed that the self-attention operation is completely independent of positions. In other words, the embedded results of self-attention would be completely identical even if, for example, we flipped the word order between "Maria" and "daba," because the operation looks only at the word itself and the aggregated embeddings from other words, regardless of where they are. This is obviously very limiting—what a natural language sentence means depends a lot on how its words are ordered. How does the Transformer encode word order, then?

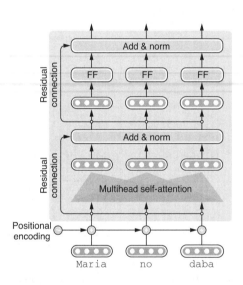

Figure 8.10 Adding positional encoding to the input to represent word order

The Transformer model solves this problem by generating some artificial embeddings that differ from position to position and adding them to word embeddings before they are fed to the layers. These embeddings, called *positional encoding* and shown in figure 8.10, are either generated by some mathematical function (such as sine curves) or learned during training per position. This way, the Transformer can distinguish between "Maria" at the first position and "Maria" at the third position, because they have different positional encoding.

Figure 8.11 shows the Transformer decoder. Although a lot is going on, make sure to notice two important things. First, you'll notice one extra mechanism called *cross-attention* inserted between the self-attention and feed-forward networks. This cross-attention mechanism is similar to the encoder-decoder attention mechanism we covered in section 8.2. This works exactly the same as self-attention, except that the values for the attention come from the encoder, not the decoder, summarizing the information extracted from the encoder.

Finally, the Transformer model generates the target sentence in exactly the same way as RNN-based Seq2Seq models we've previously learned in section 6.4. The decoder is initialized by a special token <START> and produces a probability distribution over possible next tokens. From here, you can proceed by choosing the token with the maximum probability (greedy decoding, as shown in section 6.4.3) or keeping a few tokens with the highest probability while searching for the path that maximizes the

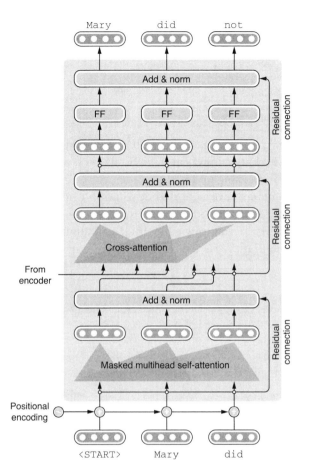

Figure 8.11 A Transformer decoder layer with self- and cross-attention

total score (beam search, as shown in section 6.4.4). In fact, if you look at the Transformer decoder as a black box, the way it produces the target sequence is exactly the same as RNNs, and you can use the same set of decoding algorithms. In other words, the decoding algorithms covered in section 6.4 are generic ones that are agnostic of the underlying decoder architecture.

8.3.3 Experiments

Now that we know how the Transformer model works, let's build a machine translation system with it. The good news is the sequence-to-sequence toolkit, Fairseq, already supports the Transformer-based models (along with other powerful models), which can be specified by the `--arch transformer` option when you train the model. Assuming that you have already preprocessed the dataset we used to build the Spanish-to-English machine translation, you need to tweak only the parameters you give to `fairseq-train`, as shown next:

```
fairseq-train \
  data/mt-bin \
```

```
--arch transformer \
--share-decoder-input-output-embed \
--optimizer adam --adam-betas '(0.9, 0.98)' --clip-norm 0.0 \
--lr 5e-4 --lr-scheduler inverse_sqrt --warmup-updates 4000 \
--dropout 0.3 --weight-decay 0.0 \
--criterion label_smoothed_cross_entropy --label-smoothing 0.1 \
--max-tokens 4096 \
--save-dir data/mt-ckpt-transformer
```

Note that this might not even run on your laptop. You really need GPUs to train the Transformer models. Also note that training can take hours even with GPUs. See section 11.5 for more information on using GPUs.

A number of cryptic parameters appear here, but you don't need to worry about them. You can see the model structure when you run this command. The entire model dump is quite long, so we are omitting some intermediate layers in listing 8.1. If you look carefully, you'll see that the structure of the layers corresponds to the figures we showed earlier.

Listing 8.1   Transformer model dump from Fairseq

```
TransformerModel(
  (encoder): TransformerEncoder(
    (embed_tokens): Embedding(16832, 512, padding_idx=1)
    (embed_positions): SinusoidalPositionalEmbedding()
    (layers): ModuleList(
      (0): TransformerEncoderLayer(
        (self_attn): MultiheadAttention(
          (out_proj): Linear(in_features=512, out_features=512, bias=True)
        )
        (self_attn_layer_norm): LayerNorm((512,), eps=1e-05, elementwise_
         affine=True)
        (fc1): Linear(in_features=512, out_features=2048, bias=True)
        (fc2): Linear(in_features=2048, out_features=512, bias=True)
        (final_layer_norm): LayerNorm((512,), eps=1e-05,
    elementwise_affine=True)
      )
      ...
      (5): TransformerEncoderLayer(
        (self_attn): MultiheadAttention(
          (out_proj): Linear(in_features=512, out_features=512, bias=True)
        )
        (self_attn_layer_norm): LayerNorm((512,), eps=1e-05,
    elementwise_affine=True)
        (fc1): Linear(in_features=512, out_features=2048, bias=True)
        (fc2): Linear(in_features=2048, out_features=512, bias=True)
        (final_layer_norm): LayerNorm((512,), eps=1e-05,
    elementwise_affine=True)
      )
    )
  )
  (decoder): TransformerDecoder(
    (embed_tokens): Embedding(11416, 512, padding_idx=1)
```

Self-attention of the encoder ← (annotation pointing to `(self_attn): MultiheadAttention`)

Feed-forward network of the encoder ← (annotation pointing to `(fc1)`/`(fc2)`)

```
(embed_positions): SinusoidalPositionalEmbedding()
(layers): ModuleList(
  (0): TransformerDecoderLayer(
    (self_attn): MultiheadAttention(
      (out_proj): Linear(in_features=512, out_features=512, bias=True)
    )
    (self_attn_layer_norm): LayerNorm((512,), eps=1e-05,
elementwise_affine=True)
    (encoder_attn): MultiheadAttention(
      (out_proj): Linear(in_features=512, out_features=512, bias=True)
    )
    (encoder_attn_layer_norm): LayerNorm((512,), eps=1e-05, elementwise_
     affine=True)
    (fc1): Linear(in_features=512, out_features=2048, bias=True)
    (fc2): Linear(in_features=2048, out_features=512, bias=True)
    (final_layer_norm): LayerNorm((512,), eps=1e-05,
elementwise_affine=True)
  )
  ...
  (5): TransformerDecoderLayer(
    (self_attn): MultiheadAttention(
      (out_proj): Linear(in_features=512, out_features=512, bias=True)
    )
    (self_attn_layer_norm): LayerNorm((512,), eps=1e-05,
elementwise_affine=True)
    (encoder_attn): MultiheadAttention(
      (out_proj): Linear(in_features=512, out_features=512, bias=True)
    )
    (encoder_attn_layer_norm): LayerNorm((512,), eps=1e-05, elementwise_
     affine=True)
    (fc1): Linear(in_features=512, out_features=2048, bias=True)
    (fc2): Linear(in_features=2048, out_features=512, bias=True)
    (final_layer_norm): LayerNorm((512,), eps=1e-05,
elementwise_affine=True)
  )
)
)
)
```

Self-attention of the decoder

Encoder-decoder of the decoder

Feed-forward network of the decoder

When I ran this, the validation loss converges after around epoch 30, at which point you can stop the training. The result I got by translating the same set of Spanish sentences into English follows:

```
¡ Buenos días !
S-0      ¡ Buenos días !
H-0      -0.0753164291381836    Good morning !
P-0      -0.0532 -0.0063 -0.1782 -0.0635
¡ Hola !
S-1      ¡ Hola !
H-1      -0.17134985327720642    Hi !
P-1      -0.2101 -0.2405 -0.0635
¿ Dónde está el baño ?
S-2      ¿ Dónde está el baño ?
H-2      -0.2670585513114929    Where &apos;s the toilet ?
P-2      -0.0163 -0.4116 -0.0853 -0.9763 -0.0530 -0.0598
```

```
¿ Hay habitaciones libres ?
S-3     ¿ Hay habitaciones libres ?
H-3     -0.26301929354667664     Are there any rooms available ?
P-3     -0.1617 -0.0503 -0.2078 -1.2516 -0.0567 -0.0532 -0.0598
¿ Acepta tarjeta de crédito ?
S-4     ¿ Acepta tarjeta de crédito ?
H-4     -0.06886537373065948     Do you accept credit card ?
P-4     -0.0140 -0.0560 -0.0107 -0.0224 -0.2592 -0.0606 -0.0594
La cuenta , por favor .
S-5     La cuenta , por favor .
H-5     -0.08584468066692352     The bill , please .
P-5     -0.2542 -0.0057 -0.1013 -0.0335 -0.0617 -0.0587
Maria no daba una bofetada a la bruja verde .
S-6     Maria no daba una bofetada a la bruja verde .
H-6     -0.3688890039920807     Mary didn &apos;t slapped the green witch .
P-6     -0.2005 -0.5588 -0.0487 -2.0105 -0.2672 -0.0139 -0.0099 -0.1503 -
        0.0602
```

You can see most of these English translations here are almost perfect. It is quite surprising that the model translated the most difficult sentence ("Maria no daba . . .")
almost perfectly. This is probably enough to convince us that the Transformer is a
powerful translation model. After its advent, this model became the de facto standard
in research and commercial machine translation.

8.4   *Transformer-based language models*

In section 5.5, we introduced language models, which are statistical models that give a
probability to a piece of text. By decomposing text into a sequence of tokens, language models can estimate how "probable" the given text is. In section 5.6, we demonstrated that by leveraging this property, language models can also be used to generate
new texts out of thin air!

The Transformer is a powerful model that achieves impressive results in Seq2Seq
tasks (such as machine translation), although its architecture can also be used for
modeling and generating language. In this section, we learn how to use the Transformer for modeling language and generating realistic texts.

8.4.1   *Transformer as a language model*

In section 5.6, we built a language-generation model based on a character LSTM-
RNN. To recap, given a prefix (a partial sentence generated so far), the model uses an
LSTM-based RNN (a neural network with a loop) to produce a probability distribu-
tion over possible next tokens, as shown in figure 8.12.

We noted earlier that, by regarding the Transformer decoder as a black box, you can
use the same set of decoding algorithms (greedy, beam search, and so on) as we introduced earlier for RNNs. This is also the case for language generation—by thinking of
the neural network as a black box that produces some sort of score given a prefix, you
can use the same logic to generate texts, no matter the underlying model. Figure 8.13
shows how an architecture similar to the Transformer can be used for language gener-

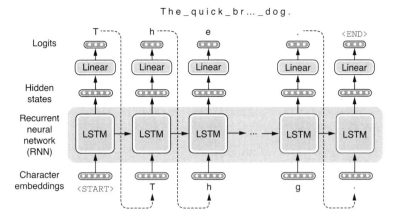

Figure 8.12   Generating text using an RNN

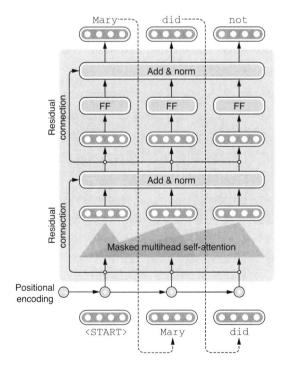

Figure 8.13   Using the Transformer for language generation

ation. Except for a few minor differences (such as lack of cross-attention), the structure is almost identical to the Transformer decoder.

The following snippet shows Python-like pseudocode for generating text with the Transformer model. Here, `model()` is the main function where the model computation happens—it takes the tokens, converts them to embeddings, adds positional encoding, and passes them through all the Transformer layers, returning the final hidden states back to the caller. The caller then passes them through a linear layer to convert them to logits, which in turn get converted to a probability distribution by softmax:

```
def generate():
    token = <START>
    tokens = [<START>]
    while token != <END>:
        hidden = model(tokens)
        probs = softmax(linear(hidden))
        token = sample(probs)
        tokens.append(token)
    return tokens
```

In fact, decoding for Seq2Seq models and language generation with language models are very similar tasks, where the output sequence is produced token by token, feeding itself back to the network, as shown in the previous code snippet. The only difference is that the former has some form of input (the source sentence) whereas the latter does not (the model feeds itself). These two tasks are also called *unconditional* and *conditional generation*, respectively. Figure 8.14 illustrates these three components (network, task, and decoding) and how they can be combined to solve a specific problem.

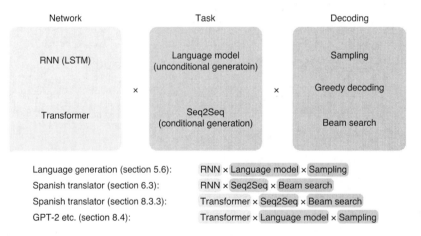

Figure 8.14   Three components of language generation and Seq2Seq tasks

In the rest of this section, we are going to experiment with some Transformer-based language models and generate natural language texts using them. We'll be using the `transformers` library (https://huggingface.co/transformers/) developed by Hugging Face, which has become a standard, go-to library for NLP researchers and engineers working with Transformer models in the past few years. It comes with a number of state-of-the-art model implementations including GPT-2 (this section) and BERT (next chapter), along with pretrained model parameters that you can load and use right away. It also provides a simple, consistent interface through which you can interact with powerful NLP models.

8.4.2 *Transformer-XL*

In many cases, you want to load and use pretrained models provided by third parties (most often the developer of the model), instead of training them from scratch. Recent Transformer models are fairly complex (usually with hundreds of millions of parameters) and are trained with huge datasets (tens of gigabytes of text). This would require GPU resources that only large institutions and tech giants can afford. It is not completely uncommon that some of these models take days to train, even with more than a dozen GPUs! The good news is the implementation and pretrained model parameters for these huge Transformer models are usually made publicly available by their creators so that anyone can integrate them into their NLP applications.

In this section, we'll first check out Transformer-XL, a variant of the Transformer developed by the researchers at Google Brain. Because there is no inherent "loop" in the original Transformer model, unlike RNNs, the original Transformer is not good at dealing with super-long context. In training language models with the Transformer, you first split long texts into shorter chunks of, say, 512 words, and feed them to the model separately. This means the model is unable to capture dependencies longer than 512 words. Transformer-XL[4] addresses this issue by making a few improvements over the vanilla Transformer model ("XL" means extra-long). Although the details of these changes are outside the scope of this book, in a nutshell, the model reuses its hidden states from the previous segment, effectively creating a loop that passes information between different segments of texts. It also improves the positional encoding scheme we touched on earlier to make it easier for the model to deal with longer texts.

You can install the `transformers` library just by running `pip install transformers` from the command line. The main abstractions you'll be interacting with are tokenizers and models. The tokenizers split a raw string into a sequence of tokens, whereas the model defines the architecture and implements the main logic. The model and the pretrained weights usually depend on a specific tokenization scheme, so you need to make sure you are using the tokenizer that is compatible with the model.

The easiest way to initialize a tokenizer and a model with some specified pretrained weights is use the `AutoTokenizer` and `AutoModelWithLMHead` classes and call their `from_pretrained()` methods as follows:

```
import torch
from transformers import AutoModelWithLMHead, AutoTokenizer

tokenizer = AutoTokenizer.from_pretrained('transfo-xl-wt103')
model = AutoModelWithLMHead.from_pretrained('transfo-xl-wt103')
```

---

[4] Dai et al., "Transformer-XL: Attentive Language Models Beyond a Fixed-Length Context," (2019). https://arxiv.org/abs/1901.02860.

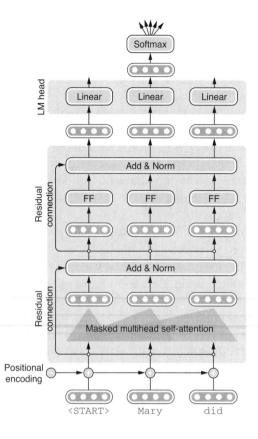

Figure 8.15   Using a language model head with the Transformer

The parameter to from_pre-trained() is the name of the model/pretrained weights. This is a Transformer-XL model trained on a dataset called wt103 (WikiText103).

You may be wondering what this "LMHead" part in AutoModelWith-LMHead means. An LM (language model) head is a specific layer added to a neural network that converts its hidden states to a set of scores that determine which tokens to generate next. These scores (also called *logits*) are then fed to a softmax layer to obtain a probability distribution over possible next tokens (figure 8.15). We would like a model with an LM head because we are interested in generating text by using the Transformer as a language model. However, depending on the task, you may also want a Transformer model without an LM head and just want to use its hidden states. That's what we'll do in the next chapter.

The next step is to initialize the prefix for which you would like your language model to write the rest of the story. You can use tokenizer.encode() to convert a string into a list of token IDs, which are then converted to a tensor. We'll also initialize a variable past for caching the internal states and making the inference faster, as shown next:

```
generated = tokenizer.encode("On our way to the beach")
context = torch.tensor([generated])
past = None
```

Now you are ready to generate the rest of the text. Notice the next code is similar to the pseudocode we showed earlier. The idea is simple: get the output from the model, sample a token using the output, and feed it back to the model. Rinse and repeat.

```
for i in range(100):
    output = model(context, mems=past)
    token = sample_token(output.prediction_scores)

    generated.append(token.item())
    context = token.view(1, -1)
    past = output.mems
```

You need to do some housekeeping to make the shape of the tensors compatible with the model, which we can ignore for now. The `sample_token()` method here takes the output of the model, converts it to a probability distribution, and samples a single token from it. I'm not showing the entire code for the method, but you can check the Google Colab notebook (http://realworldnlpbook.com/ch8.html#xformer-nb) for more details. Also, here we wrote the generation algorithm from scratch, but if you need more full-fledged generation (such as beam search), check out the official example script from the developers of the library: http://mng.bz/wQ6q.

After finishing the generation, you can convert the token IDs back into a raw string by calling `tokenizer.decode()` as follows:

```
print(tokenizer.decode(generated))
```

The following "story" is what I got when I ran this:

```
On our way to the beach, she finds, she finds the men who are in the group to
    be " in the group ". This has led to the perception that the " group "
    in the group is " a group of people in the group with whom we share a
    deep friendship, and which is a common cause to the contrary. " <eos>
    <eos> = = Background = = <eos> <eos> The origins of the concept of "
    group " were in early colonial years with the English Civil War. The
    term was coined by English abolitionist John
```

This is not a bad start. I like the way the story is trying to be consistent by sticking with the concept of "group." However, because the model is trained on Wikipedia text only, its generation is not realistic and looks a little bit too formal.

8.4.3   *GPT-2*

GPT-2 (which stands for generative pretraining), developed by OpenAI, is probably the most famous language model to date. You may have heard the story about a language model generating natural language texts that are so realistic that you cannot tell them from those written by humans. Technically, GPT-2 is just a huge Transformer model, just like the one we introduced earlier. The main difference is its size (the largest model has 48 layers!) and the fact that the model is trained on a huge amount of natural language text collected from the web. The OpenAI team publicly released the implementation and the pretrained weights, so we can easily try out the model.

Initialize the tokenizer and the model for GPT-2 as you have done for Transformer-XL, as shown next:

```
tokenizer = AutoTokenizer.from_pretrained('gpt2-large')
model = AutoModelWithLMHead.from_pretrained('gpt2-large')
```

Then generate text using the next code snippet:

```
generated = tokenizer.encode("On our way to the beach")
context = torch.tensor([generated])
past = None
```

```
for i in range(100):
    output = model(context, past_key_values=past)
    token = sample_token(output.logits)

    generated.append(token.item())
    context = token.unsqueeze(0)
    past = output.past_key_values

print(tokenizer.decode(generated))
```

You may have noticed how little this code snippet changed from the one for Transformer-XL. In many cases, you don't need to make any modifications when switching between different models. This is why the `transformers` library is so powerful—you can try out and integrate a variety of state-of-the-art Transformer-based models into your application with a simple, consistent interface. As we'll see in the next chapter, this library is also integrated into AllenNLP, which makes it easy to build powerful NLP applications with state-of-the-art models.

When I tried this, the GPT-2 generated the following beautifully written passage:

```
On our way to the beach, there was a small island that we visited for the
    first time. The island was called 'A' and it is a place that was used by
    the French military during the Napoleonic wars and it is located in the
    south-central area of the island.

A is an island of only a few hundred meters wide and has no other features to
    distinguish its nature. On the island there were numerous small beaches
    on which we could walk. The beach of 'A' was located in the...
```

Notice how naturally it reads. Also, the GPT-2 model is good at staying consistent—you can see the name of the island, "A," is consistently used throughout the passage. As far as I checked, there is no real island named A in the world, meaning that this is something the model simply made up. It is a great feat that the model remembered the name it just coined and successfully wrote a story around it!

Here's another passage that GPT-2 generated with a prompt: `'Real World Natural Language Processing'` is the name of the book:

```
'Real World Natural Language Processing' is the name of the book. It has all
    the tools you need to write and program natural language processing
    programs on your computer. It is an ideal introductory resource for
    anyone wanting to learn more about natural language processing. You can
    buy it as a paperback (US$12), as a PDF (US$15) or as an e-book
    (US$9.99).

The author's blog has more information and reviews.

The free 'Real World Natural Language Processing' ebook has all the necessary
    tools to get started with natural language processing. It includes a
    number of exercises to help you get your feet wet with writing and
    programming your own natural language processing programs, and it
    includes a few example programs. The book's author, Michael Karp has
    also written an online course about Natural Language Processing.
```

```
'Real World Natural Language Processing: Practical Applications' is a free
    e-book that explains how to use natural language processing to solve
    problems of everyday life (such as writing an email, creating and
```

As of February 2019, when GPT-2 was released, I had barely begun writing this book, so I doubt GPT-2 knew anything about it. For a language model that doesn't have any prior knowledge about the book, this is an amazing job, although I have to note that it got the price and the name of the author wrong.

8.4.4   XLM

Finally, as an interesting example, we will experiment with multilingual language generation. XLM (cross-lingual language model), proposed by researchers at Facebook AI Research, is a Transformer-based cross-lingual language model that can generate and encode texts in multiple languages.[5] By learning how to encode multilingual texts, the model can be used for transfer learning between different languages. We'll cover transfer learning in chapter 9.

You can start by initializing the tokenizer and the model and initialize it with the pretrained weights as follows:

```
tokenizer = AutoTokenizer.from_pretrained('xlm-clm-enfr-1024')
model = AutoModelWithLMHead.from_pretrained('xlm-clm-enfr-1024')
```

Here, we are loading an XLM model (xlm), trained with a *causal language modeling* (CLM) *objective* (clm) in English and French (enfr). CLM is just a fancier way to describe what we've been doing in this chapter—predicting the next token based on a prefix. XLM is usually used for encoding multilingual texts for some downstream tasks such as text classification and machine translation, but we are simply using it as a language model to generate texts. See listing 8.2 for the code snippet for generating multilingual text with XLM. You can again reuse most of the earlier code snippet, although you also need to specify what language you are working in (note the lang = 0 line). Also, here we are generating text from scratch by supplying just the BOS token (whose index is zero).

Listing 8.2   Generating multilingual text with XLM

```
generated = [0] # start with just <s>
context = torch.tensor([generated])
lang = 0 # English

for i in range(100):
    langs = torch.zeros_like(context).fill_(lang)
    output = model(context, langs=langs)
    token = sample_token(output)
```

---

[5] Lample and Conneau, "Cross-Lingual Language Model Pretraining," (2019). https://arxiv.org/abs/1901.07291.

```
        generated.append(token.item())
        context = torch.tensor([generated])

print(tokenizer.decode(generated))
```

When I ran this, I got the following:

```
<s>and its ability to make decisions on the basis of its own. " </s>The
    government has taken no decisions on that matter, " Mr Hockey said. </
    s>A lot of the information is very sensitive. </s>The new research and
    information on the Australian economy, which is what we're going to get
    from people, and the information that we are going to be looking at,
    we're going to be able to provide and we 'll take it forward. </s>I'm
    not trying to make sure we're not
```

Then, let's change `lang` to 1 (which means French) and run the same snippet again, which gives you the next bit of text:

```
<s></s>En revanche, les prix des maisons individuelles n' ont guère augmenté
    ( - 0,1 % ). </s>En mars dernier, le taux de la taxe foncière, en légère
    augmentation à la hausse par rapport à février 2008. </s>" Je n' ai
    jamais eu une augmentation " précise ". </s>" Je me suis toujours dit
    que ce n' était pas parce que c' était une blague. </s>En effet, j'
    étais un gars de la rue " </s>Les jeunes sont des gens qui avaient beau-
    coup d' humour... "
```

Although the quality of generation is not as great as GPT-2, which we experimented with earlier, it is refreshing to see that a single model can produce texts both in English and French. These days, it is increasingly common to build multilingual Transformer-based NLP models to solve NLP problems and tasks in multiple languages at the same time. This also became possible thanks to the Transformer's powerful capacity to model the complexity of language.

8.5   *Case study: Spell-checker*

In the final section of this chapter, we will build a practical NLP application—a spell-checker—with the Transformer. In the modern world, spell-checkers are everywhere. Chances are your web browser is equipped with a spell-checker that tells you when you make a spelling mistake by underlining misspelled words. Many word processors and editors also run spell-checkers by default. Some applications (including Google Docs and Microsoft Word) even point out simple grammatical errors, too. Ever wondered how they work? We'll learn how to formulate this as an NLP problem, prepare the dataset, train, and improve the model next.

8.5.1   *Spell correction as machine translation*

Spell-checkers receive a piece of text such as "tisimptant too spll chck ths dcment," detect spelling and grammatical errors, if any, and fix all errors: "It's important to spell-check this document." How can you solve this task with NLP technologies? How can such systems be implemented?

The simplest thing you could do is tokenize the input text into words and check if each word is in a dictionary. If it's not, you look for the closest valid word in the dictionary according to some measure such as the edit distance and replace with that word. You repeat this until there are no words to fix. This word-by-word fixing algorithm is widely used by many spell-checkers due to its simplicity.

However, this type of spell-checker has several issues. First, just like the first word in the example, "tisimptant," how do you know which part of the sentence is actually a word? The default spell-checker for my copy of Microsoft Word indicates it's a misspelling of "disputant," although it would be obvious to any English speakers that it is actually a misspelling of two (or more) words. The fact that users can also misspell punctuation (including whitespace) makes everything complicated. Second, just because some word is in a dictionary doesn't mean it's not an error. For example, the second word in the example, "too" is a misspelling of "to," but both are valid words that are in any English dictionary. How can you tell if the former is wrong in this context? Third, all these decisions are made out of context. One of the spell-checkers I tried shows "thus" as a candidate to replace "ths" in this example. However, from this context (before a noun), it is obvious that "this" is a more appropriate candidate, although both "this" and "thus" are one edit distance away from "ths," meaning they are equally valid options according to the edit distance.

You would be able to solve some of these issues by adding some heuristic rules. For example, "too" is more likely a misspelling of "to" before a verb, and "this" is more likely before a noun than "thus." But this method is obviously not scalable. Remember the poor junior developer from section 1.1.2? Language is vast and full of exceptions. You cannot just keep writing such rules to deal with the full complexity of language. Even if you are able to write rules for such simple words, how would you tell that "tisimptant" is actually two words? Would you try to split this word at every possible position to see if split words resemble existing words? What if the input was in a language that is written without whitespace, like Chinese and Japanese?

At this point, you may realize this "split and fix" approach is going nowhere. In general, when designing an NLP application, you should think in terms of the following three aspects:

- *Task*—What is the task being solved? Is it a classification, sequential-labeling, or sequence-to-sequence problem?
- *Model*—What model are you going to use? Is it a feed-forward network, an RNN, or the Transformer?
- *Dataset*—Where are you obtaining the dataset to train and validate your model?

Based on my experience, a vast majority of NLP applications nowadays can be solved by combining these aspects. How about spell-checkers? Because they take a piece of text as the input and produce the fixed string, it'd be most straightforward if we solve this as a Seq2Seq task using the Transformer model. In other words, we will be building a machine translation system that translates noisy inputs with spelling/grammatical

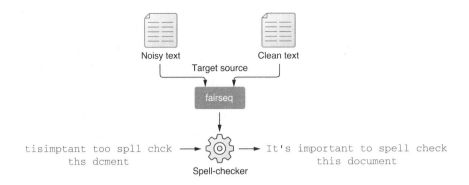

Figure 8.16   Training a spell-checker as an MT system that translates "noisy" sentences into "clean" ones

errors into clean, errorless outputs as shown in figure 8.16. You can regard these two sides as two different "languages" (or "dialects" of English).

At this point, you may be wondering where we are obtaining the dataset. This is often the most important (and the most difficult) part in solving real-world NLP problems. Fortunately, we can use a public dataset for this task. Let's dive in and start building a spell-checker.

8.5.2   *Training a spell-checker*

We will be using GitHub Typo Corpus (https://github.com/mhagiwara/github-typo -corpus) as the dataset to train a spell-checker. The dataset, created by my collaborator and me, consists of hundreds of thousands of "typo" edits automatically harvested from GitHub. It is the largest dataset of spelling mistakes and their corrections to date, which makes it a perfect choice for training a spell-checker.

One decision we need to make before preparing the dataset and training a model is what to use as the atomic linguistic unit on which the model operates. Many NLP models use tokens as the smallest unit (i.e., RNN/Transformer is fed a sequence of tokens), but a growing number of NLP models use *word or sentence pieces* as the basic units (section 10.4). What should we use as the smallest unit for spelling correction? As with many other NLP models, using words as the input sounds like a good "default" thing to do at first. However, as we saw earlier, the concept of tokens is not well suited for spelling correction—users can mess up with punctuation, which makes everything overly complex if you are dealing with tokens. More importantly, because NLP models need to operate on a fixed vocabulary, the spell-corrector vocabulary would need to include every single misspelling of every single word it encountered during the training. This would make it unnecessarily expensive to train and maintain such an NLP model.

For these reasons, we will be using *characters* as the basic unit for our spell-checker, as we did in section 5.6. Using characters has several advantages—it can keep the size of the vocabulary quite small (usually less than one hundred for a language with a small set of alphabets such as English). You don't need to worry about bloating your vocabulary, even with a noisy dataset full of typos, because typos are just different arrangements of characters. You can also treat punctuation marks (even whitespace) as one of the characters in the vocabulary. This makes the preprocessing step extremely easy because you don't need any linguistic toolkits (such as tokenizers) for doing this.

> **NOTE** Using characters is not without disadvantages. One main issue is using them will increase the length of sequences, because you need to break everything up into characters. This makes the model large and slower to train.

First, let's prepare the dataset for training a spell-checker. All the necessary data and code for building a spell-checker are included in this repository: https://github.com/mhagiwara/xfspell. The tokenized and split datasets are located under data/gtc (as train.tok.fr, train.tok.en, dev.tok.fr, dev.tok.en). The suffixes en and fr are a commonly used convention in machine translation—"fr" means "foreign language" and "en" means English, because many MT research projects were originally motivated by people wanting to translate some foreign language into English. Here, we are using "fr" and "en" to mean just "noisy text before spelling correction" and "clean text after spelling correction."

Figure 8.17 shows an excerpt from the dataset for spelling correction created from GitHub Typo Corpus. Notice that text is segmented into individual characters, even whitespaces (replaced by "_"). Any characters outside common alphabets (upper- and lowercase letters, numbers, and some common punctuation marks) are replaced with "#." You can see that the dataset contains diverse corrections, including simple typos (pubilc -> public on line 670, HYML -> HTML on line 672), trickier errors (mxnet as not -> mxnet is not on line 681, 22th -> 22nd on line 682), and even lines without any corrections (line 676). This looks like a good resource to use for training a spell-checker.

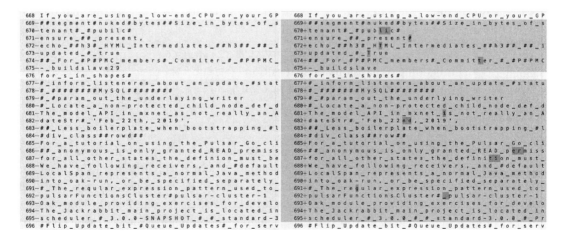

Figure 8.17　Training data for spelling correction

The first step for training a spell-checker (or any other Seq2Seq model) is to preprocess the datasets. Because the dataset is already split and formatted, all you need to do
is run `fairseq-preprocess` to convert the datasets into a binary format as follows:

```
fairseq-preprocess --source-lang fr --target-lang en \
    --trainpref data/gtc/train.tok \
    --validpref data/gtc/dev.tok \
    --destdir bin/gtc
```

Then you can start training your model right away using the following code.

Listing 8.3 Training a spell-checker

```
fairseq-train \
    bin/gtc \
    --fp16 \
    --arch transformer \
    --encoder-layers 6 --decoder-layers 6 \
    --encoder-embed-dim 1024 --decoder-embed-dim 1024 \
    --encoder-ffn-embed-dim 4096 --decoder-ffn-embed-dim 4096 \
    --encoder-attention-heads 16 --decoder-attention-heads 16 \
    --share-decoder-input-output-embed \
    --optimizer adam --adam-betas '(0.9, 0.997)' --adam-eps 1e-09 --clip-norm
     25.0 \
    --lr 1e-4 --lr-scheduler inverse_sqrt --warmup-updates 16000 \
    --dropout 0.1 --attention-dropout 0.1 --activation-dropout 0.1 \
    --weight-decay 0.00025 \
    --criterion label_smoothed_cross_entropy --label-smoothing 0.2 \
    --max-tokens 4096 \
    --save-dir models/gtc01 \
    --max-epoch 40
```

You don't need to worry about most of the hyperparameters here—this set of parameters worked fairly well for me, although some other combinations of parameters may
work better. However, you may want to pay attention to some of the parameters
related to the size of the model, namely:

- Number of layers (`--[encoder|decoder]-layers`)
- Embedding dimension of self-attention (`--[encoder|decoder]-embed-dim`)
- Embedding dimension of feed-forward layers (`--[encoder/decoder]-ffn-
  embed-dim`)
- Number of attention heads (`--[encoder|decoder]-attention-heads`)

These parameters determine the capacity of the model. In general, the larger these
parameters are, the larger capacity the model would have, although as a result the
model would also require more data, time, and GPU resources to train. Another
important parameter is `--max-tokens`, which specifies the number of tokens loaded
onto a single batch. If you are experiencing out-of-memory errors on a GPU, try
adjusting this parameter.

After the training is finished, you can run the following command to make predictions using the trained model:

```
echo "tisimptant too spll chck ths dcment." \
    | python src/tokenize.py \
    | fairseq-interactive bin/gtc \
    --path models/gtc01/checkpoint_best.pt \
    --source-lang fr --target-lang en --beam 10 \
    | python src/format_fairseq_output.py
```

Because the `fairseq-interactive` interface can also take source text from the standard input, we are directly providing the text using the `echo` command. The Python script `src/format_fairseq_output.py`, as its name suggests, formats the output from `fairseq-interactive` and shows the predicted target text. When I ran this, I got the following:

```
tisimplement too spll chck ths dcment.
```

This is rather disappointing. The spell-checker learned to somehow fix "imptant" to "implement," although it failed to correct any other words. I suspect a couple of reasons for this. The training data used, GitHub Typo Corpus, is heavily biased toward software-related language and corrections, which might have led to the wrong correction (imptant -> implement). Also, the training data might have just been too small for the Transformer to be effective. How could we improve the model so that it can fix spellings more accurately?

8.5.3 Improving a spell-checker

As we discussed earlier, one main reason the spell-checker is not working as expected might be because the model wasn't exposed to a more diverse, larger amount of misspellings during training. But as far as I know, no such large datasets of diverse misspellings are publicly available for training a general-domain spell-checker. How could we obtain more data for training a better spell-checker?

This is where we need to be creative. One idea is to artificially generate noisy text from clean text. If you think of it, it is very difficult (especially for a machine learning model) to fix misspellings, whereas it is very easy to "corrupt" clean text to simulate how people make typos, even for a computer. For example, we can take some clean text (which is available from, for example, scraped web text almost indefinitely) and replace some letters at random. If you pair artificially generated noisy text created this way with the original, clean text, this will effectively create a new, larger dataset on which you can train an even better spell-checker!

The remaining issue we need to address is how to "corrupt" clean text to generate realistic spelling errors that look like the ones made by humans. You can write a Python script that, for example, replaces, deletes, and/or swaps letters at random, although there is no guarantee that typos made this way are similar to those made by humans and that the resulting artificial dataset will provide useful insights for the

Transformer model. How can we model the fact that, for example, humans are more likely to type "too" in place of "to" than they do "two"?

This is starting to sound familiar again. We can use the data to simulate the typos! But how? This is where we need to be creative again—if you "flip" the direction of the original dataset we used to train the spell-checker, you can observe how humans make typos. If you treat the clean text as the source language and the noisy text as the target and train a Seq2Seq model for that direction, you are effectively training a "spell-corruptor"—a Seq2Seq model that inserts realistic-looking spelling errors into clean text. See Figure 8.18 for an illustration.

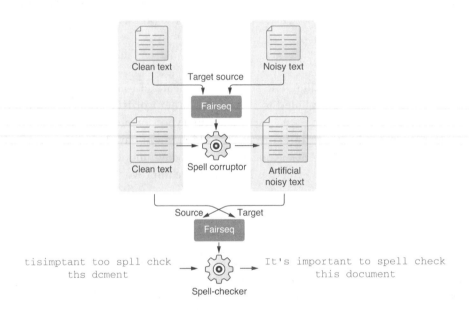

Figure 8.18   Using back-translation to generate artificial noisy data

This technique of using the "inverse" of the original training data to artificially generate a large amount of data in the source language from a real corpus in the target language is called *back-translation* in the machine learning literature. It is a popular technique to improve the quality of machine translation systems. As we'll show next, it is also effective for improving the quality of spell-checkers.

You can easily train a spell corruptor just by swapping the source and the target languages. You can do this by supplying "en" (clean text) as the source language and "fr" (noisy text) as the target language when you run `fairseq-preprocess` as follows:

```
fairseq-preprocess --source-lang en --target-lang fr \
    --trainpref data/gtc/train.tok \
    --validpref data/gtc/dev.tok \
    --destdir bin/gtc-en2fr
```

We are not going over the training process again—you can use almost the same `fairseq-train` command to start the training. Just don't forget to specify a different directory for `--save-dir`. After you finish training, you can check whether the spelling corrupter can indeed corrupt the input text as expected:

```
$ echo 'The quick brown fox jumps over the lazy dog.' | python src/
    tokenize.py \
    | fairseq-interactive \
    bin/gtc-en2fr \
    --path models/gtc-en2fr/checkpoint_best.pt \
    --source-lang en --target-lang fr \
    --beam 1 --sampling --sampling-topk 10 \
    | python src/format_fairseq_output.py
The quink brown fox jumps ove-rthe lazy dog.
```

Note the extra options that I added earlier, which are shown in bold. It means that the `fairseq-interactive` command uses sampling (from top 10 tokens with largest probabilities) instead of beam search. When corrupting clean text, it is often better to use sampling instead of beam search. To recap, sampling picks the next token randomly according to the probability distribution after the softmax layer, whereas beam search tries to find the "best path" that maximizes the score of the output sequence. Although beam search can find better solutions when translating some text, we want noisy, more diverse output when corrupting clean text. Past research[6] has also shown that sampling (instead of beam search) works better for augmenting data via back-translation.

From here, the sky's the limit. You can collect as much clean text as you want, generate noisy text from it using the corruptor you just trained, and increase the size of the training data. There is no guarantee that the artificial errors look like the real ones made by humans, but this is not a big deal because 1) the source (noisy) side is used only for encoding, and 2) the target (clean) side data is always "real" data written by humans, from which the Transformer can learn how to generate real text. The more text data you collect, the more confident the model will get about what error-free, real text looks like.

I won't go over every step I took to increase the size of the data, but here's the summary of what I did and what you can also do. Collect as much clean and diverse text data from publicly available datasets, such as Tatoeba and Wikipedia dumps. My favorite way to do this is to use OpenWebTextCorpus (https://skylion007.github.io/Open-WebTextCorpus/), an open source project to replicate the dataset on which GPT-2 was originally trained. It consists of a huge amount (40 GB) of high-quality web text crawled from all outbound links from Reddit. Because the entire dataset would take days, if not weeks, just to preprocess and run the corruptor on, you can take a subset (say, 1/1000th) and add it to the dataset. I took 1/100th of the dataset, preprocessed it, and ran the corruptor to obtain the noisy-clean parallel dataset. This 1/100th subset

---

[6] Edunov et al.,"Understanding Back-Translation at Scale," (2018). https://arxiv.org/abs/1808.09381.

alone added more than five million pairs (in comparison, the original training set contains only ~240k pairs). Instead of training from scratch, you can download the pretrained weights and try the spell-checker from the repository.

The training took several days, even on multiple GPUs, but when it was done, the result was very encouraging. Not only can it accurately fix spelling errors, as shown here

```
$ echo "tisimptant too spll chck ths dcment." \
    | python src/tokenize.py \
    | fairseq-interactive \
    bin/gtc-bt512-owt1k-upper \
    --path models/bt05/checkpoint_best.pt \
    --source-lang fr --target-lang en --beam 10 \
    | python src/format_fairseq_output.py
    It's important to spell check this document.
```

but the spell-checker also appears to understand the grammar of English to some degree, as shown here:

```
$ echo "The book wer about NLP." |
    | python src/tokenize.py \
    | fairseq-interactive \
    ...
The book was about NLP.

$ echo "The books wer about NLP." |
    | python src/tokenize.py \
    | fairseq-interactive \
    ...
The books were about NLP.
```

This example alone may not prove that the model really understands the grammar (namely, using the correct verb depending on the number of the subject). It might just be learning some association between consecutive words, which can be achieved by any statistical NLP model, such as n-gram language models. However, even after you make the sentences more complicated, the spell-checker shows amazing resilience, as shown in the next code snippet:

```
$ echo "The book Tom and Jerry put on the yellow desk yesterday wer about NLP." |
    | python src/tokenize.py \
    | fairseq-interactive \
    ...
The book Tom and Jerry put on the yellow desk yesterday was about NLP.

$ echo "The books Tom and Jerry put on the yellow desk yesterday wer about
    NLP." |
    | python src/tokenize.py \
    | fairseq-interactive \
    ...
The books Tom and Jerry put on the yellow desk yesterday were about NLP.
```

From these examples, it is clear that the model learned how to ignore irrelevant noun phrases (such as "Tom and Jerry" and "yellow desk") and focus on the noun ("book(s)") that determines the form of the verb ("was" versus "were"). We are more confident that it understands the basic sentence structure. All we did was collect a large amount of clean text and trained the Transformer model on it, combined with the original training data and the corruptor. Hopefully through these experiments, you were able to feel how powerful the Transformer model can be!

Summary

- Attention is a mechanism in neural networks that focuses on a specific part of the input and computes its context-dependent summary. It works like a "soft" version of a key-value store.
- Encoder-decoder attention can be added to Seq2Seq models to improve their translation quality.
- Self-attention is an attention mechanism that produces the summary of the input by summarizing itself.
- The Transformer model applies self-attention repeatedly to gradually transform the input.
- High-quality spell-checkers can be built using the Transformer and a technique called back-translation.

Transfer learning with pretrained language models

This chapter covers

- Using transfer learning to leverage knowledge from unlabeled textual data
- Using self-supervised learning to pretrain large language models such as BERT
- Building a sentiment analyzer with BERT and the Hugging Face Transformers library
- Building a natural language inference model with BERT and AllenNLP

The year 2018 is often called "an inflection point" in the history of NLP. A prominent NLP researcher, Sebastian Ruder (https://ruder.io/nlp-imagenet/), dubbed this change "NLP's ImageNet moment," where he used the name of a popular computer vision dataset and powerful models pretrained on it, pointing out that similar changes were underway in the NLP community as well. Powerful pretrained language models such as ELMo, BERT, and GPT-2 achieved state-of-the-art performance in many NLP tasks and completely changed how we build NLP models within months.

One important concept underlying these powerful pretrained language models is *transfer learning*, a technique for improving the performance of one task using a model trained on another task. In this chapter, we'll first introduce the concept, then move on to introducing BERT, the most popular pretrained language model proposed for NLP. We'll cover how BERT is designed and pretrained, as well as how to use the model for downstream NLP tasks including sentiment analysis and natural language inference. We'll also touch on other popular pretrained models including ELMo and RoBERTa.

9.1 Transfer learning

We start this chapter by introducing *transfer learning*, a powerful machine learning concept fundamental to many pretrained language models (PLMs) in this chapter.

9.1.1 Traditional machine learning

In traditional machine learning, before the advent of pretrained language models, NLP models were trained on a per-task basis, and they were useful only for the type of the task they were trained for (figure 9.1). For example, if you wanted a sentiment analysis model, you needed to use a dataset annotated with the desired output (e.g., negative, neutral, and positive labels), and the trained model was useful only for sentiment analysis. If you needed to build another model for part-of-speech (POS) tagging (an NLP task to identify the part of speech of words; see section 5.2 for a review), you needed to do this all over again by collecting training data and training a POS tagging model from scratch. You could not "reuse" your sentiment analysis model for POS tagging, no matter how good your model was, because these two were trained for two fundamentally different tasks. However, these tasks both operated on the same language and all this seemed wasteful. For example, knowing that "wonderful," "awesome," and "great" are all adjectives that have positive meaning would help both sentiment analysis

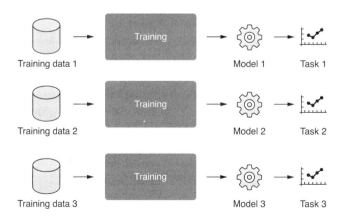

Figure 9.1 In traditional machine learning, each trained model was used for just one task.

and part-of-speech tagging. Under the traditional machine learning paradigm, not only did we need to prepare training data large enough to teach "common sense" like this to the model, but individual NLP models also needed to learn such facts about the language from scratch, solely from the given data.

9.1.2   Word embeddings

At this point, you may realize this sounds somewhat familiar. Recall our discussion in section 3.1 on word embeddings and why they are important. To recap, word embeddings are vector representations of words that are learned so that semantically similar words share similar representations. As a result, vectors for "dog" and "cat," for example, end up being located in a close proximity in a high-dimensional space. These representations are trained on an independent, large textual corpus without any training signals, using algorithms such as Skip-gram and CBOW, often collectively called *Word2vec* (section 3.4).

After these word embeddings are trained, downstream NLP tasks can use them as the input to their models (which are often neural networks, but not necessarily). Because these embeddings already capture semantic relationship between words (e.g., dogs and cats are both animals), these tasks no longer need to learn how the language works from scratch, which gives them the upper hand in the task they are trying to solve. The model can now focus on learning higher-level concepts that cannot be captured by word embeddings (e.g., phrases, syntax, and semantics) and the task-specific patterns learned from the given annotated data. This is why using word embeddings gives a performance boost to many NLP models.

In chapter 3, we likened this to teaching a baby (= an NLP model) how to dance. By letting babies learn how to walk steadily first (= training word embeddings), dance teachers (= task-specific datasets and training objectives) can focus on teaching specific dance moves without worrying whether babies can even stand and walk properly. This "phased training" approach makes everything easier if you want to teach another skill to the baby (e.g., teaching martial arts) because they already have a good grasp of the fundamental skill (walking).

The beauty of all this is that word embeddings can be learned independently of the downstream tasks. These word embeddings are *pretrained*, meaning their training happens before the training of downstream NLP tasks. Using the dancing baby analogy, dance teachers can safely assume that all the incoming dance students have already learned how to stand and walk properly. Pretrained word embeddings created by the developers of the algorithm are often freely available, and anyone can download and integrate them into their NLP applications. This process is illustrated in figure 9.2.

9.1.3   What is transfer learning?

If you generalize what you did with word embeddings earlier, you took the outcome of one task (i.e., predicting word cooccurrence with embeddings) and transferred the knowledge gleaned from it to another one (i.e., sentiment analysis, or any other NLP

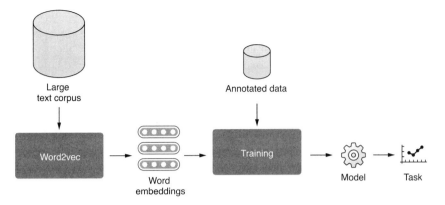

Figure 9.2 Leveraging word embeddings helps build a better NLP model.

tasks). In machine learning, this process is called *transfer learning*, which is a collection of related techniques to improve the performance of a machine learning model in a task using data and/or models trained in a different task. Transfer learning always consists of two or more steps—a machine learning model is first trained for one task (called *pretraining*), which is then adjusted and used in another (called *adaptation*). If the same model is used for both tasks, the second step is called *fine-tuning*, because you are tuning the same model slightly but for a different task. See figure 9.3 for an illustration of transfer learning in NLP.

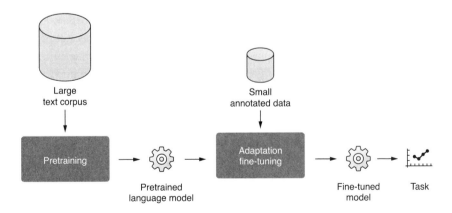

Figure 9.3 Leveraging transfer learning helps build a better NLP model.

Transfer learning has become the dominant way for building high-quality NLP models in the past few years for two main reasons. Firstly, thanks to powerful neural network models such as the Transformer and self-supervised learning (see section 9.2.2), it became possible to bootstrap high-quality embeddings from an almost unlimited amount of natural language text. These embeddings take into account the structure, context, and semantics of natural language text to a great extent. Secondly, thanks to transfer learning, anyone can incorporate these powerful pretrained language models into their NLP applications, even without access to a lot of textual resources, such as web-scale corpora, or compute resources, such as powerful GPUs. The advent of these new technologies (the Transformer, self-supervised learning, pretrained language models, and transfer learning) moved the field of NLP to a completely new stage and pushed the performance of many NLP tasks to a near-human level. In the following subsections, we'll see transfer learning in action by actually building NLP models while leveraging PLMs such as BERT.

Note that the concept called *domain adaptation* is closely related to transfer learning. Domain adaptation is a technique where you train a machine learning model in one domain (e.g., news) and adapt it to another domain (e.g., social media), but these are for the *same task* (e.g., text classification). On the other hand, the transfer learning we cover in this chapter is applied to *different tasks* (e.g., language modeling versus text classification). You can achieve the same effect using the transfer learning paradigm covered in this chapter, and we do not specifically cover domain adaptation as a separate topic. Interested readers can learn more about domain adaptation from a recent review paper.[1]

9.2   BERT

In this section, we will cover BERT in detail. BERT (Bidirectional Encoder Representations from Transformers)[2] is by far the most popular and most influential pretrained language model to date that revolutionized how people train and build NLP models. We will first introduce *contextualized embeddings* and why they are important, then move on to explaining self-supervised learning, which is an important concept in pretraining language models. We'll cover two self-supervised tasks used for pretraining BERT, namely, masked language models and next-sentence prediction, and cover ways to adapt BERT for your applications.

9.2.1   *Limitations of word embeddings*

Word embeddings are a powerful concept that can give your application a boost in the performance, although they are not without limitation. One obvious issue is that they cannot take context into account. Words you see in natural language are often polysemous, meaning they may have more than one meaning, depending on their context. However, because word embeddings are trained per token type, all the different meanings are compressed into a single vector. For example, training a single vector

---

for "dog" or "apple" cannot deal with the fact that "hot dog" or "Big Apple" are not a type of animal or fruit, respectively. As another example, consider what "play" means in these sentences: "They played games," "I play Chopin," "We play baseball," and "Hamlet is a play by Shakespeare" (these sentences are all from Tatoeba.org). These occurrences of "play" have different meanings, and assigning a single vector wouldn't help much in downstream NLP tasks (e.g., in classifying the topic into sports, music, and art).

Due to this limitation, NLP researchers started exploring ways to transform the entire sentence into a series of vectors that consider the context, called *contextualized embeddings* or simply *contextualization*. With these representations, all the occurrences of "play" in the previous examples would have different vectors assigned, helping downstream tasks disambiguate different uses of the word. Notable milestones in contextualized embeddings include CoVe[3] and ELMo (section 9.3.1), although the biggest breakthrough was achieved by BERT, a Transformer-based pretrained language model, which is the focus of this section.

We learned the Transformer uses a mechanism called *self-attention* to gradually transform the input sequence by summarizing it. The core idea of BERT is simple: it uses the Transformer (the Transformer encoder, to be precise) to transform the input into contextualized embeddings. The Transformer transforms the input through a series of layers by gradually summarizing the input. Similarly, BERT contextualizes the input through a series of Transformer encoder layers. This is illustrated in figure 9.4.

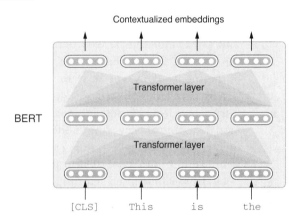

Figure 9.4   BERT processes input through attention layers to produce contextualized embeddings.

Because BERT is based on the Transformer architecture, it inherits all the strengths of the Transformer. Its self-attention mechanism enables it to "random access" over the input and capture long-term dependencies among input tokens. Unlike traditional language models (such as the one based on LSTM that we covered in section 5.5) that can make predictions in only one direction, the Transformer can take into account the context in both directions. Using the sentence "Hamlet is a play by Shakespeare" as an example, the contextualized embedding for "play" can incorporate the information from both "Hamlet" and "Shakespeare," which makes it easier to capture its "dramatic work for the stage" meaning of "play."

---

[3] Bryan McCann, James Bradbury, Caiming Xiong, and Richard Socher, "Learned in Translation: Contextualized Word Vectors," in NIPS 2017.

If this concept is as simple as "BERT is just a Transformer encoder," why does it deserve an entire section here? Because we haven't answered two important practical questions yet: how to train and adapt the model. Neural network models, no matter how powerful, are useless without specific strategies for training and where to get the training data. Also, transfer learning is useless without specific strategies for adapting the pretrained model. We will discuss these questions in the following subsections.

9.2.2 *Self-supervised learning*

The Transformer, which was originally proposed for machine translation, is trained using parallel text. Its encoder and decoder are optimized to minimize the loss function, which is the cross entropy defined by the difference between the decoder output and the expected, correct translation. However, the purpose of pretraining BERT is to derive high-quality contextualized embeddings, and BERT has only an encoder. How can we "train" BERT so that it is useful for downstream NLP tasks?

If you think of BERT just as another way of deriving embeddings, you can draw inspiration from how word embeddings are trained. Recall that in section 3.4, to train word embeddings, we make up a "fake" task where surrounding words are predicted with word embeddings. We are not interested in the prediction per se but rather the "by-product" of the training, which is the word embeddings derived as the parameters of the model. This type of training paradigm where the data itself provides training signals is called *self-supervised learning*, or simply *self-supervision*, in modern machine learning. Self-supervised learning is still one type of supervised learning from the model's point of view—the model is trained in such a way that it minimizes the loss function defined by the training signal. It is where the training signal comes from that is different. In supervised learning, training signals usually come from human annotations. In self-supervised learning, training signals come from the data itself with no human intervention.

With increasingly larger datasets and more powerful models, self-supervised learning has become a popular way to pretrain NLP models in the past several years. But why does it work so well? Two factors contribute to this—one is that the type of self-supervision here is trivially simple to create (just extracting surrounding words for Word2vec), but it requires deep understanding of the language to solve it. For example, reusing the example from the language model we discussed in chapter 5, to answer "My trip to the beach was ruined by bad ___," not only does the system need to understand the sentence but it also needs to be equipped with some sort of "common sense" for what type of things could ruin a trip to a beach (e.g., bad weather, heavy traffic). The knowledge required to predict the surrounding words ranges from simple collocation/association (e.g., The Statue of ____ in New ____), syntactic and grammatical (e.g., "My birthday is ___ May"), and semantic (the previous example). Second, there is virtually no limit on the amount of data used for self-supervision, because all you need is clean, plain text. You can download large datasets (e.g., Wikipedia dump) or crawl and filter web pages, which is a popular way to train many pretrained language models.

9.2.3 *Pretraining BERT*

Now that we all understand how useful self-supervised learning can be for pretraining language models, let's see how we can use it for pretraining BERT. As mentioned earlier, BERT is just a Transformer encoder that transforms the input into a series of embeddings that take context into account. For pretraining word embeddings, you could simply predict surrounding words based on the embeddings of the target word. For pretraining unidirectional language models, you could simply predict the next token based on the tokens that come before the target. But for bidirectional language models such as BERT, you cannot use these strategies, because the input for the prediction (contextualized embeddings) also depends on what comes before and after the input. This sounds like a chicken-and-egg problem.

The inventors of BERT solved this with a brilliant idea called *masked language model* (MLM), where they drop (mask) words randomly in a given sentence and let the model predict what the dropped word is. Specifically, after replacing a small percentage of words in a sentence with a special placeholder, BERT uses the Transformer to encode the input and then uses a feed-forward layer and a softmax layers to derive a probability distribution over possible words that can fill in that blank. Because you already know the answer (because you dropped the words in the first place), you can use the regular cross entropy to train the model, as illustrated in figure 9.5.

Masking and predicting words is not a completely new idea—it's closely related to *cloze tests*, where the test-taker is asked to replace the removed words in a sentence. This test form is often used to assess how well stu-

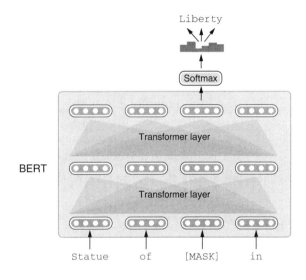

Figure 9.5   Pretraining BERT with a masked language model

dents can understand the language. As we saw earlier, completing missing words in a natural language text requires deep understanding of the language, ranging from simple associations to semantic relationships. As a result, by telling the model to solve this fill-in-the-blank type of task over a huge amount of textual data, the neural network model is trained so that it can produce contextualized embeddings that incorporate deep linguistic knowledge.

You may be wondering what this input [MASK] is and what you actually need to do if you want to implement pretraining BERT yourself. In training neural networks, people often use special tokens such as [MASK] that we mentioned here. These special tokens are just like other (naturally occurring) tokens such as the words "dog" and "cat," except they don't occur in text naturally (you can't find any [MASK] in natural language corpora, no matter how hard you look) and the designers of the neural networks define what they mean. The model will learn to give representations to these tokens so that it can solve the task at hand. Other special tokens include BOS (beginning of sentence), EOS (end of sentence), and UNK (unknown word), which we already encountered in earlier chapters.

Finally, BERT is pretrained not just with the masked language model but also with another type of task called *next-sentence prediction (NSP)*, where two sentences are given to BERT and the model is asked to predict whether the second sentence is the "real" next sentence of the first. This is another type of self-supervised learning ("fake" task) for which the training data can be created in an unlimited manner without much human intervention, because you can extract two consecutive sentences (or just stitch together two sentences at random) from any corpus and make the training data for this task. The rationale behind this task is that by training with this objective, the model will learn how to infer the relationship of two sentences. However, the effectiveness of this task has been actively debated (e.g., RoBERTa dropped this task whereas ALBERT replaced it with another task called *sentence-order prediction*), and we will not go into the details of this task here.

All this pretraining sounds somewhat complex, but good news is that you rarely need to implement this step yourself. Similar to word embeddings, developers and researchers of these language models pretrain their models on a huge amount of natural language text (usually 10 GB-plus or even 100 GB-plus of uncompressed text) with many GPUs and make the pretrained models publicly available so that anyone can use them.

9.2.4 *Adapting BERT*

At the second (and final) stage of transfer learning, a pretrained model is adapted to the target task so that the latter can leverage signals learned by the former. There are two main ways to adapt BERT to individual downstream tasks: *fine-tuning* and *feature extraction*. In fine-tuning, the neural network architecture is slightly modified so that it can produce the type of predictions for the task in question, and the entire network is continuously trained on the training data for the task so that the loss function is minimized. This is exactly the way you train a neural network for NLP tasks, such as sentiment analysis, with one important difference—BERT "inherits" the model weights learned through pretraining, instead of being initialized randomly and trained from scratch. In this way, the downstream task can leverage the powerful representations learned by BERT through pretraining on a large amount of data.

The exact way the BERT architecture is modified varies, depending on the final task, but here I'm going to describe the simplest case where the task is to predict some sort of label for a given sentence. This is also called a *sentence-prediction task*, which includes sentiment analysis, which we covered in chapter 2. For downstream tasks to be able to extract representations for a sentence, BERT prepends a special token [CLS] (for *classification*) to every sentence at the pretraining phase. You can extract the hidden states of BERT with this token and use them as the representation of the sentence. As with other classification tasks, a linear layer can compress this representation into a set of "scores" that correspond to how likely each label is the correct answer. You can then use softmax to derive a probability distribution. For example, if you are working on a sentiment analysis dataset with five labels (strongly negative to strongly positive), you'll use a linear layer to reduce the dimensionality to 5. This type of linear layer combined with softmax, which is plugged into a larger pretrained model such as BERT, is often called a *head*. In other words, we are attaching a *classification head* to BERT to solve a sentence-prediction task. The weights for the entire network (the head and BERT) are adjusted so that the loss function is minimized. This means that the BERT weights initialized with pretrained ones also are adjusted (fine-tuned) through backpropagation. See figure 9.6 for an illustration.

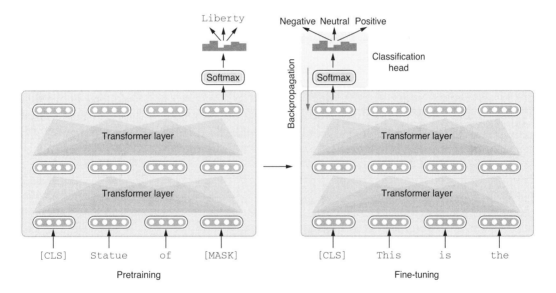

Figure 9.6 Pretraining and fine-tuning BERT with an attached classification head

Another variation in fine-tuning BERT uses all the embeddings, averaged over the input tokens. In this method, called *mean over time* or *bag of embeddings*, all the embeddings produced by BERT are summed up and divided by the length of input, just like the bag-of-words model, to produce a single vector. This method is less popular than using the CLS special token but may work better depending on the task. Figure 9.7 illustrates this.

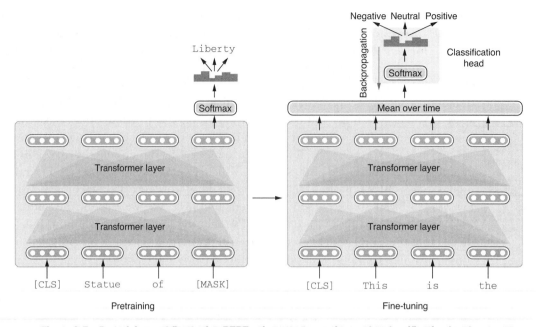

Figure 9.7   Pretraining and fine-tuning BERT using mean over time and a classification head

Another way to adapt BERT for downstream NLP tasks is *feature extraction*. Here BERT is used to extract features, which are simply a sequence of contextualized embeddings produced by the final layer of BERT. You can simply feed these vectors to another machine learning model as features and make predictions, as shown in figure 9.8.

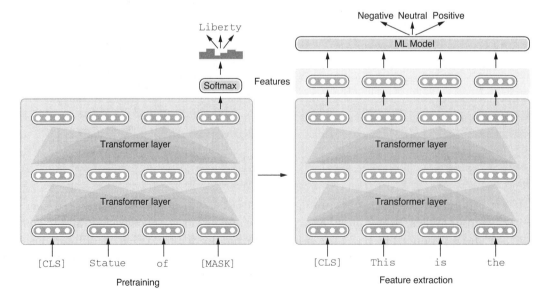

Figure 9.8   Pretraining and using BERT for feature extraction

Graphically, this approach looks similar to fine-tuning. After all, you are feeding the output from BERT to another ML model. However, there are two subtle but important differences: first, because you are no longer optimizing the neural network, the second ML model doesn't have to be a neural network. Some machine learning tasks (e.g., unsupervised clustering) are not what neural networks are good at solving, and feature extraction offers a perfect solution in these situations. Also, you are free to use more "traditional" ML algorithms, such as SVMs (support vector machines), decision trees, and gradient-boosted methods (such as GBDT, or gradient-boosted decision trees), which may offer a better tradeoff in terms of computational cost and performance. Second, because BERT is used only as a feature extractor, there is no backpropagation and its internal parameters won't be updated during the adaptation phase. In many cases, you get better accuracy in the downstream task if you fine-tune the BERT parameters, because by doing so, you are also teaching BERT to get better at the task at hand.

Finally, note that these two are not the only ways to adapt BERT. Transfer learning is an actively researched topic, not just in NLP but also in many fields of artificial intelligence, and we have many other ways to use pretrained language models to make the best of them. If you are interested in learning more, I recommend checking out the tutorial given at NAACL 2019 (one of the top NLP conferences) titled "Transfer Learning in Natural Language Processing" (http://mng.bz/o8qp).

9.3 *Case study 1: Sentiment analysis with BERT*

In this section, we will build a sentiment analyzer (again), but this time with BERT. Instead of AllenNLP, we will use the Transformers library developed by Hugging Face, which we used for making predictions with language models in the previous chapter. All the code here is accessible on a Google Colab notebook (http://www.realworldnlp-book.com/ch9.html#sst). The code snippets you see in this section all assume that you import related modules, classes, and methods as follows:

```
import torch
from torch import nn, optim
from transformers import AutoTokenizer, AutoModel, AdamW,
    get_cosine_schedule_with_warmup
```

In the Transformers library, you specify the pretrained models by their names. We'll use the cased BERT-base model (`'bert-base-cased'`) throughout this section, so let's define a constant first as follows:

```
BERT_MODEL = 'bert-base-cased'
```

The Transformers library also supports other pretrained BERT models, which you can see in their documentation (https://huggingface.co/transformers/pretrained_models.html). If you want to use other models, you can simply replace this constant with the name of the model you want to use, and the rest of the code works as-is in many cases (but not always).

9.3.1   *Tokenizing input*

The first step we took for building an NLP model is to build a dataset reader. Although AllenNLP (or more precisely speaking, the `allennlp-modules` package) is shipped with a dataset reader for the Stanford Sentiment Treebank, the dataset reader's output is compatible only with AllenNLP. In this section, we are going to write a simple method that reads the dataset and returns a sequence of batched input instances.

Tokenization is one of the most important steps in processing natural language input. As we saw in the previous chapter, tokenizers in the Transformers library can be initialized with the `AutoTokenizer.from_pretrained()` class method as follows:

```
tokenizer = AutoTokenizer.from_pretrained(BERT_MODEL)
```

Because different pretrained models use different tokenizers, it is important to initialize the one that matches the pretrained model you are going to use by supplying the same model name.

You can use the tokenizer to convert between a string and a list of token IDs back and forth, as shown next:

```
>>> token_ids = tokenizer.encode('The best movie ever!')

[101, 1109, 1436, 2523, 1518, 106, 102]

>>> tokenizer.decode(token_ids)

'[CLS] The best movie ever! [SEP]'
```

Notice that BERT's tokenizer added two special tokens—`[CLS]` and `[SEP]`—to your sentence. As discussed earlier, `CLS` is a special token used to extract the embedding for the entire input, whereas `SEP` is used to separate two sentences if your task involves making predictions on a pair of sentences. Because we are making predictions for single sentences here, there's no need to pay much attention to this token. We'll discuss sentence-pair classification tasks later in section 9.5.

Deep neural networks rarely operate on single instances. They usually are trained on and make predictions for batches of instances for stability and performance reasons. The tokenizer also supports converting the given input in batches by invoking the `__call__` method (i.e., just use the object as a method) as follows:

```
>>> result = tokenizer(
>>>     ['The best movie ever!', 'Awful movie'],
>>>     max_length=10,
>>>     pad_to_max_length=True,
>>>     truncation=True,
>>>     return_tensors='pt')
```

When you run this, each string in the input list is tokenized and then resulting tensors are *padded* with 0s to have the same lengths. Padding here means adding 0s at the end of each sequence so that individual instances have the same length and can be bundled as a single tensor, which is needed for more efficient computation (we'll cover padding in more detail in chapter 10). The method call contains several other parameters that control the maximum length (max_length=10, meaning to pad everything to the length of 10), whether to pad to the maximum length, whether to truncate sequences that are too long, and the type of the returned tensors (return_tensors='pt', meaning it returns PyTorch tensors). The result of this tokenizer() call is a dictionary that contains the following three keys and three different types of packed tensors:

```
>>> result['input_ids']

tensor([[ 101, 1109, 1436, 2523, 1518,  106, 102,   0,   0,   0],
        [ 101,  138, 7921, 2365, 2523,  102,   0,   0,   0,   0]])

>>> result['token_type_ids']

tensor([[0, 0, 0, 0, 0, 0, 0, 0, 0, 0],
        [0, 0, 0, 0, 0, 0, 0, 0, 0, 0]])

>>> result['attention_mask']

tensor([[1, 1, 1, 1, 1, 1, 1, 0, 0, 0],
        [1, 1, 1, 1, 1, 1, 0, 0, 0, 0]])
```

The input_ids tensor is a packed version of token IDs converted from the texts. Notice that each row is a vectorized token ID padded with 0s so that its length is always 10. The token_type_ids tensor specifies which sentence each token comes from. As with the SEP special token earlier, this is relevant only if you are working with sentence pairs, which is why the tensor is simply filled with just 0s. The attention_mask tensor specifies which tokens the Transformer should attend to. Because there are no tokens at the padded elements (0s in input_ids), the corresponding elements in attention_mask are all 0s, and attention to these tokens is simply ignored. Masking is a common technique often used in neural networks to ignore irrelevant elements in batched tensors like the ones shown here. Chapter 10 covers masking in more detail.

As you see here, the Transformers library's tokenizers do more than just tokenizing—they take a list of strings and create batched tensors for you, including the auxiliary tensors (token_type_ids and attention_mask). You just need to create lists of strings from your dataset and pass them to tokenizer() to create batches to pass on to the model. This logic for reading datasets is rather boring and a bit lengthy, so I packaged it in a method named read_dataset, which is not shown here. If you are interested, you can check the Google Colab notebook mentioned earlier. Using this method, you can read a dataset and convert it to a list of batches as follows:

```
train_data = read_dataset('train.txt', batch_size=32, tokenizer=tokenizer,
    max_length=128)
dev_data = read_dataset('dev.txt', batch_size=32, tokenizer=tokenizer,
    max_length=128)
```

9.3.2 Building the model

In the next step, we'll build the model to classify texts into their sentiment labels. The model we build here is nothing but a thin wrapper around BERT. All it does is pass the input through BERT, take out its embedding at CLS, pass it through a linear layer to convert to a set of scores (logits), and compute the loss.

Note that we are building a PyTorch `Module`, not an AllenNLP `Model`, so make sure to inherit from `nn.Module`, although the structure of these two types of models are usually very similar (because AllenNLP's `Model`s inherit from PyTorch `Module`s). You need to implement `__init__()`, where you define and initialize submodules of the model, and `forward()`, where the main computation ("forward pass") happens. The entire code snippet is shown next.

Listing 9.1 Sentiment analysis model with BERT

```
class BertClassifier(nn.Module):
    def __init__(self, model_name, num_labels):
        super(BertClassifier, self).__init__()
        self.bert_model = AutoModel.from_pretrained(model_name)    ◁── Initializes BERT

        self.linear = nn.Linear(self.bert_model.config.hidden_size,
    num_labels)                                                    ◁── Defines a linear layer

        self.loss_function = nn.CrossEntropyLoss()

    def forward(self, input_ids, attention_mask, token_type_ids, label=None):
        bert_out = self.bert_model(              ◁── Applies BERT
            input_ids=input_ids,
            attention_mask=attention_mask,
            token_type_ids=token_type_ids)

        logits = self.linear(bert_out.pooler_output)    ◁── Applies the linear layer

        loss = None
        if label is not None:
            loss = self.loss_function(logits, label)    ◁── Computes the loss

        return loss, logits
```

The module first defines the BERT model (via the `AutoModel.from_pretrained()` class method), a linear layer (`nn.Linear`), and the loss function (`nn.CrossEntropyLoss`) in `__init__()`. Note that the module has no way of knowing the number of labels it needs to classify into, so we are passing it as a parameter (`num_labels`).

In the `forward()` method, it first calls the BERT model. You can simply pass the three types of tensors (`input_ids`, `attention_mask`, and `token_type_ids`) to the model. The model returns a data structure that contains `last_hidden_state` and `pooler_output` among other things, where `last_hidden_state` is a sequence of hidden states of the last layer, whereas `pooler_output` is a pooled output, which is basically the embedding at CLS transformed with a linear layer. Because we are interested only in the pooled output that represents the entire input, we'll pass the latter to the linear layer. Finally, the method computes the loss (if the label is supplied) and returns it, along with the logits, which are used for making predictions and measuring the accuracy.

Pay attention to the way we designed the method signature—it takes the three tensors we inspected earlier with their exact names. This lets us simply destruct a batch and pass it to the forward method, as shown here:

```
>>> model(**train_data[0])

(tensor(1.8050, grad_fn=<NllLossBackward>),
 tensor([[-0.5088,  0.0806, -0.2924, -0.6536, -0.2627],
         [-0.3816,  0.3512, -0.1223, -0.5136, -0.4421],
         ...
         [-0.4220,  0.3026, -0.1723, -0.4913, -0.4106],
         [-0.3354,  0.3871, -0.0787, -0.4673, -0.4169]],
        grad_fn=<AddmmBackward>))
```

Notice that the return value of the forward pass is a tuple of the loss and the logits. Now you are ready to train your model!

9.3.3 Training the model

In the third and the final step of this case study, we will train and validate the model. Although AllenNLP took care of the training process in the previous chapters, in this section we'll write our own training loop from scratch so we can better understand what it takes to train a model yourself. Note that you can also choose to use the library's own Trainer class (https://huggingface.co/transformers/main_classes/trainer.html), which works similarly to AllenNLP's Trainer, to run the training loop by specifying its parameters.

We covered the basics of training loops in section 2.5, but to recap, in modern machine learning, every training loop looks somewhat similar. If you write it in pseudocode, it would look like the one shown as follows.

Listing 9.2 Pseudocode for the neural network training loop

```
MAX_EPOCHS = 100
model = Model()

for epoch in range(MAX_EPOCHS):
    for batch in train_set:
        loss, prediction = model.forward(**batch)
        new_model = optimizer(model, loss)
        model = new_model
```

This training loop is almost identical to listing 2.2, except it operates on batches instead of single instances. The dataset yields a series of batches, which are then passed to the forward method of the model. The method returns the loss, which is then used to optimize the model. It is also common for the model to return the predictions so that the caller can use the result to compute some metrics, such as accuracy.

Before we move on to writing our own training loop, we need to note two things—it is customary to alternate between training and validation during each epoch. In the training phase, the model is optimized (the "magic constants" are changed) based on the loss function and the optimizer. The training data is used during this phase. In the validation phase, the model's parameters are fixed, and its accuracy of prediction is measured against validation data. Although the loss is not used for optimization during validation, it is common to compute it to monitor how the loss changes during the course of the training, as we did in section 6.3.

Another thing to note is that when training Transformer-based models such as BERT, we usually use *warm-up*, a process where the learning rate (how much to change the magic constants) is gradually increased for the first few thousand steps. A step here is just another name for one execution of backpropagation, which corresponds to the inner loop of listing 9.2. This is useful for stabilizing training. We are not going into the mathematical details of warm-up and controlling the learning rate here—we just note that a learning rate scheduler is usually used for controlling the learning rate over the course of the training. With the Transformers library, you can define an optimizer (`AdamW`) and a learning controller as follows:

```
optimizer = AdamW(model.parameters(), lr=1e-5)
scheduler = get_cosine_schedule_with_warmup(
    optimizer,
    num_warmup_steps=100,
    num_training_steps=1000)
```

The controller we are using here (`get_cosine_schedule_with_warmup`) increases the learning rate from zero to the maximum during the first 100 steps, then gradually decreases it afterward (based on the cosine function, which is where it got its name). If you plot how the learning rate changes over time, it'll look like the graph in figure 9.9.

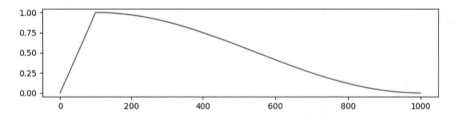

Figure 9.9 **With a cosine learning rate schedule with warm-up, the learning rate ramps up first, then declines following a cosine function.**

Now we are ready to train our BERT-based sentiment analyzer. The next listing shows our training loop.

Listing 9.3 Training loop for the BERT-based sentiment analyzer

```
for epoch in range(epochs):
    print(f'epoch = {epoch}')

    model.train()                              Turns on the
                                               training mode
    losses = []
    total_instances = 0
    correct_instances = 0
    for batch in train_data:
        batch_size = batch['input_ids'].size(0)    Moves the batch to
        move_to(batch, device)                      GPU (if available)

        optimizer.zero_grad()              Remember to reset the gradients
                                           (in PyTorch gradients accumulate).
        loss, logits = model(**batch)
        loss.backward()            Backpropagation
        optimizer.step()
        scheduler.step()

        losses.append(loss)

        total_instances += batch_size
        correct_instances += torch.sum(torch.argmax(logits, dim=-1)
            == batch['label']).item()         Computes the accuracy by counting
    avr_loss = sum(losses) / len(losses)      the number of correct instances
    accuracy = correct_instances / total_instances
    print(f'train loss = {avr_loss}, accuracy = {accuracy}')
```

Forward pass → `loss, logits = model(**batch)`

When you train a model using PyTorch (and, consequently, AllenNLP and Transformers, two libraries that are built on top of it), remember to call `model.train()` to turn on the "training mode" of the model. This is important because some layers such as BatchNorm and dropout behave differently between training and evaluation (we'll cover dropout in chapter 10). On the other hand, when you validate or test your model, be sure to call `model.eval()`.

The code in listing 9.3 does not show the validation phase, but the code for validation would look almost the same as that for training. When you validate/test your model, pay attention to the following:

- As mentioned previously, make sure to call `model.eval()` before validating/testing your model.
- Optimization calls (`loss.backward()`, `optimizer.step()`, and `scheduler.step()`) are not necessary because you are not updating the model.
- Losses are still recorded and reported for monitoring. Be sure to wrap your forward pass call with `with torch.no_grad()`—this will disable gradient computation and save memory.
- Accuracy is computed in exactly the same way (this is the point of validation!).

When I ran this, I got the following output to `stdout` (with intermediate epochs omitted):

```
epoch = 0
train loss = 1.5403757095336914, accuracy = 0.31624531835205993
dev loss = 1.7507736682891846, accuracy = 0.2652134423251589
epoch = 1
...
epoch = 8
train loss = 0.4508829712867737, accuracy = 0.8470271535580525
dev loss = 1.687158465385437, accuracy = 0.48319709355131696
epoch = 9
...
```

The dev accuracy peaked around 0.483 at epoch 8 and didn't improve after that. Compared to the result we got from LSTM (dev accuracy ~0.35, in chapter 2) and CNN (dev accuracy ~0.40, in chapter 7), this is the best result we have achieved on this dataset. We've done very little hyperparameter tuning, so it's too early to conclude that BERT is the best model of the three we compared, but we at least know that it is a strong baseline to start from!

9.4   *Other pretrained language models*

BERT is neither the first nor the last of popular pretrained language models (PLMs) commonly used in the NLP community nowadays. In this section, we'll learn several other popular PLMs and how they are different from BERT. Most of these models are already implemented and publicly available from the Transformers library, so you can integrate them with your NLP application by changing just a couple of lines of your code.

9.4.1   *ELMo*

ELMo (Embeddings from Language Models), proposed[4] in early 2018, is one of the earliest PLMs for deriving contextualized embeddings using unlabeled texts. Its core idea is simple—train an LSTM-based language model (similar to the one we trained back in chapter 5) and use its hidden states as additional "features" for downstream NLP tasks. Because the language model is trained to predict the next token given the previous context, the hidden states can encode the information needed to "understand the language." ELMo does the same with another, backward LM and combines the embeddings from both directions so that it can also encode the information in both directions. See figure 9.10 for an illustration.

After pretraining LMs in both directions, downstream NLP tasks can simply use the ELMo embeddings as features. Note that ELMo uses multilayer LSTM, so the features are the sum of hidden states taken from different layers, weighted in a task-specific way. The inventors of ELMo showed that adding these features improves the performance

---

[4] Peters et al., "Deep Contextualized Word Representations," (2018). https://arxiv.org/abs/1802.05365.

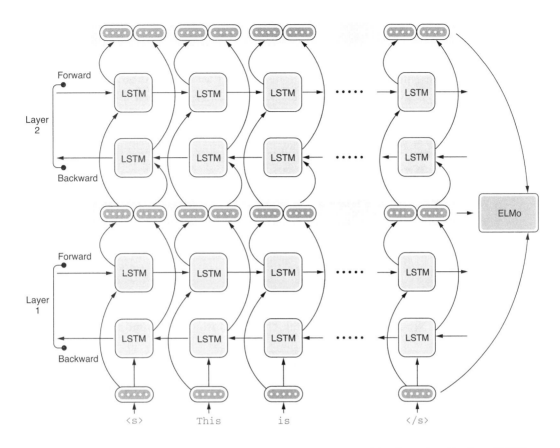

Figure 9.10 ELMo computes contextualized embeddings by combining forward and backward LSTMs.

of a wide range of NLP tasks, including sentiment analysis, named entity recognition, and question answering. Although ELMo is not implemented in Hugging Face's Transformers library, you can use it with AllenNLP fairly easily.[5]

ELMo is a historically important PLM, although it is not often used in research or production anymore today—it predates BERT (and the advent of the Transformer) and there are other PLMs (including BERT) that outperform ELMo and are widely available today.

9.4.2 XLNet

XLNet, proposed in 2019, is an important successor of BERT and often referenced as one of the most powerful PLMs as of today. XLNet addresses two main issues of how BERT is trained: train-test skew and the independence of masks. The first issue has to

---

[5] See here for the detailed documentation on how to use ELMo with AllenNLP: https://allennlp.org/elmo.

do with how BERT is pretrained using the masked language model (MLM) objective. During training time, BERT is trained so that it can accurately predict masked tokens, whereas during prediction, it just sees the input sentence, which does not contain any masks. This means that there's a discrepancy of information to which BERT is exposed to between training and testing, and that creates the train-test skew problem.

The second issue has to do with how BERT makes predictions for masked tokens. If there is more than one [MASK] token in the input, BERT makes predictions for them in parallel. There doesn't seem to be anything wrong with this approach at first glance—for example, if the input was "The Statue of [MASK] in New [MASK]," the model wouldn't have difficulties answering this as "Liberty" and "York." If the input was "The Statue of [MASK] in Washington, [MASK]," most of you (and probably a language model) would predict "Lincoln" and "DC." However, what if the input was the following:

The Statue of [MASK] *in* [MASK] [MASK]

Then there is no information to bias your prediction one way or the other. BERT won't learn the fact that "The Statue of Liberty in Washington, DC" or "The Statue of Lincoln in New York" don't make much sense during the training from this example, because these predictions are all made in parallel. This is a good example showing that you cannot simply make independent predictions on tokens and combine them to create a sentence that makes sense.

> **NOTE** This issue is related to the multimodality of natural language, which means there are multiple modes in the joint probability distribution, and combinations of best decisions made independently do not necessarily lead to globally best decisions. Multimodality is a big challenge in natural language generation.

To address this issue, instead of making predictions in parallel, you can make predictions sequentially. In fact, this is exactly what typical language models do—generate tokens from left to right, one by one. However, here we have a sentence interspersed with masked tokens, and predictions depend not only on the tokens on the left (e.g., "The Statue of" in the previous example) but also on the right ("in"). XLNet solves this by generating missing tokens in a random order, as shown in figure 9.11. For example, you can choose to generate "New" first, which gives a strong clue for the next words, "York" and "Liberty," and so on. Note that prediction is still made based on all the tokens generated previously. If the model chose to generate "Washington" first, then the model would proceed to generate "DC" and "Lincoln" and would never mix up these two.

XLNet is already implemented in the Transformers library, and you can use the model with only a few lines of code change.[6]

---

[6]   See https://huggingface.co/transformers/model_doc/xlnet.html for the documentation.

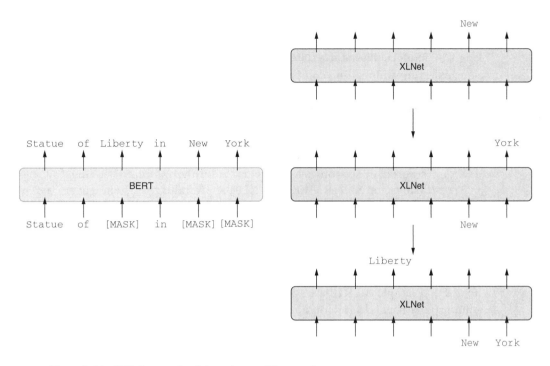

Figure 9.11   XLNet generates tokens in an arbitrary order.

9.4.3   *RoBERTa*

RoBERTa (from "robustly optimized BERT")[7] is another important PLM that is commonly used in research and industry. RoBERTa revisits and modifies many training decisions of BERT, which makes it match or even exceed the performance of post-BERT PLMs, including XLNet, which we covered earlier. My personal impression is that RoBERTa is the second most referenced PLM after BERT as of this writing (mid-2020), and it shows robust performance in many downstream NLP tasks in English.

RoBERTa makes several improvements over BERT, but the most important (and the most straightforward) is the amount of its training data. The developers of RoBERTa collected five English corpora of varying sizes and domains, which total over 160 GB of text (versus 16 GB used for training BERT). Simply by using a lot more data for training, RoBERTa overperforms some of the other powerful PLMs, including XLNet, in downstream tasks after fine-tuning. The second modification has to do with the next-sentence prediction (NSP) objective we touched on in section 9.2.3, where BERT is pretrained to classify whether the second sentence is the "true" sentence that follows the first one in a corpus. The developers of RoBERTa found that, by removing NSP (and training with the MLM objective only), the performance of downstream

[7] Liu et al., "RoBERTa: A Robustly Optimized BERT Pretraining Approach," (2019). https://arxiv.org/abs/1907.11692.

tasks stays about the same or slightly improves. In addition to these, they also revisited the batch size and the way masking is done for MLM. Combined, the new pretrained language model achieved the state-of-the-art results on downstream tasks such as question answering and reading comprehension.

Because RoBERTa uses the identical architecture to BERT and both are implemented in Transformers, switching to RoBERTa is extremely easy if your application already uses BERT.

> **NOTE** Similar to BERT versus RoBERTa, the cross-lingual language model XLM (covered in section 8.4.4) has its "robustly optimized" sibling called *XLM-R* (short for XML-RoBERTa).[8] XLM-R pretrains on 100 languages and shows competitive performance on many cross-lingual NLP tasks.

9.4.4   *DistilBERT*

Although pretrained models such as BERT and RoBERTa are powerful, they are computationally expensive, not just for pretraining but also for tuning and making predictions. For example, BERT-base (the regular-sized BERT) and BERT-large (the larger counterpart) have 110 million and 340 million parameters, respectively, and virtually every input has to go through this huge network to get predictions. If you were to fine-tune and make predictions with a BERT-based model (such as the one we built in section 9.3), you'd most certainly need a GPU, which is not always available, depending on your computational environment. For example, if you'd like to run some real-time text analytics on a mobile phone, BERT wouldn't be a great choice (and it might not even fit in the memory).

To reduce the computational requirement of modern large neural networks, *knowledge distillation* (or simply *distillation*) is often used. This is a machine learning technique where, given a large pretrained model (called the *teacher model*), a smaller model (called the *student model*) is trained to mimic the behavior of the larger model. See figure 9.12 for more details. The student model is trained with the masked language model (MLM) loss (same as BERT), as well as the cross-entropy loss between the teacher and the student. This pushes the student model to produce the probability distribution over predicted tokens that are as similar to the teacher as possible.

Researchers at Hugging Face developed a distilled version of BERT called *DistilBERT*,[9] which is 40% smaller and 60% faster while retraining 97% of task performance compared to BERT. You can use DistilBERT by simply replacing the model name you pass to AutoModel.from_pretrained() for BERT (e.g., bert-base-cased) with distilled versions (e.g., distilbert-base-cased), while keeping the rest of your code the same.

---

8   Conneau et al., "Unsupervised Cross-lingual Representation Learning at Scale," (2019). https://arxiv.org/abs/1911.02116.

9   Sanh et al., "DistilBERT, a distilled version of BERT: smaller, faster, cheaper and lighter," (2019). https://arxiv.org/abs/1910.01108.

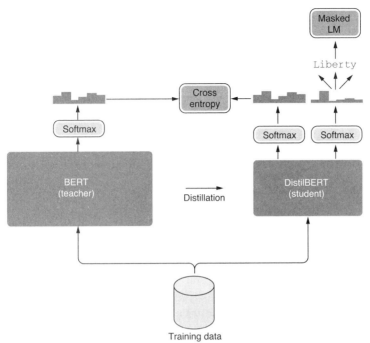

Figure 9.12 Knowledge distillation combines cross entropy and the masked LM objectives.

9.4.5 *ALBERT*

Another pretrained language model that addresses the computational complexity problem of BERT is ALBERT,[10] short for "A Lite BERT." Instead of resorting to knowledge distillation, ALBERT makes a few changes to its model and the training procedure.

One design change ALBERT makes to its model is how it handles word embeddings. In most deep NLP models, word embeddings are represented by and stored in a big lookup table that contains one word embedding vector per word. This way of managing embeddings is usually fine for smaller models such as RNNs and CNNs. However, for Transformer-based models such as BERT, the dimensionality (i.e., the length) of input needs to match that of the hidden states, which is usually as big as 768 dimensions. This means that the model needs to maintain a big lookup table of size *V* times 768, where *V* is the number of unique vocabulary items. Because in many NLP models *V* is also large (e.g., 30,000), the resulting lookup table becomes huge and takes up a lot of memory and computation.

ALBERT addresses this issue by decomposing word embedding lookup into two stages, as shown in figure 9.13. The first stage is similar to how word embeddings are retrieved from a mapping table, except that the output dimensionality of word embedding vectors is smaller (say, 128 dimensions). In the next stage, these shorter

---

[10] Lan et al., "ALBERT: A Lite BERT for Self-Supervised Learning of Language Representations," (2020). https://arxiv.org/abs/1909.11942.

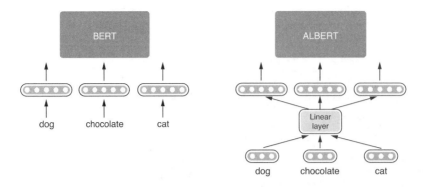

Figure 9.13 ALBERT (right) decomposes word embeddings into two smaller projections.

vectors are expanded using a linear layer so that they match the desired input dimensionality of the model (say, 768). This is similar to how we expanded word embeddings with the Skip-gram model (section 3.4). Thanks to this decomposition, ALBERT needs to store only two smaller lookup tables ($V \times 128$, plus 128×768) instead of one big look-up table ($V \times 768$).

Another design change that ALBERT implements is parameter sharing between Transformer layers. Transformer models use a series of self-attention layers to transform the input vector. The way these layers transform the input is usually different from layer to layer—the first layer may transform the input one way (e.g., capture basic phrases), and the second one may do so another way (e.g., capture some syntactic information). However, this means that the model needs to retain all the necessary parameters (projections for keys, queries, and values) per each layer, which is expensive and takes up a lot of memory. Instead, ALBERT's layers all share the same set of parameters, meaning that the model applies the same transformation repeatedly to the input. These parameters are adjusted in such a way that the series of transformations are effective for predicting the objective, even though they are identical.

Finally, ALBERT uses a training objective called *sentence-order prediction* (SOP) for pretraining, instead of the next-sentence prediction (NSP) adopted by BERT. As mentioned earlier, the developers of RoBERTa and some others found out that the NSP objective is basically useless and decided to eliminate it. ALBERT replaces NSP with sentence-order prediction (SOP), a task where the model is asked to predict the ordering of two consecutive segments of text. For example:[11]

- (A) She and her boyfriend decided to go for a long walk. (B) After walking for over a mile, something happened.
- (C) However, one of the teachers around the area helped me get up. (D) At first, no one was willing to help me up.

---

[11] These examples are taken from ROCStories: https://cs.rochester.edu/nlp/rocstories/.

In the first example, you can tell that A happens before B. In the second, the order is flipped, and D should come before C. This is an easy feat for humans, but a difficult task for machines—an NLP model needs to learn to ignore superficial topical signals (e.g., "go for a long walk," "walking for over a mile," "helped me get up," and "help me up") and focus on discourse-level coherence. Training with this objective makes the model more robust and effective for deeper natural language understanding tasks.

As a result, ALBERT was able to scale up its training and outperform BERT-large with fewer parameters. As with DistilBERT, the model architecture of ALBERT is almost identical to that of BERT, and you can use it by simply supplying the model name when you call `AutoModel.from_pretrained()` (e.g., `albert-base-v1`).

9.5　Case study 2: Natural language inference with BERT

In this final section of this chapter, we will build an NLP model for natural language inference, a task where the system predicts logical relationship between sentences. We'll use AllenNLP for building the model while demonstrating how to integrate BERT (or any other Transformer-based pretrained models) into your pipeline.

9.5.1　What is natural language inference?

Natural language inference (or NLI, for short) is the task of determining the logical relationship between a pair of sentences. Specifically, given one sentence (called *premise*) and another sentence (called *hypothesis*), you need to determine whether the hypothesis is logically inferred from the premise. This is easier to see in the following examples.[12]

Premise	Hypothesis	Label
A man inspects the uniform of a figure in some East Asian country.	The man is sleeping.	contradiction
An older and younger man smiling.	Two men are smiling and laughing at the cats playing on the floor.	neutral
A soccer game with multiple males playing.	Some men are playing a sport.	entailment

In the first example, the hypothesis ("The man is sleeping") clearly contradicts the premise ("A man inspects . . .") because someone cannot be inspecting something while asleep. In the second example, you cannot tell if the hypothesis contradicts or is entailed by the premise (especially the "laughing at the cats" part), which makes the relationship "neutral." In the third example, you can logically infer the hypothesis from the premise—in other words, the hypothesis is entailed by the premise.

As you can guess, NLI can be tricky even for humans. The task requires not only lexical knowledge (e.g., plural of "man" is "men," soccer is one type of sport) but also

---

[12] These examples are taken from http://nlpprogress.com/english/natural_language_inference.html.

some "common sense" (e.g., you cannot inspect while sleeping). NLI is one of the most typical natural language understanding (NLU) tasks. How can you build an NLP model to solve this task?

Fortunately, NLI is a well-studied field in NLP. The most popular dataset for NLI, the Standard Natural Language Inference (SNLI) corpus (https://nlp.stanford.edu/projects/snli/), has been used in numerous NLP studies as a benchmark. In what follows, we'll build a neural NLI model with AllenNLP and learn how to use BERT for this particular task.

Before moving on, make sure that you have AllenNLP (we use version 2.5.0) and the AllenNLP model's modules installed. You can install them by running the following code:

```
pip install allennlp==2.5.0
pip install allennlp-models==2.5.0
```

This also installs the Transformers library as a dependency.

9.5.2 *Using BERT for sentence-pair classification*

Before we start building the model, notice that every input to the NLI task consists of two pieces: a premise and a hypothesis. Most of the NLP tasks we covered in this book had just one part—usually a single sentence—as the input to the model. How can we build a model that makes predictions for instances that are pairs of sentences?

We have multiple ways to deal with multipart input for NLP models. We can encode each sentence with an encoder and apply some mathematical operations (e.g., concatenation, subtractions) to the result to derive an embedding for the pair (which, by the way, is the basic idea of Siamese networks[13]). Researchers have also come up with more complex neural network models with attention (such as BiDAF[14]).

However, there's inherently nothing preventing BERT from accepting more than one sentence. Because the Transformer accepts a sequence of any tokens, you can simply concatenate the two sentences and feed them to the model. If you are worried about the model mixing up the two sentences, you can separate them with a special token, [SEP]. You can also add different values to each sentence as an extra signal to the model. BERT uses these two techniques to solve sentence-pair classification tasks such as NLI with little modification to the model.

The rest of the pipeline proceeds in a similar way to other classification tasks. A special token [CLS] is appended to every sentence pair, from which the final embedding of the input is extracted. Finally, you can use a classification head to convert the embedding into a set of values (called *logits*) corresponding to the classes. This is illustrated in figure 9.14.

---

[13] Reimers and Gurevych, "Sentence-BERT: Sentence Embeddings Using Siamese BERT-Networks," (2019). https://arxiv.org/abs/1908.10084.

[14] Seo et al., "Bidirectional Attention Flow for Machine Comprehension," (2018). https://arxiv.org/abs/1611.01603.

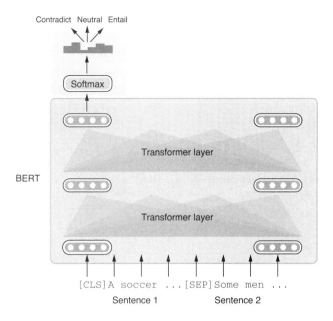

Figure 9.14 Feeding
and classifying a pair of
sentences with BERT

In practice, concatenating and inserting special tokens are both taken care of by
SnliReader, an AllenNLP dataset reader specifically built for dealing with the SNLI
dataset. You can initialize the dataset and observe how it turns the data into AllenNLP
instances with the following snippet:

```
from allennlp.data.tokenizers import PretrainedTransformerTokenizer
from allennlp_models.pair_classification.dataset_readers import SnliReader

BERT_MODEL = 'bert-base-cased'
tokenizer = PretrainedTransformerTokenizer(model_name=BERT_MODEL,
    add_special_tokens=False)

reader = SnliReader(tokenizer=tokenizer)
dataset_url = 'https://realworldnlpbook.s3.amazonaws.com/data/snli/
    snli_1.0_dev.jsonl'
for instance in reader.read():
    print(instance)
```

The dataset reader takes a JSONL (JSON line) file from the Stanford NLI corpus and
turns it into a series of AllenNLP instances. We specify the URL of a dataset file that I
put online (S3). Note that you need to specify add_special_tokens=False when
initializing the tokenizer. This sounds a little bit strange—aren't the special tokens the
very things we need to add here? This is necessary because the dataset reader (Snli-
Reader), not the tokenizer, will take care of the special tokens. If you were to use the
Transformer library only (without AllenNLP), you wouldn't need this option.

The previous snippet produces the following dump of generated instances:

```
Instance with fields:
        tokens: TextField of length 29 with text:
```

```
                  [[CLS], Two, women, are, em, ##bracing, while, holding, to,
         go, packages,
                   ., [SEP], The, sisters, are, hugging, goodbye, while, hold-
         ing, to, go,
                   packages, after, just, eating, lunch, ., [SEP]]
                   and TokenIndexers : {'tokens': 'SingleIdTokenIndexer'}
              label: LabelField with label: neutral in namespace: 'labels'.'

Instance with fields:
         tokens: TextField of length 20 with text:
                   [[CLS], Two, women, are, em, ##bracing, while, holding, to,
         go, packages,
                   ., [SEP], Two, woman, are, holding, packages, ., [SEP]]
                   and TokenIndexers : {'tokens': 'SingleIdTokenIndexer'}
              label: LabelField with label: entailment in namespace: 'labels'.'

Instance with fields:
         tokens: TextField of length 23 with text:
                   [[CLS], Two, women, are, em, ##bracing, while, holding, to,
         go, packages,
                   ., [SEP], The, men, are, fighting, outside, a, del, ##i, .,
         [SEP]]
                   and TokenIndexers : {'tokens': 'SingleIdTokenIndexer'}
              label: LabelField with label: contradiction in namespace: 'labels'.'
...
```

Notice that every sentence is tokenized, and the sentences are concatenated and separated by [SEP] special tokens. Each instance also has a label field containing the gold label.

NOTE   You may have noticed some weird characters in the tokenized results, such as ##bracing and ##i. These are the results of byte-pair encoding (BPE), a tokenization algorithm for splitting words into what's called *subword units*. We'll cover BPE in detail in chapter 10.

9.5.3   *Using Transformers with AllenNLP*

Now we are ready to build our model with AllenNLP. The good news is you don't need to write any Python code to build an NLI model thanks to AllenNLP's built-in modules—all you need to do is write a Jsonnet config file (as we did in chapter 4). AllenNLP also integrates Hugging Face's Transformer library seamlessly, so you usually need to make little change, even if you want to integrate Transformer-based models such as BERT into your existing models.

You need to make changes to the following four components when integrating BERT into your model and pipeline:

- *Tokenizer*—As you did in section 9.3 earlier, you need to use a tokenizer that matches the pretrained model you are using.
- *Token indexer*—Token indexers turn tokens into integer indices. Because pretrained models come with their own predefined vocabularies, it is important that you use a matching token indexer.

- *Token embedder*—Token embedders turn tokens into embeddings. This is where the main computation of BERT happens.
- *Seq2Vec encoder*—The raw output from BERT is a sequence of embeddings. You need a Seq2Vec encoder to turn it into a single embedding vector.

Don't worry if this sounds intimidating—in most cases, all you need to do is remember to initialize the right modules with the name of the model you want. I'll walk you through these steps next.

First, let's define the dataset we use for reading and converting the SNLI dataset. We already did this with Python code earlier, but here we will write the corresponding initialization in Jsonnet. First, let's define the model name we'll use throughout the pipeline using the following code. One of the cool features of Jsonnet over vanilla JSON is you can define and use variables:

```
local bert_model = "bert-base-cased";
```

The first section of the config file where the dataset is initialized looks like the following:

```
"dataset_reader": {
    "type": "snli",
    "tokenizer": {
        "type": "pretrained_transformer",
        "model_name": bert_model,
        "add_special_tokens": false
    },
    "token_indexers": {
        "bert": {
            "type": "pretrained_transformer",
            "model_name": bert_model,
        }
    }
},
```

At the top level, this is initializing a dataset reader specified by the type `snli`, which is the `SnliReader` we experimented with previously. The dataset reader takes two parameters—`tokenizer` and `token_indexers`. For the tokenizer, we initialize a `PretrainedTransformerTokenizer` (type: `pretrained_transformer`) with a model name. Again, this is the tokenizer we initialized and used earlier in the Python code. Notice how the Python code and the Jsonnet config file correspond to each other nicely. Most of AllenNLP modules are designed in such a way that there's nice correspondence between these two, as shown in the following table.

Python code	Jsonnet config

`tokenizer =`
`PretrainedTransformerTokenizer(`
`    model_name=BERT_MODEL,`
`    add_special_tokens=False)`
	`"tokenizer": {`
	`    "type": "pretrained_transformer",`
	`    "model_name": bert_model,`
	`    "add_special_tokens": false`
	`}`

The section for initializing a token indexer may look a bit confusing. It is initializing a `PretrainedTransformerIndexer` (type: `pretrained_transformer`) with a model name. The indexer will store the indexed result to a section named `bert` (the key corresponding to the token indexer). Fortunately, this code is a boilerplate that changes little from model to model, and chances are you can simply copy and paste this section when you work on a new Transformer-based model.

As for the training/validation data, we can use the ones in this book's S3 repository, shown here:

```
"train_data_path": "https://realworldnlpbook.s3.amazonaws.com/data/snli/
    snli_1.0_train.jsonl",
"validation_data_path": "https://realworldnlpbook.s3.amazonaws.com/data/snli/
    snli_1.0_dev.jsonl",
```

Now we are ready to move on to defining our model:

```
"model": {
    "type": "basic_classifier",

    "text_field_embedder": {
        "token_embedders": {
            "bert": {
                "type": "pretrained_transformer",
                "model_name": bert_model
            }
        }
    },
    "seq2vec_encoder": {
        "type": "bert_pooler",
        "pretrained_model": bert_model
    }
},
```

At the top level, this section is defining a `BasicClassifier` model (type: `basic_classifier`). It is a generic text classification model that embeds the input, encodes it with a Seq2Vec encoder, and classifies it with a classification head (with a softmax layer). You can "plug in" embedders and encoders of your choice as the subcomponents of the model. For example, you can embed the tokens via word embeddings and encode the sequence with an RNN (this is what we did in chapter 4). Alternatively, you can encode the sequence with a CNN, as we did in chapter 7. This is where the design of AllenNLP excels—the generic model specifies only *what* (e.g., a `TextFieldEmbedder` and a `Seq2VecEncoder`) but not exactly *how* (e.g., word embeddings, RNNs, BERT). You can use any submodules for embedding/encoding input, as long as those submodules conform to the specified interfaces (i.e., they are subclasses of the required classes).

In this case study, we will use BERT to embed the input sequence first. This is achieved by a special token embedder, `PretrainedTransformerEmbedder` (type: `pretrained_transformer`), which takes the result of a Transformer tokenizer, puts it through a pretrained BERT model, and produces the embedded input. You need to pass this embedder as the value for the `bert` key (the one you specified for `token_indexers` earlier) of the `token_embedders` parameter.

The raw output from BERT, however, is a sequence of embeddings. Because we are interested in classifying the given pair of sentences, we need to extract the embeddings for the entire sequence, which can be done by taking out the embeddings corresponding to the CLS special token. AllenNLP implements a type of `Seq2VecEncoder` called `BertPooler` (type: `bert_pooler`) that does exactly this.

After embedding and encoding the input, the basic classifier model takes care of the rest—the embeddings go through a linear layer that converts them into a set of logits, and the entire network is trained with a cross-entropy loss, just like other classification models. The entire config file is shown here.

Listing 9.4 Config file for training an NLI model with BERT

```
local bert_model = "bert-base-cased";

{
    "dataset_reader": {
        "type": "snli",
        "tokenizer": {
            "type": "pretrained_transformer",
            "model_name": bert_model,
            "add_special_tokens": false
        },
        "token_indexers": {
            "bert": {
                "type": "pretrained_transformer",
                "model_name": bert_model,
            }
        }
    },
    "train_data_path": "https://realworldnlpbook.s3.amazonaws.com/data/snli/
     snli_1.0_train.jsonl",
    "validation_data_path": "https://realworldnlpbook.s3.amazonaws.com/data/
     snli/snli_1.0_dev.jsonl",

    "model": {
        "type": "basic_classifier",

        "text_field_embedder": {
            "token_embedders": {
                "bert": {
                    "type": "pretrained_transformer",
                    "model_name": bert_model
                }
            }
        },
        "seq2vec_encoder": {
            "type": "bert_pooler",
            "pretrained_model": bert_model,
        }
    },
```

```
    "data_loader": {
        "batch_sampler": {
            "type": "bucket",
            "sorting_keys": ["tokens"],
            "padding_noise": 0.1,
            "batch_size" : 32
        }
    },
    "trainer": {
        "optimizer": {
            "type": "huggingface_adamw",
            "lr": 5.0e-6
        },
        "validation_metric": "+accuracy",
        "num_epochs": 30,
        "patience": 10,
        "cuda_device": 0
    }
}
```

It's OK if you are not familiar with what's going on in the data_loader and trainer sections. We'll discuss these topics (batching, padding, optimizing, hyperparameter tuning) in chapter 10. After saving this config file under examples/nli/snli_ transformers.jsonnnet, you can start the training process by running the following code:

```
allennlp train examples/nli/snli_transformers.jsonnet --serialization-dir
    models/snli
```

This will run for a while (even on a fast GPU such as Nvidia V100) and produce a large amount of log messages on stdout. The following is a snippet of log messages I got after four epochs:

```
...
allennlp.training.trainer - Epoch 4/29
allennlp.training.trainer - Worker 0 memory usage MB: 6644.208
allennlp.training.trainer - GPU 0 memory usage MB: 8708
allennlp.training.trainer - Training
allennlp.training.trainer - Validating
allennlp.training.tensorboard_writer -                     Training | Validation
allennlp.training.tensorboard_writer - accuracy          |    0.933 |   0.908
allennlp.training.tensorboard_writer - gpu_0_memory_MB   | 8708.000 |    N/A
allennlp.training.tensorboard_writer - loss              |    0.190 |   0.293
allennlp.training.tensorboard_writer - reg_loss          |    0.000 |   0.000
allennlp.training.tensorboard_writer - worker_0_memory_MB | 6644.208 |    N/A
allennlp.training.checkpointer - Best validation performance so far. Copying weights
to 'models/snli/best.th'.
allennlp.training.trainer - Epoch duration: 0:21:39.687226
allennlp.training.trainer - Estimated training time remaining: 9:04:56
...
```

Pay attention to the validation accuracy (0.908). This looks very good considering that this is a three-class classification and the random baseline would be just 0.3. In comparison, when I replaced BERT with an LSTM-based RNN, the best validation accuracy I got was around ~0.68. We need to run experiments more carefully to make a fair comparison between different models, but this result seems to suggest that BERT is a powerful model for solving natural language understanding problems.

Summary

- Transfer learning is a machine learning concept where a model learned for one task is applied to another by transferring knowledge between them. It is an underlying concept for many modern, powerful, pretrained models.

- BERT is a Transformer encoder pretrained with masked language modeling and next-sentence prediction objectives to produce contextualized embeddings, a series of word embeddings that take context into account.

- ELMo, XLNet, RoBERTa, DistilBERT, and ALBERT are other popular pretrained models commonly used in modern deep NLP.

- You can build BERT-based NLP applications by using Hugging Face's Transformers library directly, or by using AllenNLP, which integrates the Transformers library seamlessly.

Part 3

Putting into production

In parts 1 and 2, we learned a lot about the "modeling" part of the modern NLP, including word embeddings, RNNs, CNNs, and the Transformer. However, you still need to learn how to effectively train, serve, deploy, and interpret those models for building robust and practical NLP applications.

Chapter 10 touches upon important machine learning techniques and best practices when developing NLP applications, including batching and padding, regularization, and hyperparameter optimization.

Finally, if chapters 1 to 10 are about building NLP models, chapter 11 covers everything that happens *outside* NLP models. The chapter covers how to deploy, serve, explain, and interpret NLP models.

10

Best practices in developing NLP applications

This chapter covers

- Making neural network inference more efficient by sorting, padding, and masking tokens
- Applying character-based and BPE tokenization for splitting text into tokens
- Avoiding overfitting via regularization
- Dealing with imbalanced datasets by using upsampling, downsampling, and loss weighting
- Optimizing hyperparameters

We've covered a lot of ground so far, including deep neural network models such as RNNs, CNNs, and the Transformer, and modern NLP frameworks such as AllenNLP and Hugging Face Transformers. However, we've paid little attention to the details of training and inference. For example, how do you train and make predictions efficiently? How do you avoid having your model overfit? How do you optimize hyperparameters? These factors could make a huge impact on the final performance and generalizability of your model. This chapter covers these important topics that you need to consider to build robust and accurate NLP applications that perform well in the real world.

10.1 Batching instances

In chapter 2, we briefly mentioned *batching*, a machine learning technique where instances are grouped together to form batches and sent to the processor (CPU or, more often, GPU). Batching is almost always necessary when training large neural networks—it is critical for efficient and stable training. In this section, we'll dive into some more techniques and considerations related to batching.

10.1.1 Padding

Training large neural networks requires a number of linear algebra operations such as matrix addition and multiplication, which involve executing basic mathematical operations on many, many numbers at once. This is why it requires specialized hardware such as GPUs, processors designed to execute such operations in a highly parallelized manner. Data is sent to the GPU as tensors, which are just high-dimensional arrays of numbers, along with some instructions as to what types of mathematical operations it needs to execute. The result is sent back as another tensor.

In chapter 2, we likened GPUs to factories overseas that are highly specialized and optimized for manufacturing the same type of products in a large quantity. Because there is considerable overhead in communicating and shipping products, it is more efficient if you make a small number of orders for manufacturing a large quantity of products by shipping all the required materials in batches, rather than shipping materials on demand.

Materials and products are usually shipped back and forth in standardized containers. If you have ever loaded a moving pod or trailer yourself (or observed someone else do it), you may know that there are many considerations that are important for safe and reliable shipping. You need to put furniture and boxes in tightly so that they don't shift around in transition. You need to wrap them with blankets and fix them with ropes to prevent them from being damaged. You need to put heavy stuff at the bottom so that lighter stuff won't get crushed, and so on.

Batches in machine learning are similar to containers for shipping stuff in the real world. Just like shipping containers are all the same size and rectangular, batches in machine learning are just rectangular tensors packed with numbers of the same type. If you want to "ship" multiple instances of different shapes in a single batch to the GPU, you need to pack them so that the packed numbers form a rectangular tensor.

In NLP, we often deal with sequences of text in different lengths. Because batches have to be rectangular, we need to do *padding*, (i.e., append special tokens, <PAD>, to each sequence so that each row of the tensor has the same length. You need as many padding tokens as necessary to make the sequences the same length, which means that you need to pad short sequences until they are all as long as the longest sequence in the same batch. This is illustrated in figure 10.1.

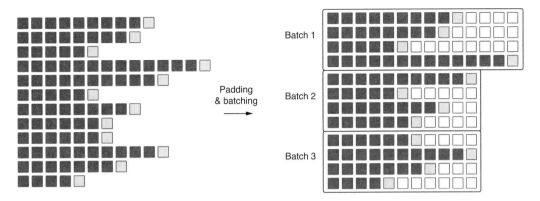

Figure 10.1 Padding and batching. Black squares are tokens, gray ones are EOS tokens, and white ones are padding.

In reality, each token in natural language text is often represented as a vector of length D, generated by the word embeddings method. This means that each batched tensor is a three-dimensional tensor that has a "depth" of D. In many NLP models, sequences are represented as batches of size $N \times L \times D$ (see figure 10.2), where N, L, D are the number of instances per batch, the maximum length of the sequences, and the dimension of word embeddings, respectively.

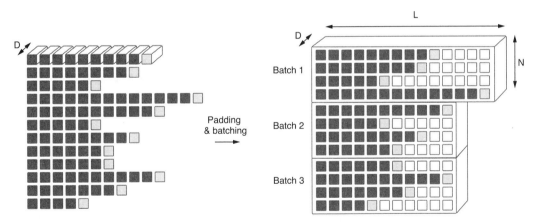

Figure 10.2 Padding and batching of embedded sequences create rectangular, three-dimensional tensors.

This is starting to look more like real containers!

10.1.2 *Sorting*

Because each batch has to be rectangular, if one batch happens to include both short sequences and long sequences, you need to add a lot of padding to short sequences so that they are as long as the longest sequence in the same batch. This often leads to some wasted space in the batch—see "batch 1" in figure 10.3 for an illustration. The shortest sequence (six tokens) needs to be padded with eight more tokens to be equally long as the longest sequence (14 tokens). Wasted space in a tensor means wasted memory and computation, so it is best avoided, but how?

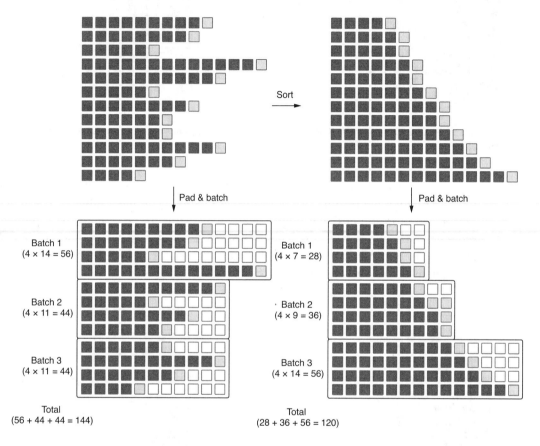

Figure 10.3 Sorting instances before batching (right) reduces the total number of tensors.

You can reduce the amount of padding by putting instances of similar size in the same batch. If shorter instances are batched only with other equally shorter ones, they don't need to get padded with many padding tokens. Similarly, if longer instances are batched only with other longer ones, they don't need a lot of padding either, because they are already long. One idea is to sort instances by their length and batch accordingly. Figure 10.3 compares two situations—one in which the instances are batched in their original order, and the other where instances are first sorted before batching. The numbers below each batch indicate how many tokens are required to represent the batch, including the padding tokens. Notice that the number of total tokens is reduced from 144 to 120 by sorting. Because the number of tokens in the original sentences doesn't change, this is purely because sorting reduced the number of padding tokens. Smaller batches require less memory to store and less computation to process, so sorting instances before batching improves the efficiency of training.

All these techniques sound somewhat complicated, but the good news is, you rarely need to write code for sorting, padding, and batching instances yourself as long as you use high-level frameworks such as AllenNLP. Recall that we used a combination of `DataLoader` and `BucketBatchSampler` for building our sentiment analysis model back in chapter 2 as follows:

```
train_data_loader = DataLoader(train_dataset,
                    batch_sampler=BucketBatchSampler(
                        train_dataset,
                        batch_size=32,
                        sorting_keys=["tokens"]))
```

The `sorting_keys` given to `BucketBatchSampler` specifies which field to use for sorting. As you can guess from its name, by specifying "tokens" you are telling the data loader to sort the instances by the number of tokens (which is what you want in most cases). The pipeline will take care of padding and batching automatically, and the data loader will give you a series of batches you can feed into your model.

10.1.3 *Masking*

One final detail that you need to pay attention to is *masking*. Masking is an operation where you ignore some part of the network that corresponds to padding. This becomes relevant especially when you are dealing with a sequential-labeling or a language-generation model. To recap, sequential labeling is a task where the system assigns a label per token in the input sequence. We built a POS tagger with a sequential labeling model (RNN) in chapter 5.

As shown in figure 10.4, sequential-labeling models are trained by minimizing the per-token loss aggregated across all tokens in a given sentence. We do this because we'd like to minimize the number of "errors" the network makes per token. This is fine as long as we are dealing with "real" tokens

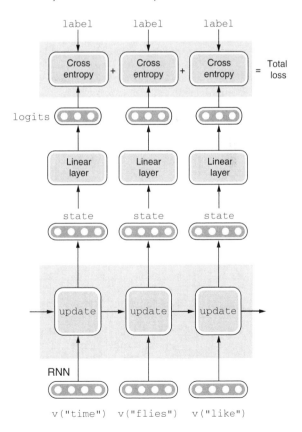

Figure 10.4 Loss for a sequence is the sum of per-token cross entropy.

("time," "flies," and "like" in the figure), although it becomes an issue when the input batch includes padded tokens. Because they exist just to pad the batch, they should be ignored when computing the total loss.

We usually do this by creating an extra vector for masking the loss. The vector for masking has the same length as the input, whose elements are 1s for "real" tokens and 0s for padding. When computing the total loss, you can simply take an element-wise product between the per-token loss and the mask and then sum up the result.

Fortunately, as long as you are building standard sequential-labeling models with AllenNLP, you rarely need to implement masking yourself. Remember, in chapter 5, we wrote the forward pass of the POS tagger model as shown in listing 10.1. Here, we get the mask vector from the get_text_field_mask() helper function and compute the final loss with sequence_cross_entropy_with_logits().

Listing 10.1   Forward pass of the POS tagger

```
def forward(self,
            words: Dict[str, torch.Tensor],
            pos_tags: torch.Tensor = None,
            **args) -> Dict[str, torch.Tensor]:
    mask = get_text_field_mask(words)

    embeddings = self.embedder(words)
    encoder_out = self.encoder(embeddings, mask)
    tag_logits = self.linear(encoder_out)

    output = {"tag_logits": tag_logits}
    if pos_tags is not None:
        self.accuracy(tag_logits, pos_tags, mask)
        output["loss"] = sequence_cross_entropy_with_logits(
            tag_logits, pos_tags, mask)

    return output
```

If you take a peek at what's inside mask (e.g., by inserting a print statement in this forward method), you'll see the following tensor made of binary (True or False) values:

```
tensor([[ True,  True,  True,  True,  True,  True,  True,  True, False],
        [ True,  True,  True,  True,  True,  True,  True,  True,  True],
        [ True,  True,  True,  True,  True,  True,  True,  True, False],
        [ True,  True,  True,  True,  True,  True,  True,  True,  True],
        [ True,  True,  True,  True,  True,  True,  True,  True, False],
        [ True,  True,  True,  True,  True,  True,  True,  True, False],
        [ True,  True,  True,  True,  True,  True,  True,  True, False],
        [ True,  True,  True,  True,  True,  True,  True,  True,  True],
        [ True,  True,  True,  True,  True,  True,  True,  True, False],
        [ True,  True,  True,  True,  True,  True,  True,  True,  True],
        [ True,  True,  True,  True,  True,  True,  True,  True,  True],
```

Each row of this tensor corresponds to one sequence of tokens, and locations with `False` are where padding occurred. The loss function (`sequence_cross_entropy _with_logits`) receives the prediction, the ground truth (the correct labels), and the mask and computes the final loss while ignoring all the elements marked as `False`.

10.2 *Tokenization for neural models*

In chapter 3, we covered the basic linguistic units (words, characters, and n-grams) and how to compute their embeddings. In this section, we will go deeper and focus on how to analyze texts and obtain these units—a process called *tokenization*. Neural network models pose a set of unique challenges on how to deal with tokens, and we'll cover some of the modern models to deal with these challenges.

10.2.1 *Unknown words*

A vocabulary is a set of tokens that an NLP model deals with. Many neural NLP models operate within a fixed, finite set of tokens. For example, when we built a sentiment analyzer in chapter 2, the AllenNLP pipeline first tokenized the training dataset and constructed a `Vocabulary` object that consists of all unique tokens that appeared more than, say, three times. The model then uses an embedding layer to convert tokens into word embeddings, which are some abstract representation of the input tokens.

So far, so good, right? But the number of all words in the world is not finite. We constantly make up new words that didn't exist before (I don't think people talked about "NLP" a hundred years ago). What if the model receives a word that it has never seen during training? Because the word is not part of the vocabulary, the model cannot even convert it to an index, let alone look up its embeddings. Such words are called *out-of-vocabulary* (OOV) *words*, and they are one of the biggest problems when building NLP applications.

By far the most common (but not the best) way to deal with this problem is to represent all the OOV tokens as a special token, which is conventionally named `UNK` (for "unknown"). The idea is that every time the model sees a token that is not part of the vocabulary, it pretends it saw a special token `UNK` instead and proceeds as usual. This means that the vocabulary and the embedding table both have a designated "slot" for `UNK` so that the model can deal with words that it has never seen. The embeddings (and any other parameters) for `UNK` are trained in the same manner as other regular tokens.

Do you see any problems with this approach? Treating all OOV tokens with a single `UNK` token means that they are collapsed into a single embedding vector. It doesn't matter if the word is "NLP" or "doggy"—as long as it's something unseen, it always gets treated as a `UNK` token and assigned the same vector, which becomes a generic, catchall representation of various words. Because of this, the model cannot tell the differences among OOV words, no matter what the identity of the words is.

This may be fine if you are building, for example, a sentiment analyzer. OOV words are, by definition, very rare and might not affect the prediction of most of the input sentences. However, this becomes a huge problem if you are building a machine translation system or a conversational engine. It wouldn't be a usable MT system or a chatbot if it produces "I don't know" every time it sees new words! In general, the OOV problem is more serious for language-generation systems (including machine translation and conversational AI) compared to NLP systems for prediction (sentiment analysis, POS tagging, and so on).

How can we do better? OOV tokens are such a big problem in NLP that there has been a lot of research work on how to deal with them. In the following subsections, we'll cover character-based and subword-based models, two techniques commonly used for building robust neural NLP models.

10.2.2 Character models

The simplest yet effective solution for dealing with the OOV problem is to treat characters as tokens. Specifically, we break the input text into individual characters, even including punctuation and whitespace, and treat them as if they are regular tokens. The rest of the application is unchanged—"word" embeddings are assigned to characters, which are further processed by the model. If the model produces text, it does so character-by-character.

In fact, we used a character-level model in chapter 5 when we built a language generator. Instead of generating text word-by-word, the RNN produces text one character at a time, as illustrated in figure 10.5. Thanks to this strategy, the model was able to produce words that look like English but actually aren't. Notice a number of peculiar words (*despoit, studented, redusention, distaples*) that resemble English words in the output shown in listing 10.2. If the model operated on words, it produces only known words (or UNKs when unsure), and this wouldn't have been possible.

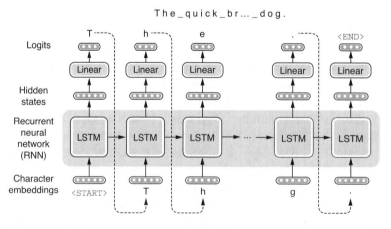

Figure 10.5 A language-generation model that generates text character-by-character (including whitespace)

Listing 10.2 Generated sentences by a character-based language model

```
You can say that you don't know it, and why decided of yourself.
Pike of your value is to talk of hubies.
The meeting despoit from a police?
That's a problem, but us?
The sky as going to send nire into better.
We'll be look of the best ever studented.
There's you seen anything every's redusention day.
How a fail is to go there.
It sad not distaples with money.
What you see him go as famous to eat!
```

Character-based models are versatile and put few assumptions on the structure of the language. For languages with small sets of alphabets (like English), it effectively eradicates unknown words, because almost any words, no matter how rare they are, can be broken down into characters. Tokenizing into characters is also an effective strategy for languages with large alphabets (like Chinese), although you need to watch out for "unknown character" problems.

However, this strategy is not without drawbacks. The biggest issue is its inefficiency. To encode a sentence, the network (be it an RNN or the Transformer) needs to go over all the characters in it. For example, a character-based model needs to process "t," "h," "e," and "_" (whitespace) to process a single word "the," whereas a word-based model can finish this in a single step. This inefficiency takes its biggest toll on the Transformers, where the attention computation increases quadratically when the input sequence gets longer.

10.2.3 Subword models

So far, we studied two extremes—the word-based approach is efficient but not great at dealing with unknown words. The character-based approach is great at dealing with unknown words but is inefficient. Is there something in between? Can we use some tokenization that is both efficient and robust to unknown words?

Subword models are a recent invention that addresses this problem for neural networks. In subword models, the input text is segmented into a unit called *subwords*, which simply means something smaller than words. There is no formal linguistic definition as to what subwords actually are, but they roughly correspond to part of words that appear frequently. For example, one way to segment "dishwasher" is "dish + wash + er," although some other segmentation is possible.

Some varieties of algorithms (such as WordPiece[1] and SentencePiece[2]) tokenize input into subwords, but by far the most widely used is *byte-pair encoding* (BPE).[3] BPE was

---

[1] Wu et al., "Google's Neural Machine Translation System: Bridging the Gap between Human and Machine Translation," (2016). https://arxiv.org/abs/1609.08144.

[2] Kudo, "Subword Regularization: Improving Neural Network Translation Models with Multiple Subword Candidates," (2018). https://arxiv.org/abs/1804.10959.

[3] Sennrich et al., "Neural Machine Translation of Rare Words with Subword Units," (2016). https://arxiv.org/abs/1508.07909.

originally invented as a compression algorithm,[4] but since 2016, it's been widely used as a tokenization method for neural models, particularly in machine translation.

The basic concept of BPE is to keep frequent words (such as "the" and "you") and n-grams (such as "-able" and "anti-") unsegmented, while breaking up rarer words (such as "dishwasher") into subwords ("dish + wash + er"). Keeping frequent words and n-grams together helps the model process those tokens efficiently, whereas breaking up rare words ensures there are no UNK tokens, because everything can be ultimately broken up into individual characters, if necessary. By flexibly choosing where to tokenize based on the frequency, BPE achieves the best of two worlds—being efficient while addressing the unknown word problem.

Let's see how BPE determines where to tokenize with real examples. BPE is a purely statistical algorithm (it doesn't use any language-dependent information) and operates by merging the most frequently occurring pair of consecutive tokens, one at a time. First, BPE tokenizes all the input texts into individual characters. For example, if your input is four words low, lowest, newer, and wider, it will tokenize them into l o w _, l o w e s t _, n e w e r _, w i d e r _. Here, "_" is a special symbol that indicates the end of each word. Then, the algorithm identifies any two consecutive elements that appear most often. In this example, the pair l o appears most often (two times), so these two characters are merged, yielding lo w _, lo w e s t _, n e w e r _, w i d e r _. Then, lo w will be merged into low, e r into er, er _ into er_, at which time you have low _, low e s t _, n e w er_, w i d er_. This process is illustrated in figure 10.6.

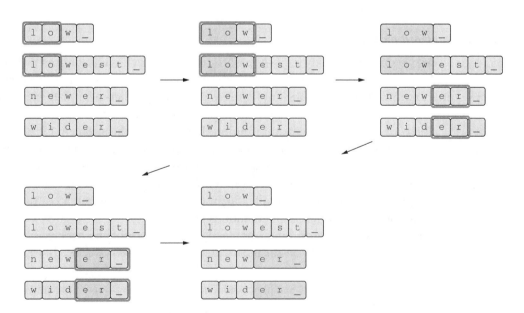

Figure 10.6   BPE learns subword units by iteratively merging consecutive units that cooccur frequently.

---

4   See https://www.derczynski.com/papers/archive/BPE_Gage.pdf.

Notice that, after four merge operations, `lowest` is segmented into `low e s t` where frequent substrings such as `low` are merged together whereas infrequent ones such as `est` are broken apart. To segment a new input (e.g., `lower`), the same sequence of merge operations is applied in order, yielding `low e r _`. If you start from 52 unique letters (26 upper- and lowercase letters), you will end up with $52 + N$ unique tokens in your vocabulary, where N is the number of merge operations executed. In this way, you have complete control over the size of the vocabulary.

In practice, you rarely need to implement BPE (or any other subword tokenization algorithms) yourself. These algorithms are implemented in many open source libraries and platforms. Two popular options are Subword-NMT (https://github.com/rsenn-rich/subword-nmt) and SentencePiece (https://github.com/google/sentencepiece) (which also supports a variant of subword tokenization using a unigram language model). Many of the default tokenizers shipped with NLP frameworks, such as the one implemented in Hugging Face Transformers, support subword tokenization.

10.3 Avoiding overfitting

Overfitting is one of the most common and important issues you need to address when building any machine learning applications. An ML model is said to overfit when it fits the given data so well that it loses its generalization ability to unseen data. In other words, the model may capture the training data very well and show good performance on it, but it may not be able to capture its inherent patterns well and shows poor performance on data that the model has never seen before.

Because overfitting is so prevalent in machine learning, researchers and practitioners have come up with a number of algorithms and techniques to combat overfitting in the past. In this section, we'll learn two such techniques—regularization and early stopping. These are popular in any ML applications (not just NLP) and worth getting under your belt.

10.3.1 Regularization

Regularization in machine learning refers to techniques that encourage the simplicity and the generalization of the model. You can think of it as one form of penalty you impose on your ML model to ensure that it is as generic as possible. What does it mean? Say you are building an "animal classifier" by training word embeddings from a corpus and by drawing a line between animals and other stuff in this embedding space (i.e., you represent each word as a multidimensional vector and classify whether the word describes an animal based on the coordinates of the vector). Let's simplify this problem a lot and assume that each word is a two-dimensional vector, and you end up with the plot shown in figure 10.7. You can now visualize how a machine learning model makes a classification decision by drawing lines where

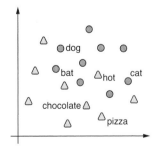

Figure 10.7 Animal vs. non-animal classification plot

the decision flips between different classes (animals and non-animals), which is called the *classification boundary*. How would you draw a classification boundary so that animals (blue circles) are separated from everything else (triangles)?

One simple way to separate animals is to draw one straight line, as in the first plot in figure 10.8. This simple classifier makes several mistakes (in classifying words like "hot" and "bat"), but it correctly classifies the majority of data points. This sounds like a good start.

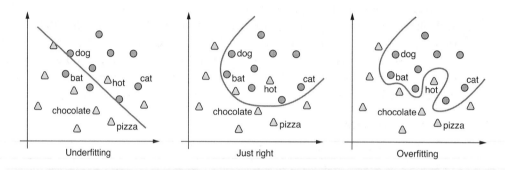

Figure 10.8   Classification boundaries with increasing complexity

What if you are told that the decision boundary doesn't have to be a straight line? You may want to draw something like the one shown in the middle in figure 10.8. This one looks better—it makes fewer mistakes than the first one, although it is still not perfect. It appears tractable for a machine learning model because the shape is simple.

But there's nothing that stops you here. If you want to make as few errors as possible, you can also draw something wiggly like the one shown in the third plot. That decision boundary doesn't even make any classification errors, which means that we achieved 100% classification accuracy!

Not so fast—remember that up until here, we've been thinking only about the training time, but the main purpose of machine learning models is to achieve good classification performance *at the test time* (i.e., they need to classify unobserved, new instances as correctly as possible). Now let's think about how the three decision boundaries described earlier fare at test time. If we assume the test instances are distributed similarly to the training instances we saw in figure 10.8, the new "animal" points are most likely to fall in the upper-right region of the plot. The first two decision boundaries will achieve decent accuracy by classifying the majority of new instances correctly. But how about the third one? Training instances such as "hot" shown in the plot are most likely exceptions rather than the norm, so the curved sections of the decision boundary that tried to accommodate as many training instances as possible may do more harm than good at the test time by inadvertently misclassifying test instances. This is exactly what overfitting looks like—the model fits the training data so well that it sacrifices its generalization ability, which is what's happening here.

Then, the question is, how can we avoid having your model look like the third decision boundary? After all, it is doing a very good job correctly classifying the training data. If you looked only at the training accuracy and/or the loss, there would be nothing to stop you from choosing it. One way to avoid overfitting is to use a separate, held-out dataset (called a *validation set*; see section 2.2.3) to validate the performance of your model. But can we do this even without using a separate dataset?

The third decision boundary just doesn't look right—it's overly complex. With all other things being equal, we should prefer simpler models, because in general, simpler models generalize better. This is also in line with Occam's razor, which states that a simpler solution is preferable to a more complex one. How can we balance between the training fit and the simplicity of the model?

This is where regularization comes into play. Think of regularization as additional constraints imposed on the model so that simpler and/or more general models are preferred. The model is optimized so that it achieves the best training fit while being as generic as possible.

Numerous regularization techniques have been proposed in machine learning because overfitting is such an important topic. We are going to introduce only a few of the most important ones—L2 regularization (weight decay), dropout, and early stopping.

L2 REGULARIZATION

L2 regularization, also called *weight decay*, is one of the most common regularization methods not just for NLP or deep learning but for a wide range of ML models. We are not going into its mathematical details, but in short, L2 regularization adds a penalty for the complexity of a model measured by how large its parameters are. To represent a complex classification boundary, an ML model needs to adjust a large number of parameters (the "magic constants") to extreme values, measured by the L2 loss, which captures how far away they are from zero. Such models incur a larger L2 penalty, which is why L2 encourages simpler models. If you are interested in learning more about L2 regularization (and other related topics about NLP in general), check out textbooks such as *Speech and Language Processing* by Jurafsky and Martin (https://web.stanford .edu/~jurafsky/slp3/5.pdf) or Goodfellow et al.'s *Deep Learning* (https://www.deep learningbook.org/contents/regularization.html).

DROPOUT

Dropout is another popular regularization technique commonly used with neural networks. Dropout works by randomly "dropping" neurons during training, where a "neuron" is basically a dimension of an intermediate layer and "dropping" means to mask it with zeros. You can think of dropout as a penalty to the model's structural complexity and its reliance on particular features and values. As a result, the network tries to make the best guess with the remaining smaller number of values, which forces it to generalize well. Dropout is easy to implement and effective in practice and is used as a default regularization method in many deep learning models. For more information on dropout, the regularization chapter of the Goodfellow book mentioned earlier provides a good introduction and mathematical details of regularization techniques.

10.3.2 *Early stopping*

Another popular approach for combatting overfitting in machine learning is *early stopping*. Early stopping is a relatively simple technique where you stop training your model when the model performance stops improving, usually measured by the validation set loss. In chapter 6, we plotted learning curves when we built an English-Spanish machine translation model (shown again in figure 10.9). Notice that the validation loss curve flattens out around the eighth epoch and starts to creep up after that, which is a sign of overfitting. Early stopping would detect this, stop the training, and use the result from the best epoch when the loss is lowest. In general, early stopping has a "patience" parameter, which is the number of nonimproving epochs for early stopping to kick in. When patience is 10 epochs, for example, the training pipeline will wait 10 epochs after the loss stops improving to stop the training.

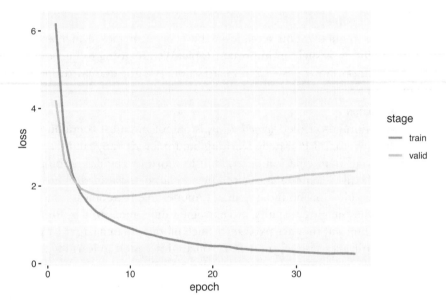

Figure 10.9 The validation loss curve flattens out around the eighth epoch and creeps back up.

Why does early stopping help mitigate overfitting? What does it have to do with model complexity? Without getting into mathematical details, it takes some time (training epochs) for the model to learn complex, overfitted decision boundaries. Most models start from something simple (e.g., straight decision lines) and gradually increase their complexity over the course of training. By stopping the training early, early stopping can prevent the model from becoming overly complex.

Many machine learning frameworks have built-in support for early stopping. For example, AllenNLP's trainer supports early stopping by default. Recall that we used the following configuration in section 9.5.3 when we trained a BERT-based natural language inference model, where we used early stopping (with patience = 10) without paying much attention. This allows the trainer to stop if the validation metric doesn't improve for 10 epochs:

```
"trainer": {
    "optimizer": {
        "type": "huggingface_adamw",
        "lr": 1.0e-5
    },
    "num_epochs": 20,
    "patience": 10,
    "cuda_device": 0
}
```

10.3.3 Cross-validation

Cross-validation is not exactly a regularization method, but it is one of the techniques commonly used in machine learning. A common situation in building and validating a machine learning model is this—you have only a couple of hundred instances available for training. As we've seen so far in this book, you can't train a reliable ML model just on the training set—you need a separate set for validation, and preferably another separate set for testing. How much you use for validation/testing depends on the task and the data size, but in general, it is advised that you set aside 5–20% of your training instances for validation and testing. This means that if your training data is small, your model is validated and tested on just a few dozen instances, which can make the estimated metrics unstable. Also, how you choose these instances has a large impact on the evaluation metrics, which is not ideal.

The basic idea of cross-validation is to iterate this phase (splitting the dataset into training and validation portions) multiple times with different splits to improve the stability of the result. Specifically, in a typical setting called *k-fold cross validation*, you first split the dataset into k different portions of equal size called *folds*. You use one of the folds for validation while training the model on the rest ($k - 1$ folds), and repeat this process k times, using a different fold for validation every time. See figure 10.10 for an illustration.

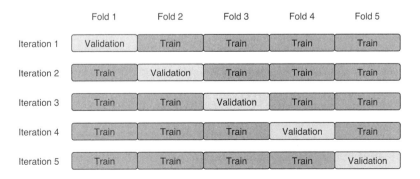

Figure 10.10   In *k*-fold cross validation, the dataset is split into *k* equally sized folds and one is used for validation.

The validation metrics are computed for every fold, and the final metrics are averaged over all iterations. This way, you can obtain a more stable estimate of the evaluation metrics that are not impacted heavily by the way the dataset is split.

The use of cross-validation in deep learning models is not common, because these models require a large amount of data, and you don't need cross-validation if you have a large dataset, although its use is more common for more traditional and industrial settings where the amount of training data is limited.

10.4 Dealing with imbalanced datasets

In this section, we'll focus on one of the most common problems you may encounter in building NLP and ML models—the class imbalance problem. The goal of a classification task is to assign one of the classes (e.g., spam or nonspam) to each instance (e.g., an email), but these classes are rarely distributed evenly. For example, in spam filtering, the number of nonspam emails is usually larger than the number of spam emails. In document classification, some topics (such as politics or sports) are usually more popular than other topics. Classes are said to be imbalanced when some classes have way more instances than others (see figure 10.11 for an example).

Many classification datasets have imbalanced classes, which poses some additional challenges when you train your classifier. The signals your model gets from smaller classes are overwhelmed by larger classes, which causes your model to perform poorly on minority classes. In the following subsections, I'm going to discuss some techniques you can consider when faced with an imbalanced dataset.

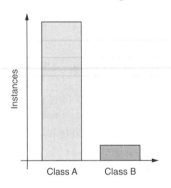

Figure 10.11   Imbalanced dataset

10.4.1 Using appropriate evaluation metrics

Before you even begin tweaking your dataset or your model, make sure you are validating your model with an appropriate metric. In section 4.3, we discussed why it is a bad idea to use accuracy as your evaluation metric when the dataset is imbalanced. In one extreme case, if 90% of your instances belong to class A and the other 10% belong to class B, even a stupid classifier that assigns class A to everything can achieve 90% accuracy. This is called a *majority class baseline*. A slightly more clever (but still stupid) classifier that randomly assigns label A 90% of the time and label B 10% of the time without even looking at the instance will achieve 0.9 * 0.9 + 0.1 * 0.1 = 82% accuracy. This is called a *random baseline*, and the more imbalanced your dataset is, the higher the accuracy of these baseline models will become.

But this kind of random baseline is rarely a good model for minority classes. Imagine what would happen to class B if you used the random baseline. Because it will assign class A 90% of the time no matter what, 90% of the instances belonging to class B will be assigned class A. In other words, the accuracy of this random baseline for class B is only 10%. If this was a spam filter, it would let 90% of spam emails go through, no matter what the content is, just because 90% of emails you receive are not spam! This would make a terrible spam filter.

If your dataset is imbalanced and you care about the classification performance on the minority class, you should consider using metrics that are more appropriate for such settings. For example, if your task is a "needle in a haystack" type of setting, where the goal is to find a very small number of instances among others, you may want to use the F1-measure instead of accuracy. As we saw in chapter 4, the F-measure is some sort of average between precision (how hay-free your prediction is) and recall (how much of the needle you actually found). Because the F1-measure is calculated per class, it does not underrepresent minority classes. If you'd like to measure the model's overall performance including majority classes, you can compute the macro-averaged F-measure, which is simply an arithmetic average of F-measures computed per class.

10.4.2 *Upsampling and downsampling*

Now let's look at concrete techniques that can mitigate the class imbalance problem. First of all, if you can collect more labeled training data, you should seriously consider doing that first. Unlike academic and ML competition settings where the dataset is fixed while you tweak your model, in a real-world setting you are free to do whatever is necessary to improve your model (of course, as long as it's lawful and practical). Often, the best thing you can do to improve a model's generalization is expose it to more data.

If your dataset is imbalanced and the model is making biased predictions, you can either *upsample* or *downsample* your data so that classes have roughly equal representations.

In upsampling (see the second figure in figure 10.12), you artificially increase the size of the minority class by copying the instances multiple times. Take the scenario we discussed earlier for example—if you duplicate the instances of class B and add eight extra copies of each instance to the dataset, they have an equal number of instances.

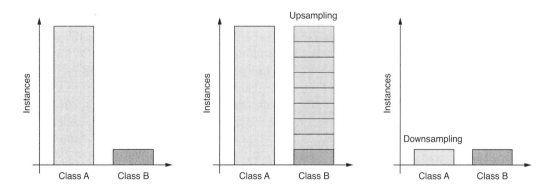

Figure 10.12   Upsampling and downsampling

This can mitigate the biased prediction issue. More sophisticated data augmentation algorithms such as SMOTE[5] are available, although they are not widely used in NLP, due to the inherent difficulty in generating linguistic examples artificially.

If your model is biased not because the minority class is too small but because the majority class is too large, you can instead choose to downsample (the third figure in figure 10.12). In downsampling, you artificially decrease the size of the majority class by choosing a subset of the instances belonging to that class. For example, if you sample one out of nine instances from class A, you'll end up with the equal number of instances in classes A and B. You can downsample in multiple ways—the easiest is to randomly choose the subset. If you would like to make sure that the downsampled dataset still preserves the diversity in the original data, you can try *stratified sampling*, where you sample some number of instances per group defined by some attributes. For example, if you have too many nonspam emails and want to downsample, you can group them by the sender's domain first, then sample a fixed number of emails per domain. This will ensure that your sampled dataset will contain a diverse set of domains.

Note that neither upsampling nor downsampling is a magic bullet. If you "correct" the distribution of classes too aggressively, you risk making unfair predictions for the majority class, if that's what you care about. Always make sure to check your model with a held-out validation set with appropriate evaluation metrics.

10.4.3 *Weighting losses*

Another approach for mitigating the class imbalance problem is to use weighting when computing the loss, instead of making modification to your training data. Remember that the loss function is used to measure how "off" the model's prediction for an instance is compared against the ground truth. When you measure how bad the model's prediction is, you can tweak the loss so that it penalizes more when the ground truth belongs to the minority class.

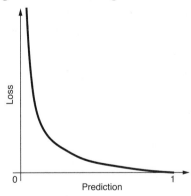

Let's take a look at a concrete example. The binary cross-entropy loss, a common loss function used for training a binary classifier, looks like the curve shown in figure 10.13, when the correct label is 1. The x-axis is the predicted probability of the target class, and the y-axis is the amount of loss the prediction will incur. When the prediction is perfectly correct (probability = 1), there's no penalty, whereas as the prediction gets worse (probability < 1), the loss goes up.

If you care more about the model's performance on the minority class, you can tweak this loss. Specifically, you can change the shape of this loss (by simply multiplying it by a constant

Figure 10.13   Binary cross-entropy loss (when the correct label is 1)

---

5 Chawla et al., "SMOTE: Synthetic Minority Over-Sampling Technique," (2002). https://arxiv.org/abs/ 1106.1813.

number) just for that class so that the model incurs a larger loss when it makes mistakes on the minority class. One such tweaked loss curve is shown in the figure 10.14 as the top curve. This weighting has the same effect as upsampling the minority class, although modifying the loss is computationally cheaper because you don't need to actually increase the amount of training data.

It is easy to implement loss weighting in PyTorch and AllenNLP. PyTorch's binary cross-entropy implementation `BCEWithLogitLoss` already supports different weights for different classes. You simply need to pass the weight as the `pos_weight` parameter as follows:

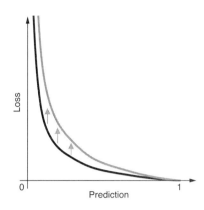

Figure 10.14 Weighted binary cross entropy loss

```
>>> import torch
>>> import torch.nn as nn

>>> input = torch.randn(3)
>>> input
tensor([-0.5565,  1.5350, -1.3066])

>>> target = torch.empty(3).random_(2)
>>> target
tensor([0., 0., 1.])

>>> loss = nn.BCEWithLogitsLoss(reduction='none')
>>> loss(input, target)
tensor([0.4531, 1.7302, 1.5462])

>>> loss = nn.BCEWithLogitsLoss(reduction='none',
      pos_weight=torch.tensor(2.))
>>> loss(input, target)
tensor([0.4531, 1.7302, 3.0923])
```

In this code snippet, we randomly generate prediction (`input`) and the ground truth (`target`). There are three instances in total, two of which are of class 0 (majority) and one belongs to class 1 (minority). We first compute the loss without weighting by calling the `BCEWithLogitsLoss` object, which returns the three loss values, one for each instance. We then compute the loss with weighting by passing the weight 2—this means that the wrong prediction will be penalized twice as much if the target class is positive (class 1). Notice that the third element corresponding to class 1 is twice as large as the one returned by the unweighted loss function.

10.5 *Hyperparameter tuning*

In this final section of this chapter, we'll discuss hyperparameter tuning. *Hyperparameters* are parameters about the model and the training algorithm. This term is used in contrast with *parameters*, which are numbers that are used by the model to make predictions from the input. This is what we've been calling "magic constants" throughout this book—they work like constants in programming languages, although their exact values are automatically adjusted by optimization so that the prediction matches the desired output as closely as possible.

Correctly tuning hyperparameters is critical for many machine learning models to work properly and achieve their highest potential, and ML practitioners spend a lot of time tuning hyperparameters. Knowing how to tune hyperparameters effectively has a huge impact on your productivity in building NLP and ML systems.

10.5.1 *Examples of hyperparameters*

Hyperparameters are "meta"-level parameters—unlike model parameters, they are used not to make predictions but for controlling the structure of the model and how the model is trained. For example, if you are working on word embeddings or an RNN, how many hidden units (dimensions) to use for representing words is one important hyperparameter. The number of RNN layers to use is another hyperparameter. In addition to these two hyperparameters (the number of hidden units and layers), the Transformer model we covered in chapter 9 has a number of other parameters, such as the number of attention heads and the dimension of the feedforward network. Even the type of architecture you use, such as RNN versus Transformer, can be thought of as one hyperparameter.

Besides, the optimization algorithm you use may have hyperparameters, too. For example, the learning rate (section 9.3.3), one of the most important hyperparameters in many ML settings, determines how much to tweak the model parameters per optimization step. The number of epochs (iterations through the training dataset) is also an important hyperparameter, too.

So far, we have been paying little attention to those hyperparameters, let alone optimizing them. However, hyperparameters can have a huge impact on the performance of machine learning models. In fact, many ML models have a "sweet spot" of hyperparameters that makes them most effective, whereas using a set of hyperparameters outside of this spot may make the model perform poorly.

Many ML practitioners tune hyperparameters by hand. This means that you start from a set of hyperparameters that look reasonable and measure the model's performance on a validation set. Then you change one or more of the hyperparameters slightly and measure the performance again. You repeat this process several times until you hit the "plateau," where any change of hyperparameters provides only a marginal improvement.

One issue with this manual tuning approach is that it is slow and arbitrary. Let's say you start from one set of hyperparameters. How do you know which ones to adjust next, and how much? How do you know when to stop? If you have experience tuning a wide range of ML models, you might have some "hunch" about how these models respond to certain hyperparameter changes, but if not, it's like shooting in the dark. Hyperparameter tuning is such an important topic that ML researchers have been working on better and more organized ways to optimize them.

10.5.2 *Grid search vs. random search*

We understand that manual optimization of hyperparameters is inefficient, but how should we go about optimizing them, then? We have two more-organized ways of tuning hyperparameters—grid search and random search.

In *grid search*, you simply try every possible combination of the hyperparameter values you want to optimize. For example, let's assume your model has just two hyperparameters—the number of RNN layers and the embedding dimension. You first define reasonable ranges for these two hyperparameters, for example, [1, 2, 3] for the number of layers and [128, 256, 512] for the dimensionality. Then grid search measures the model's validation performance for every combination—(1, 128), (1, 256), (1, 512), (2, 128), . . . , (3, 512)—and simply picks the best-performing combination. If you plot these combinations on a 2-D plot, it looks like a grid (see the illustration in figure 10.15), which is why this is called *grid search.*

Grid search is a simple and intuitive way to optimize the hyperparameters. However, if you have many hyperparameters and/or their ranges are large, this method gets out of hand. The number of possible combinations is exponential, which makes it impossible to explore all of them in a reasonable amount of time.

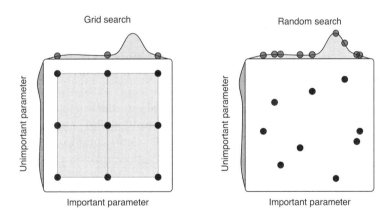

Figure 10.15   Grid search vs. random search for hyperparameter tuning. (Adapted from Bergstra and Bengio, 2012; https://www.jmlr.org/papers/ volume13/bergstra12a/bergstra12a.pdf.)

A better alternative to grid search is *random search.* In random search, instead of trying every possible combination of hyperparameter values, you randomly sample the values and measure the model's performance on a specified number of combinations (which are called *trials*). For example, in the previous example, random search may choose (2, 87), (1, 339), (2, 101), (3, 254), and so on until it hits the specified number of trials. See the illustration in figure 10.15 (right).

Unless your hyperparameter search space is very small (like the first example), random search is usually recommended over grid search if you want to optimize hyperparameters efficiently. Why? In many machine learning settings, not every hyperparameter is made equal—there are usually only a small number of hyperparameters that actually matter for the performance, whereas many others do not. Grid search will waste a lot of computation searching for the best combination of hyperparameters that do not really matter, while being unable to explore the few hyperparameters that do matter in detail (figure 10.15, left). On the other hand, random search can explore many possible points on the axis that matters for the performance (figure 10.15, right). Notice that random search can find a better model by exploring more points on the *x*-axis with the same number of trials (total of nine trials).

10.5.3 *Hyperparameter tuning with Optuna*

OK, we've covered some ways to tune hyperparameters including manual, grid, and random search, but how should you go about implementing it in practice? You can always write your own for-loop (or "for-loops," in the case of grid search), although it would quickly get tiring if you need to write this type of boilerplate code for every model and task you work on.

Hyperparameter optimization is such a universal topic that many ML researchers and engineers have been working on better algorithms and software libraries. For example, AllenNLP has its own library called *Allentune* (https://github.com/allenai/allentune) that you can easily integrate with your AllenNLP training pipeline. In the remainder of this section, however, I'm going to introduce another hyperparameter tuning library called *Optuna* (https://optuna.org/) and show how to use it with AllenNLP to optimize your hyperparameters. Optuna implements state-of-the-art algorithms that search for optimal hyperparameters efficiently and provides integration with a wide range of machine learning frameworks, including TensorFlow, PyTorch, and AllenNLP.

First, we assume that you have installed AllenNLP (1.0.0+) and the Optuna plugin for AllenNLP. These can be installed by running the following:

```
pip install allennlp
pip install allennlp_optuna
```

Also, as instructed by the official documentation (https://github.com/himkt/allennlp-optuna), you need to register the plugin with AllenNLP by running the next code:

```
echo 'allennlp_optuna' >> .allennlp_plugins
```

We are going to use the LSTM-based classifier for the Stanford Sentiment Treebank dataset we built in chapter 2. You can find the AllenNLP config file in the book repository (http://www.realworldnlpbook.com/ch10.html#config). Note that you need to reference the variables (`std.extVar`) for Optuna to have control over the parameters. Specifically, you need to define them at the beginning of the config file:

```
local embedding_dim = std.parseJson(std.extVar('embedding_dim'));
local hidden_dim = std.parseJson(std.extVar('hidden_dim'));
local lr = std.parseJson(std.extVar('lr'));
```

Then, you need to tell Optuna which parameters to optimize. You can do this by writing a JSON file (hparams.json (http://www.realworldnlpbook.com/ch10.html# hparams)). You need to specify every hyperparameter you want Optuna to optimize with its types and ranges as follows:

```json
[
    {
        "type": "int",
        "attributes": {
            "name": "embedding_dim",
            "low": 64,
            "high": 256
        }
    },
    {
        "type": "int",
        "attributes": {
            "name": "hidden_dim",
            "low": 64,
            "high": 256
        }
    },
    {
        "type": "float",
        "attributes": {
            "name": "lr",
            "low": 1e-4,
            "high": 1e-1,
            "log": true
        }
    }
]
```

Next, invoke this command to start the optimization:

```
allennlp tune \
    examples/tuning/sst_classifier.jsonnet \
    examples/tuning/hparams.json \
    --include-package examples \
    --serialization-dir result \
    --study-name sst-lstm \
    --n-trials 20 \
    --metrics best_validation_accuracy \
    --direction maximize
```

Note that we are running 20 trials (--n-trials) with validation accuracy (--metrics best_validation_accuracy) as the metric to maximize (--direction maximize). If you do not specify the metric and the direction, by default Optuna tries to minimize the validation loss.

This will take a while, but after all the trials are finished you will see the following one-line summary of the optimization:

```
Trial 19 finished with value: 0.3469573115349682 and parameters:
    {'embedding_dim': 120, 'hidden_dim': 82, 'lr': 0.00011044322486693224}.
    Best is trial 14 with value: 0.3869209809264305.
```

Finally, Optuna supports a wide range of visualization of the optimization result, including very nice contour plots (http://www.realworldnlpbook.com/ch10.html#contour), but here we'll simply use its web-based dashboard to quickly inspect the optimization process. All you need to do is invoke its dashboard from the command line as follows:

```
optuna dashboard --study-name sst-lstm --storage sqlite:///allennlp_optuna.db
```

Now you can access `http://localhost:5006/dashboard` to see the dashboard, shown in figure 10.16.

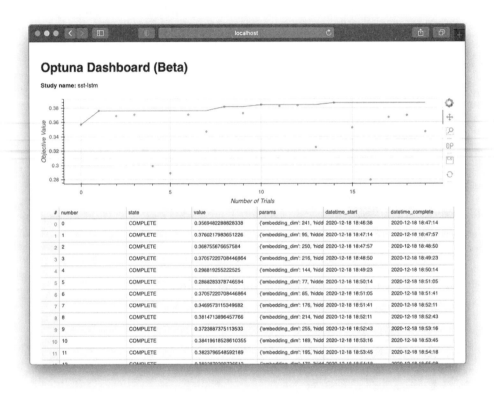

Figure 10.16   The Optuna dashboard shows the evaluation metrics of the parameters for each trial.

From this dashboard you can quickly see not only that your optimal trial was trial #14 but also the optimal hyperparameters at each trial.

Summary

- Instances are sorted, padded, and batched together for more efficient computation.
- Subword tokenization algorithms such as BPE split words into units smaller than words to mitigate the out-of-vocabulary problem in neural network models.

- Regularization (such as L2 and dropout) is a technique to encourage model simplicity and generalizability in machine learning.
- You can use data upsampling, downsampling, or loss weights for addressing the data imbalance issue.
- Hyperparameters are parameters about the model or the training algorithm. They can be optimized using manual, grid, or random search. Even better, use hyperparameter optimization libraries such as Optuna, which integrates easily with AllenNLP.

Deploying and serving NLP applications

This chapter covers

- Choosing the right architecture for your NLP application
- Version-controlling your code, data, and model
- Deploying and serving your NLP model
- Interpreting and analyzing model predictions with LIT (Language Interpretability Tool)

Where chapters 1 through 10 of this book are about building NLP models, this chapter covers everything that happens *outside* NLP models. Why is this important? Isn't NLP all about building high-quality ML models? It may come as a surprise if you don't have much experience with production NLP systems, but a large portion of an NLP system has very little to do with NLP at all. As shown in figure 11.1, only a tiny fraction of a typical real-world ML system is the ML code, but the "ML code" part is supported by numerous components that provide various functionalities, including data collection, feature extraction, and serving. Let's use a nuclear power plant as an analogy. In operating a nuclear power plant, only a tiny fraction concerns nuclear

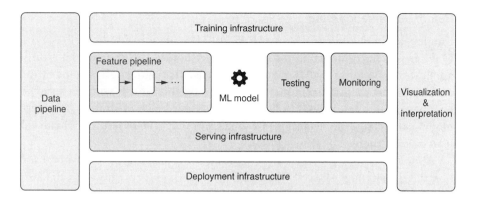

Figure 11.1 A typical ML system consists of many different components, and the ML code is only a tiny fraction of it. We cover the highlighted components in this chapter.

reaction. Everything else is a vast and complex infrastructure that supports safe and efficient generation and transportation of materials and electricity—how to use the generated heat to turn the turbine to make electricity, how to cool and circulate water safely, how to transmit the electricity efficiently, and so on. All those supporting infrastructures have little to do with nuclear physics.

Partly due to the "AI hype" in popular media, I personally think people pay too much attention to the ML modeling part and too little attention to how to serve the model in a useful way. After all, the goal of your product is to deliver values to the users, not provide them with the raw predictions of the model. Even if your model is 99% accurate, it's not useful if you cannot make the most of the prediction so that users can benefit from them. Using the previous analogy, users want to power their appliances and light their houses with electricity and do not care much how exactly the electricity is generated in the first place.

In the rest of this chapter, we'll discuss how to architect your NLP applications—we focus on some of the best practices when it comes to designing and developing NLP applications in a reliable and effective manner. Then we talk about deploying your NLP models—this is how we bring the NLP models to production and serve their predictions.

11.1 Architecting your NLP application

Machine learning engineering is still software engineering. All the best practices (decoupled software architectures, well-designed abstractions, clean and readable code, version control, continuous integration, etc.) apply to ML engineering as well. In this section, we'll discuss some best practices specific to designing and building NLP/ML applications.

11.1.1 *Before machine learning*

I understand this is a book about NLP and ML, but you should seriously think about whether you need ML at all for your product before you start working on your NLP application. Building an ML system is no easy feat—it requires a lot of money and time to collect data, train models, and serve predictions. If you can solve your problem by writing some rules, by all means do so. As a rule of thumb, if a deep learning model can achieve an accuracy of 80%, a simpler, rule-based model can take you at least halfway there.

Also, you should consider using existing solutions, if any. Many open source NLP libraries (including AllenNLP and Transformers, the two libraries that we've been using extensively throughout the book) exist that come with a wide range of pretrained models. Cloud service providers (such as AWS AI services (https://aws.amazon.com/machine-learning/ai-services/), Google Cloud AutoML (https://cloud.google.com/automl), and Microsoft Azure Cognitive Services (https://azure.microsoft.com/en-us/services/cognitive-services/)) offer a wide range of ML-related APIs for many domains, including NLP. If your task is something that can be solved using their offerings with no or little modification, that'd usually be a cost-efficient way to build your NLP application. After all, the most expensive component of any NLP application is usually highly skilled talent (i.e., your salary), and you should think twice before you go all-in and build in-house NLP solutions.

In addition, you shouldn't rule out "traditional" machine learning approaches. We've paid little attention to traditional ML models in this book, but you can find rich literature of statistical NLP models that were mainstream before the advent of deep NLP methods. Quickly building a prototype with statistical features (such as n-grams) and ML models (such as SVM) is often a great start. Non-deep algorithms such as *gradient-boosted decision trees* (GBDTs) often work almost as well as, if not better than, deep learning methods at a fraction of the cost.

Finally, I always recommend that practitioners start by developing the validation set and choosing the right evaluation metric first, even before starting to choose the right ML approach. A validation set doesn't need to be big, and most people can afford to sit down for a couple of hours and manually annotate a couple of hundred instances. Doing this offers many benefits—first, by solving the task manually, you get a feel of what's important when it comes to solving the problem and whether it's something that a machine can really solve automatically. Second, by putting yourself in the machine's shoes, you gain a lot of insights into the task (what the data looks like, how the input and output data are distributed, and how they are related), which become valuable when it comes to actually designing an ML system to solve it.

11.1.2 *Choosing the right architecture*

Except for rare occasions where the output of an ML system is the end product itself (such as machine translation), NLP modules usually interact with a larger system that collectively provide some values to the end users. For example, a spam filter is usually implemented as a module or a microservice embedded in a larger application (email service). Voice assistant systems are usually large, complex combinations of many ML/NLP subcomponents, including voice recognition, sentence-intent classification, question answering, and speech generation, that interact with each other. Even machine translation models can be one tiny component in a larger complex system if you include data pipelines, the backend, and the translation interface that the end users interact with.

An NLP application can take many forms. Surprisingly, many NLP components can be structured as a one-off task that takes some static data as its input and produces transformed data as its output. For example, if you have a static database of some documents and you'd like to classify them by their topics, your NLP classifier can be a simple one-off Python script that runs this classification task. If you'd like to extract common entities (e.g., company names) from the same database, you can write a Python script that runs a named entity recognition (NER) model to do it. Even a text-based recommender engine that finds objects based on textual similarity can be a daily task that reads from and writes data to the database. You don't need to architect a complex software system with many services talking to each other.

Many other NLP components can be structured as a (micro)service that runs prediction in batches, which is the architecture that I recommend for many scenarios. For example, a spam filter doesn't need to classify every single email as soon as they arrive—the system can queue a certain number of emails that arrive at the system and pass the batched emails to the classifier service. The NLP application usually communicates with the rest of the system via some intermediary (e.g., a RESTful API or a queuing system). This configuration is great for applications that require some freshness for their prediction (after all, users do not want to wait for hours until their emails arrive to their inbox), but the requirement is not that strict.

Finally, NLP components can also be designed so that they serve real-time prediction. This is necessary when, for example, an audience needs real-time subtitles for a speech. Another example is when the system wants to show ads based on the user's real-time behavior. For these cases, the NLP service needs to receive a stream of input data (such as audio or user events) and produce another stream of data (such as transcribed text or ad-click probabilities). *Real-time streaming frameworks* such as Apache Flink (https://flink.apache.org/) are often used for processing such stream data. Also, if your application is based on a server-client architecture, as with typical mobile and web apps, and you want to show some real-time prediction to the users, you can choose to run ML/NLP models on the client side, such as the web browser or the smartphones. Client-side ML frameworks such as TensorFlow.js (https://www.tensorflow.org/js), Core ML (https://developer.apple.com/documentation/coreml), and ML Kit (https://developers.google.com/ml-kit) can be used for such purposes.

11.1.3 *Project structure*

Many NLP applications follow somewhat similar project structures. A typical NLP project may need to manage datasets to train a model from, intermediate files generated by preprocessing data, model files produced as a result of training, source code for training and inference, and log files that store additional information about the training and inference.

Because typical NLP applications have many components and directories in common, it'd be useful if you simply follow best practices as your default choice when starting a new project. Here are my recommendations for structuring your NLP projects:

- *Data management*—Make a directory called data and put all the data in it. It may also be helpful to subdivide this into raw, interim, and result directories. The raw directory contains the unprocessed dataset files you obtained externally (such as the Stanford Sentiment Treebank we've been using throughout this book) or built internally. It is very critical that *you do not modify any files in this raw directory by hand.* If you need to make changes, write a script that runs some processing against the raw files and then writes the result to the interim directory, which serves as a place for intermediate results. Or make a patch file that manages the "diff" you made to the raw file, and version-control the patch files instead. The final results such as predictions and metrics should be stored in the result directory.

- *Virtual environment*—It is strongly recommended that you work in a virtual environment so that your dependencies are separated and reproducible. You can use tools like Conda (https://docs.conda.io/en/latest/) (my recommendation) and venv (https://docs.python.org/3/library/venv.html) to set up a separate environment for your project and use pip to install individual packages. Conda can export the environment configuration into an environment.yml file, which you can use to recover the exact Conda environment. You can also keep track of pip packages for the project in a requirements.txt file. Even better, you can use Docker containers to manage and package the entire ML environment. This greatly reduces dependency-related issues and simplifies deployment and serving.

- *Experiment management*—Training and inference pipelines for an NLP application usually consist of several steps, such as preprocessing and joining the data, converting them into features, training and running the model, and converting the results back to a human-readable format. These steps can easily get out of hand if you try to remember to manage them manually. A good practice is to keep track of the steps for the pipeline in a shell script file so that the experiments are reproducible with a single command, or use dependency management software such as GNU Make, Luigi (https://github.com/spotify/luigi), and Apache Airflow (https://airflow.apache.org/).

- *Source code*—Python source code is usually put in a directory of the same name as the project, which is further subdivided into directories such as data (for data-processing code), model (for model code), and scripts (for putting scripts for training and other one-off tasks).

11.1.4 *Version control*

You probably don't need to be convinced that version-controlling your source code is important. Tools like Git help you keep track of the changes and manage different versions of the source code. Development of NLP/ML applications is usually an iterative process where you (often with other people) make many changes to the source code and experiment with many different models. You can easily end up with a number of slightly different versions of the same code.

In addition to version-controlling your source code, it is also important to *version-control your data and models*. This means that you should version-control your training data, source code, and models separately, as shown in the dotted-line boxes in figure 11.2. This is one of the major differences between regular software projects and ML applications. Machine learning is about improving computer algorithms through data. By definition, the behavior of any ML system depends on data it is fed. This could lead to a situation where the behavior of the system is different even if you use the same code.

Tools like Git Large File Storage (https://git-lfs.github.com/) and DVC (https://dvc.org) can version-control your data and models in a seamless way. Even if you are not using these tools, you should at least manage different versions as separate files that are named clearly.

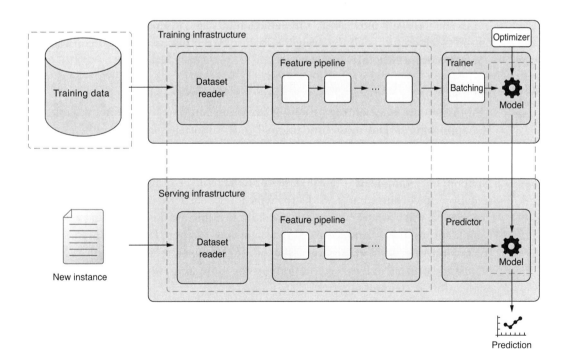

Figure 11.2 Machine learning components to version-control: training data, source code, and models

In a larger and more complex ML project, you may want to version-control your model and your feature pipeline separately, because the behavior of an ML model can be different depending on how you preprocess the input, even with the same model and input data. This will also mitigate the train-serve skew problem we'll discuss later in section 11.3.2.

Finally, when working on ML applications, you will experiment with a lot of different settings—different combinations of training datasets, feature pipelines, models, and hyperparameters—which can easily get out of control. I recommend keeping track of the training settings using some experiment management system, such as Weights & Biases (https://wandb.ai/), but you can also use something as simple as a spreadsheet in which you enter experiment information manually. When keeping track of experiments, be sure to record the following information for each experiment:

- Versions of the model code, feature pipeline, and the training data used
- Hyperparameters used to train the model
- Evaluation metrics for the training and the validation data

Platforms like AllenNLP support experiment configuration by default, which makes the first two items easy. Tools like TensorBoard, which is supported by AllenNLP and Hugging Face out of the box, make it trivial to keep track of various metrics.

11.2   *Deploying your NLP model*

In this section, we'll move on to the deployment stage, where your NLP application is put on a server and becomes available for use. We'll discuss practical considerations when deploying NLP/ML applications.

11.2.1   *Testing*

As with software engineering, testing is an important part of building reliable NLP/ML applications. The most fundamental and important tests are unit tests, which automatically check whether small units of software (such as methods and classes) are working as expected. In NLP/ML applications, it is important to unit-test your feature pipeline. For example, if you write a method that converts raw text into a tensor representation, make sure that it works for typical and corner cases with unit tests. In my experience, this is where bugs often sneak in. Reading a dataset, building a vocabulary from a corpus, tokenizing, converting tokens into integer IDs—these are all essential yet error-prone steps in preprocessing. Fortunately, frameworks such as AllenNLP offer standardized, well-tested components for these steps, which makes building NLP applications easier and bug-free.

In addition to unit tests, you need to make sure that your model learns what it's told to learn. This corresponds to testing logic errors in regular software engineering—types of errors where the software runs without crashing yet produces incorrect results. This type of error is more difficult to catch and fix in NLP/ML, because you need more insight into how the learning algorithm works mathematically. Moreover, many ML algorithms involve some randomness, such as random initialization and sampling, which makes testing even more difficult.

One recommended technique for testing NLP/ML models is sanity checks against the model output. You can start with a small and simple model and just a few toy instances with obvious labels. If you are testing a sentiment analysis model, for example, this goes as follows:

- Create a small and simple model for debugging, such as a toy encoder that simply averages the input word embeddings with a softmax layer on top.
- Prepare a few toy instances, such as "The best movie ever!" (positive) and "This is an awful movie!" (negative).
- Feed these instances to the model, and train it until convergence. Because we are using a very small dataset without a validation set, the model will heavily overfit to the instances, and that's totally fine. Check whether the training loss goes down as expected.
- Feed the same instances to the trained model, and check whether the predicted labels match the expected ones.
- Try the steps above with more toy instances and a larger model.

As a related technique, I always recommend you start with a smaller dataset, especially if the original dataset is large. Because training NLP/ML models takes a long time (hours or even days), you often find that your code has some errors only after your training is finished. You can subsample your training data, for example, by simply taking one out of every 10 instances, so that your entire training finishes quickly. Once you are sure that your model works as expected, you can gradually ramp up the amount of data you use for training. This technique is also great for quickly iterating and experimenting with many different architectures and hyperparameter settings. When you have just started building your model, you don't usually have clear understanding of the best models for your task. With a smaller dataset, you can quickly validate a large number of different options (RNN versus Transformers, different tokenizers, etc.) and narrow down the set of candidate models that work best. One caveat to this approach is that the best model architectures and hyperparameters may depend on the size of the training data. Because of this, don't forget to run the validation against the full dataset, too.

Finally, you can use integration tests to verify whether the individual components of your application work in combination. For NLP, this usually means running the whole pipeline to see if the prediction is correct. Similar to the unit tests, you can prepare a small number of instances where the expected prediction is clear and run them against the trained model. Note that these instances are not for measuring how good the model is, but rather to serve as a sanity check whether your model can produce correct predictions for "obvious" cases. It is a good practice to run integration tests every time a new model or code is deployed. This is usually part of *continuous integration* (CI) used for regular software engineering.

11.2.2 *Train-serve skew*

One common source of errors in ML applications is called *train-serve skew*, a situation where there's a discrepancy between how instances are processed at the training and the inference times. This could occur in various situations, but let's discuss a concrete example. Say you are building a sentiment-analyzer system with AllenNLP and would like to convert texts into instances. You usually start writing a data loader first, which reads the dataset and produces instances. Then you write a Python script or a config file that tells AllenNLP how the model should be trained. You train and validate your model. So far, so good. However, when it comes to using the model for prediction, things look slightly different. You need to write a predictor, which, given an input text, converts it into an instance and passes it to the model's forward method. Notice that now you have two independent pipelines that preprocess the input—one for the training in the dataset reader, and another for the inference in the predictor.

What happens if you want to modify the way the input text is processed? For example, let's say you find something you want to improve in your tokenization process, and you make changes to how input text is tokenized in your data loader. You update your data loader code, retrain the model, and deploy the model. However, you forgot to update the corresponding tokenization code in your predictor, effectively creating a discrepancy in how input is tokenized between training and serving. This is illustrated in figure 11.3.

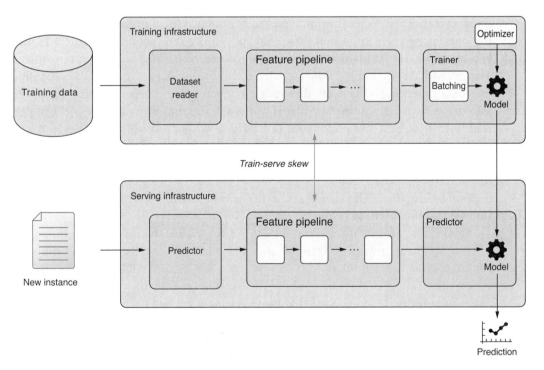

Figure 11.3   Train-serve skew is caused by discrepancies in how input is processed between training and serving.

The best way to fix this—or even better, to prevent this from happening in the first place—is to share as much of the feature pipeline as possible between the training and the serving infrastructure. A common practice in AllenNLP is to implement a method called `_text_to_instance()` in the dataset reader, which takes an input and returns an instance. By making sure that both the dataset reader and the predictor refer to the same method, you can minimize the discrepancy between the pipelines.

In NLP, the fact that input text is tokenized and converted to numerical values makes debugging your model even more difficult. For example, an obvious bug in tokenization that you can spot easily with your naked eyes can be quite difficult to identify if everything is numerical values. A good practice is to log some intermediate results into a log file that you can inspect later.

Finally, note that some behaviors of neural networks do differ between training and serving. One notable example is dropout, a regularization method we briefly covered in section 10.3.1. To recap, dropout regularizes the model by randomly masking activation values in a neural network. This makes sense in training, because by removing activations, the model learns to make robust predictions based on available values. However, remember to turn it off at the serving time, because you don't want your model to randomly drop neurons. PyTorch models implement methods—`train()` and `eval()`—that switch between the training and prediction modes, affecting how layers like dropout behave. If you are implementing a training loop manually, remember to call `model.eval()` to disable dropout. The good news is that frameworks such as AllenNLP can handle this automatically as long as you are using their default trainer.

11.2.3 Monitoring

As with other software services, deployed ML systems should be monitored continuously. In addition to the usual server metrics (e.g., CPU and memory usage), you should also monitor metrics related to the input and the output of the model. Specifically, you can monitor some higher-level statistics such as the distribution of input values and output labels. As mentioned earlier, logic errors, which are a type of error that causes the model to produce wrong results without crashing it, are the most common and hardest to find in ML systems. Monitoring those high-level statistics makes it easier to find them. Libraries and platforms like PyTorch Serve and Amazon SageMaker (discussed in section 11.3) support monitoring by default.

11.2.4 Using GPUs

Training large modern ML models almost always requires hardware accelerators such as GPUs. Recall that back in chapter 2, we used overseas factories as an analogy for GPUs, which are designed to execute a huge number of arithmetic operations such as vector and matrix addition and multiplications in parallel. In this subsection, we'll cover how to use GPUs to accelerate the training and prediction of ML models.

If you don't own GPUs or have never used cloud-based GPU solutions before, the easiest way to "try" GPUs for free is to use Google Colab. Go to its URL (https:// colab.research.google.com/), create a new notebook, go to the Runtime menu, and choose "Change runtime type." This will bring up the dialog box shown in figure 11.4.

Figure 11.4   Google Colab allows you to choose the type of hardware accelerator.

Choose GPU as the type of the hardware accelerator, and type !nvidia-smi in a code block and execute it. Some detailed information about your GPU is displayed, as shown next:

```
+-----------------------------------------------------------------------------+
| NVIDIA-SMI 460.56       Driver Version: 460.32.03    CUDA Version: 11.2      |
|-------------------------------+----------------------+----------------------+
| GPU  Name        Persistence-M| Bus-Id        Disp.A | Volatile Uncorr. ECC |
| Fan  Temp  Perf  Pwr:Usage/Cap|         Memory-Usage | GPU-Util  Compute M. |
|                               |                      |               MIG M. |
|===============================+======================+======================|
|   0  Tesla T4            Off  | 00000000:00:04.0 Off |                    0 |
| N/A   39C    P8     9W /  70W |     3MiB / 15109MiB  |      0%      Default |
|                               |                      |                  N/A |
+-------------------------------+----------------------+----------------------+

+-----------------------------------------------------------------------------+
| Processes:                                                                  |
|  GPU   GI   CI        PID   Type   Process name                  GPU Memory |
|        ID   ID                                                   Usage      |
|=============================================================================|
|  No running processes found                                                 |
+-----------------------------------------------------------------------------+
```

The nvidia-smi command (short for Nvidia System Management Interface) is a handy tool for checking information about Nvidia GPUs on the machine. From the previous snippet, you can see the version of the driver and CUDA (an API and a library for interacting with GPUs), type of GPUs (Tesla T4), available and used memory (15109 MiB and 3 MiB), and the list of processes that currently use GPUs (there aren't any). The most typical use of this command is to check how much memory your current process(es) use, because in GPU programming, you can easily get an out-of-memory error if your program uses more memory than is available.

If you use cloud infrastructures such as AWS (Amazon Web Services) and GCP (Google Cloud Platform), you'll find a wide array of virtual machine templates that you can use to quickly create cloud instances that support GPUs. For example, GCP has Nvidia's official GPU-optimized images for PyTorch and TensorFlow, which you can use as templates to launch your GPU instances. AWS offers Deep Learning AMIs (Amazon Machine Images), which preinstall basic GPU libraries such as CUDA, as well as deep learning libraries such as PyTorch. With these templates, you don't need to install necessary drivers and libraries manually—you can start building your ML applications right away. Note that although these templates are free, you do need to pay for the infrastructure. The price for GPU-enabled virtual machines is usually significantly higher than CPU machines. Make sure to check their price before you keep them running for an extended period of time.

If you are setting up GPU instances from scratch, you can find detailed instructions[1] for how to set up necessary drivers and libraries. To build NLP applications with the libraries that we covered in this book (namely, AllenNLP and Transformers), you need to install CUDA drivers and toolkits, as well as a PyTorch version that supports GPU.

If your machine has GPU(s), you can enable GPU acceleration by specifying `cuda_device` in an AllenNLP config file as follows:

```
"trainer": {
    "optimizer": {
        "type": "huggingface_adamw",
        "lr": 1.0e-5
    },
    "num_epochs": 20,
    "patience": 10,
    "cuda_device": 0
}
```

This tells the trainer to use the first GPU for training and validating the AllenNLP model.

If you are writing PyTorch code from scratch, you need to manually transfer your model and tensors to the GPU. Using an analogy, this is when your materials get shipped to an overseas factory in container ships. First, you can specify the device (GPU ID) to use, and invoke the `to()` method of tensors and models to move them

---

[1] GCP: https://cloud.google.com/compute/docs/gpus/install-drivers-gpu; AWS: https://docs.aws.amazon .com/AWSEC2/latest/UserGuide/install-nvidia-driver.html.

between devices. For example, you can use the following code snippet to run text generation on a GPU with Hugging Face Transformers:

```
device = torch.device('cuda:0')
tokenizer = AutoTokenizer.from_pretrained("gpt2-large")
model = AutoModelWithLMHead.from_pretrained("gpt2-large")

generated = tokenizer.encode("On our way to the beach ")
context = torch.tensor([generated])

model = model.to(device)
context = context.to(device)
```

The rest is identical to the code we used in section 8.4.

11.3 *Case study: Serving and deploying NLP applications*

In this section, we will go over a case study where we serve and deploy an NLP model built with Hugging Face. Specifically, we'll take a pretrained language generation model (DistilGPT2), serve it with TorchServe, and deploy it to a cloud server using Amazon SageMaker.

11.3.1 *Serving models with TorchServe*

As you have seen, deploying an NLP application is more than just writing an API for your ML model. You need to take care of a number of production-related considerations, including how to deal with high traffic by parallelizing model inference with multiple workers, how to store and manage different versions of multiple ML models, how to consistently handle pre- and postprocessing of the data, and how to monitor the health of the server as well as various metrics about the data.

Because these problems are so common, ML practitioners have been working on general-purpose platforms for serving and deploying ML models. In this section, we'll use TorchServe (https://github.com/pytorch/serve), an easy-to-use framework for serving PyTorch models jointly developed by Facebook and Amazon. TorchServe is shipped with many functionalities that can address the issues mentioned earlier.

TorchServe can be installed by running the following:

```
pip install torchserve torch-model-archiver
```

In this case study, we'll use a pretrained language model called *DistilGPT2*. DistilGPT2 is a smaller version of GPT-2 built using a technique called *knowledge distillation*. Knowledge distillation (or simply *distillation*) is a machine learning technique where a smaller model (called a *student*) is trained in such a way that it mimics the predictions produced by a larger model (called a *teacher*). It is a great way to train a smaller model that produces high quality output, and it often produces a better model than training a smaller model from scratch.

First, let's download the pretrained DistilGPT2 model from the Hugging Face repository by running the following commands. Note that you need to install Git

Large File Storage (https://git-lfs.github.com/), a Git extension for handling large files under Git:

```
git lfs install
git clone https://huggingface.co/distilgpt2
```

This creates a subdirectory called distilgpt2, which contains files such as config.json and pytorch_model.bin.

As the next step, you need write a handler for TorchServe, a lightweight wrapper class that specifies how to initialize your model, preprocess and postprocess the input, and run the inference on the input. Listing 11.1 shows the handler code for serving the DistilGPT2 model. In fact, nothing in the handler is specific to the particular model we use (DistilGPT2). You can use the same code for other GPT-2–like models, including the original GPT-2 models, as long as you use the Transformers library.

Listing 11.1 Handler for TorchServe

```python
from abc import ABC
import logging

import torch
from ts.torch_handler.base_handler import BaseHandler

from transformers import GPT2LMHeadModel, GPT2Tokenizer

logger = logging.getLogger(__name__)

class TransformersLanguageModelHandler(BaseHandler, ABC):
    def __init__(self):
        super(TransformersLanguageModelHandler, self).__init__()
        self.initialized = False
        self.length = 256
        self.top_k = 0
        self.top_p = .9
        self.temperature = 1.
        self.repetition_penalty = 1.

    def initialize(self, ctx):                        ⬅── Initializes the model
        self.manifest = ctx.manifest
        properties = ctx.system_properties
        model_dir = properties.get("model_dir")
        self.device = torch.device(
            "cuda:" + str(properties.get("gpu_id"))
            if torch.cuda.is_available()
            else "cpu"
        )

        self.model = GPT2LMHeadModel.from_pretrained(model_dir)
        self.tokenizer = GPT2Tokenizer.from_pretrained(model_dir)

        self.model.to(self.device)
        self.model.eval()
```

```
        logger.info('Transformer model from path {0} loaded
    successfully'.format(model_dir))
        self.initialized = True
```

```
    def preprocess(self, data):          ◄─┐ Preprocesses and tokenizes
        text = data[0].get("data")            the incoming data
        if text is None:
            text = data[0].get("body")
        text = text.decode('utf-8')

        logger.info("Received text: '%s'", text)

        encoded_text = self.tokenizer.encode(
            text,
            add_special_tokens=False,
            return_tensors="pt")

        return encoded_text
```

```
                                         ┐ Runs inference
    def inference(self, inputs):       ◄─┘ on the data
        output_sequences = self.model.generate(
            input_ids=inputs.to(self.device),
            max_length=self.length + len(inputs[0]),
            temperature=self.temperature,
            top_k=self.top_k,
            top_p=self.top_p,
            repetition_penalty=self.repetition_penalty,
            do_sample=True,
            num_return_sequences=1,
        )

        text = self.tokenizer.decode(
            output_sequences[0],
            clean_up_tokenization_spaces=True)

        return [text]
```

```
    def postprocess(self, inference_output):   ◄─┐ Postprocesses
        return inference_output                    the prediction
```

```
_service = TransformersLanguageModelHandler()
```

```
def handle(data, context):                 ◄─┐ The handler method
    try:                                        called by TorchServe
        if not _service.initialized:
            _service.initialize(context)

        if data is None:
            return None

        data = _service.preprocess(data)
        data = _service.inference(data)
        data = _service.postprocess(data)
```

```
      return data
  except Exception as e:
      raise e
```

Your handler needs to inherit from `BaseHandler` and override a few methods including `initialize()` and `inference()`. Your handler script also includes `handle()`, a top-level method where the handler is initialized and called.

The next step is to run `torch-model-archiver`, which is a command-line tool that packages your model and your handler, as follows:

```
torch-model-archiver \
    --model-name distilgpt2 \
    --version 1.0 \
    --serialized-file distilgpt2/pytorch_model.bin \
    --extra-files "distilgpt2/config.json,distilgpt2/vocab.json,distilgpt2/
     tokenizer.json,distilgpt2/merges.txt" \
    --handler ./torchserve_handler.py
```

The first two options specify the name and the version of the model. The next option, `serialized-file`, specifies the main weight file of the PyTorch model you want to package (which usually ends with .bin or .pt). You can also add any extra files (specified by `extra-files`) that are needed for the model to run. Finally, you need to pass the handler file you just wrote to the `handler` option.

When finished, this creates a file named `distilgpt2.mar` (`.mar` stands for "model archive") in the same directory. Let's create a new directory named `model_store` and move the .mar file there as follows. This directory serves as a model store, a place where all the model files are stored and served from:

```
mkdir model_store
mv distilgpt2.mar model_store
```

Now you are ready to spin up TorchServe and start serving your model! All you need is to run the following command:

```
torchserve --start --model-store model_store --models distilgpt2=distilgpt2.mar
```

When the server is fully up, you can start making the HTTP requests to the server. It exposes a couple of endpoints, but if you just want to run inference, you need to invoke `http://127.0.0.1:8080/predictions/` with the model name as follows:

```
curl -d "data=In a shocking finding, scientist discovered a herd of unicorns
    living in a remote, previously unexplored valley, in the Andes
    Mountains. Even more surprising to the researchers was the fact that the
    unicorns spoke perfect English." -X POST http://127.0.0.1:8080/
    predictions/distilgpt2
```

Here, we are using a prompt from OpenAI's original post about GPT-2 (https://openai.com/blog/better-language-models/). This returns the generated sentences, shown next. The generated text is of decent quality, considering that the model is a distilled, smaller version:

In a shocking finding, scientist discovered a herd of unicorns living in a remote, previously unexplored valley, in the Andes Mountains. Even more surprising to the researchers was the fact that the unicorns spoke perfect English. They used to speak the Catalan language while working there, and so the unicorns were not just part of the local herd, they were also part of a population that wasn't much less diverse than their former national-ethnic neighbors, who agreed with them.

"In a sense they learned even better than they otherwise might have been," says Andrea Rodriguez, associate professor of language at the University of California, Irvine. "They told me that everyone else was even worse off than they thought."

The findings, like most of the research, will only support the new species that their native language came from. But it underscores the incredible social connections between unicorns and foreigners, especially as they were presented with a hard new platform for studying and creating their own language.

"Finding these people means finding out the nuances of each other, and dealing with their disabilities better," Rodriguez says.

...

When you are finished, you can run the following command to stop serving:

```
torchserve --stop
```

11.3.2 *Deploying models with SageMaker*

Amazon SageMaker is a managed platform for training and deploying machine learning models. It enables you to spin up a GPU server, run a Jupyter Notebook inside it, build and train ML models there, and directly deploy them in a hosted environment. Our next step is to deploy the machine learning model as a cloud SageMaker endpoint so that production systems can make requests to it. The concrete steps for deploying an ML model with SageMaker consist of the following:

1 Upload your model to S3.
2 Register and upload your inference code to Amazon Elastic Container Registry (ECR).
3 Create a SageMaker model and an endpoint.
4 Make requests to the endpoint.

We are going to follow the official tutorial (http://mng.bz/p9qK) with a slight modification. First, let's go to the SageMaker console (https://console.aws.amazon.com/sagemaker/home) and start a notebook instance. When you open the notebook, run the following code to install the necessary packages and start a SageMaker session:

```
!git clone https://github.com/shashankprasanna/torchserve-examples.git
!cd torchserve-examples

!git clone https://github.com/pytorch/serve.git
!pip install serve/model-archiver/
```

```
import boto3, time, json
sess    = boto3.Session()
sm      = sess.client('sagemaker')
region  = sess.region_name
account = boto3.client('sts').get_caller_identity().get('Account')

import sagemaker
role = sagemaker.get_execution_role()
sagemaker_session = sagemaker.Session(boto_session=sess)

bucket_name = sagemaker_session.default_bucket()
```

The variable `bucket_name` contains a string like `sagemaker-xxx-yyy` where xxx is the region name (like `us-east-1`). Take note of this name—you need it to upload your model to S3 in the next step.

Next, you need to upload your model to an S3 bucket by running the following commands from the machine where you just created the .mar file (not from the Sage-Maker notebook instance). Before uploading, you first need to compress your .mar file into a tar.gz file, a format supported by SageMaker. Remember to replace `sagemaker-xxx-yyy` with the actual bucket name specified by `bucket_name`:

```
cd model_store
tar cvfz distilgpt2.tar.gz distilgpt2.mar
aws s3 cp distilgpt2.tar.gz s3://sagemaker-xxx-yyy/torchserve/models/
```

The next step is to register and push the TorchServe inference code to ECR. Before you start, in your SageMaker notebook instance, open `torchserve-examples/Dockerfile` and modify the following line (add `--no-cache-dir transformers`):

```
RUN pip install --no-cache-dir psutil \
                --no-cache-dir torch \
                --no-cache-dir torchvision \
                --no-cache-dir transformers
```

Now you can build a Docker container and push it to ECR as follows:

```
registry_name = 'torchserve'
!aws ecr create-repository --repository-name torchserve

image_label = 'v1'
image = f'{account}.dkr.ecr.{region}.amazonaws.com/
    {registry_name}:{image_label}'

!docker build -t {registry_name}:{image_label} .
!$(aws ecr get-login --no-include-email --region {region})
!docker tag {registry_name}:{image_label} {image}
!docker push {image}
```

Now you are ready to create a SageMaker model and create an endpoint for it, as shown next:

```
import sagemaker
from sagemaker.model import Model
```

```
from sagemaker.predictor import RealTimePredictor
role = sagemaker.get_execution_role()

model_file_name = 'distilgpt2'

model_data = f's3://{bucket_name}/torchserve/models/{model_file_name}.tar.gz'
sm_model_name = 'torchserve-distilgpt2'

torchserve_model = Model(model_data = model_data,
                        image_uri = image,
                        role = role,
                        predictor_cls=RealTimePredictor,
                        name = sm_model_name)
endpoint_name = 'torchserve-endpoint-' + time.strftime("%Y-%m-%d-%H-%M-%S",
    time.gmtime())
predictor = torchserve_model.deploy(instance_type='ml.m4.xlarge',
                                    initial_instance_count=1,
                                    endpoint_name = endpoint_name)
```

The predictor object is something you can call directly to run the inference as follows:

```
response = predictor.predict(data="In a shocking finding, scientist
    discovered a herd of unicorns living in a remote, previously unexplored
    valley, in the Andes Mountains. Even more surprising to the researchers
    was the fact that the unicorns spoke perfect English.")
```

The content of the response should look something like this:

```
b'In a shocking finding, scientist discovered a herd of unicorns living in a
    remote, previously unexplored valley, in the Andes Mountains. Even more
    surprising to the researchers was the fact that the unicorns spoke
    perfect English. The unicorns said they would take a stroll in the
    direction of scientists over the next month or so.\n\n\n\nWhen
    contacted by Animal Life and Crop.com, author Enrique Martinez explained
    how he was discovered and how the unicorns\' journey has surprised him.
    According to Martinez, the experience makes him more interested in
    research and game development.\n"This is really what I want to see this
    year, and in terms of medical research, I want to see our population
    increase."<|endoftext|>'
```

Congratulations! We just completed our journey—we started building an ML model in chapter 2 and came all the way to deploying it to a cloud platform in this chapter.

11.4   *Interpreting and visualizing model predictions*

People often talk about the metrics and leaderboard performance on standardized datasets, but analyzing and visualizing model predictions and internal states is important for NLP applications in the real world. Although deep learning models can be really good at what they do, often reaching human-level performance on some NLP tasks, those deep models are black boxes, and it is difficult to know *why* they make certain predictions.

Because of this (somewhat troubling) property of deep learning models, a growing field in AI called *explainable AI* (XAI) is working to develop methods to explain the predictions and behavior of ML models. Interpreting ML models is useful for debugging—it gives you a lot of clues if you know why it made certain predictions. In some domains such as medical applications and self-driving cars, making ML models explainable is critical for legal and practical reasons. In this final section of the chapter, we'll go over a case study where we use the *Language Interpretability Tool* (LIT) (https://pair-code.github.io/lit/) for visualizing and interpreting the predictions and behavior of NLP models.

LIT is an open source toolkit developed by Google and offers a browser-based interface for interpreting and visualizing ML predictions. Note that it is framework agnostic, meaning that it works with any Python-based ML frameworks of choice, including AllenNLP and Hugging Face Transformers.[2] LIT offers a wide range of features, including the following:

- *Saliency map*—Visualizing in color which part of the input played an important role to reach the current prediction
- *Aggregate statistics*—Showing aggregate statistics such as dataset metrics and confusion matrices
- *Counterfactuals*—Observing how model predictions change for generated new examples

In the remainder of this section, let's take one of the AllenNLP models we trained (the BERT-based sentiment analysis model in chapter 9) and analyze it via LIT. LIT offers a set of extensible abstractions such as datasets and models to make it easier to work with any Python-based ML models.

First, let's install LIT. It can be installed with a single call of pip as follows:

```
pip install lit-nlp
```

Next, you need to wrap your dataset and model with the abstract classes defined by LIT. Let's create a new script called `run_lit.py`, and import the necessary modules and classes, as shown here:

```
import numpy as np

from allennlp.models.archival import load_archive
from allennlp.predictors.predictor import Predictor
from lit_nlp import dev_server
from lit_nlp import server_flags
from lit_nlp.api import dataset as lit_dataset
from lit_nlp.api import model as lit_model
from lit_nlp.api import types as lit_types

from examples.sentiment.sst_classifier import LstmClassifier
from examples.sentiment.sst_reader import
    StanfordSentimentTreeBankDatasetReaderWithTokenizer
```

---

[2] There is another toolkit called AllenNLP Interpret (https://allennlp.org/interpret) that offers a similar set of features for understanding NLP models, although it is specifically designed to interact with AllenNLP models.

The next code shows how to define a dataset for LIT. Here, we are creating a toy dataset that consists of just four hardcoded examples, but in practice, you may want to read a real dataset that you want to explore. Remember to define the spec() method that returns the type specification of the dataset:

```
class SSTData(lit_dataset.Dataset):
    def __init__(self, labels):
        self._labels = labels
        self._examples = [
            {'sentence': 'This is the best movie ever!!!', 'label': '4'},
            {'sentence': 'A good movie.', 'label': '3'},
            {'sentence': 'A mediocre movie.', 'label': '1'},
            {'sentence': 'It was such an awful movie...', 'label': '0'}
        ]

    def spec(self):
        return {
            'sentence': lit_types.TextSegment(),
            'label': lit_types.CategoryLabel(vocab=self._labels)
        }
```

Now, we are ready to define the main model, as shown next.

Listing 11.2   Defining the main model for LIT

```
class SentimentClassifierModel(lit_model.Model):
    def __init__(self):
        cuda_device = 0
        archive_file = 'model/model.tar.gz'
        predictor_name = 'sentence_classifier_predictor'

        archive = load_archive(                    ◁─┐ Loads the
            archive_file=archive_file,               │ AllenNLP archive
            cuda_device=cuda_device
        )

        predictor = Predictor.from_archive(archive,
    predictor_name=predictor_name)
                                                   ┐ Extracts and sets
        self.predictor = predictor            ◁──┘ the predictor
        label_map =
    archive.model.vocab.get_index_to_token_vocabulary('labels')
        self.labels = [label for _, label in sorted(label_map.items())]

    def predict_minibatch(self, inputs):
        for inst in inputs:
            pred = self.predictor.predict(inst['sentence'])          ◁─┐
            tokens = self.predictor._tokenizer.tokenize(inst['sentence'])│
            yield {                                                      │
                'tokens': tokens,                           Runs the predict
                'probas': np.array(pred['probs']),                method of
                'cls_emb': np.array(pred['cls_emb'])          the predictor
            }
```

```
def input_spec(self):
    return {
        "sentence": lit_types.TextSegment(),
        "label": lit_types.CategoryLabel(vocab=self.labels,
required=False)
    }

def output_spec(self):
    return {
        "tokens": lit_types.Tokens(),
        "probas": lit_types.MulticlassPreds(parent="label",
vocab=self.labels),
        "cls_emb": lit_types.Embeddings()
    }
```

In the constructor (`__init__`), we are loading an AllenNLP model from an archive file and creating a predictor from it. We are assuming that your model is put under model/model.tar.gz and hard-coding its path, but feel free to modify this, depending on where your model is located.

The model prediction is computed in `predict_minibatch()`. Given the input (which is simply an array of dataset instances), it runs the model via the predictor and returns the result. Note that the predictions are made instance-by-instance, although in practice, you should consider making predictions in batches because it will improve throughput for larger input data. The method also returns the embeddings for predicted classes (as `cls_emb`), which will be used for visualizing embeddings (figure 11.5).

Finally, here's the code for running the LIT server:

```
model = SentimentClassifierModel()
models = {"sst": model}
datasets = {"sst": SSTData(labels=model.labels)}

lit_demo = dev_server.Server(models, datasets, **server_flags.get_flags())
lit_demo.serve()
```

After running the script above, go to `http://localhost:5432/` on your browser. You should see a screen similar to the one shown in figure 11.5. You can see an array of panels corresponding to various information about the data and predictions, including embeddings, the dataset table and editor, classification results, and saliency maps (which shows contributions of tokens computed via an automated method called *LIME*[3]).

Visualizing and interacting with model predictions are a great way to get insights into how the model works and how you should improve it.

---

[3] Ribeiro et al., "'Why Should I Trust You?': Explaining the Predictions of Any Classifier," (2016). https://arxiv.org/abs/1602.04938.

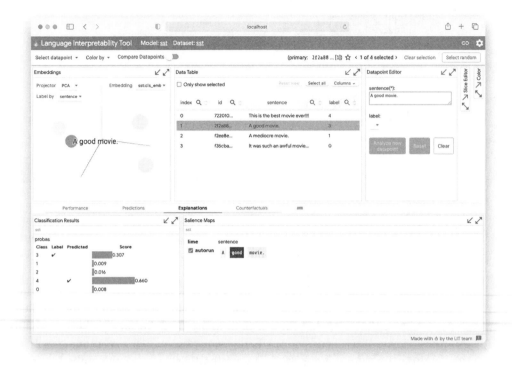

Figure 11.5   LIT can show saliency maps, aggregate statistics, and embeddings for analyzing your model and predictions.

11.5   *Where to go from here*

In this book, we've only scratched the surface of this vast, long-historied field of natural language processing. If you are interested in learning the practical aspects of NLP further, *Natural Language Processing in Action* by Hobson Lane and others (Manning Publications, 2019) and *Practical Natural Language Processing* by Sowmya Vajjala and others (O'Reilly, 2020) can be a good next step. *Machine Learning Engineering* by Andriy Burkov (True Positive Inc., 2020) is also a good book to learn engineering topics for machine learning in general.

If you are interested in learning more mathematical and theoretical aspects of NLP, I'd recommend giving some popular textbooks a try, such as *Speech and Language Processing* by Dan Jurafsky and James H. Martin (Prentice Hall, 2008)[4] and *Introduction to Natural Language Processing* by Jacob Eisenstein (MIT Press, 2019). *Foundations of Statistical Natural Language Processing* by Christopher D. Manning and Hinrich Schütze (Cambridge, 1999), though a bit outdated, is also a classic textbook that can give you a solid foundation for a wide variety of NLP methods and models.

---

[4] You can read the draft of the third edition (2021) for free at https://web.stanford.edu/~jurafsky/slp3/.

Also remember that you can often find great resources online for free. A free Allen-NLP course, "A Guide to Natural Language Processing with AllenNLP" (https://guide .allennlp.org/), and the documentation for Hugging Face Transformers (https:// huggingface.co/transformers/index.html) are great places to go to if you want to learn those libraries in depth.

Finally, the most effective way to learn NLP is actually doing it yourself. If you have problems for your hobby, work, or anything that involves dealing with natural language text, think whether any of the techniques you learned in this book are applicable. Is it a classification, tagging, or sequence-to-sequence problem? Which models do you use? How do you get the training data? How do you evaluate your model? If you don't have NLP problems laying around, don't worry—head over to Kaggle, where you can find a number of NLP-related competitions in which you can "get your hands dirty" and gain NLP experience while working on real-world problems. NLP conferences and workshops often host shared tasks, where participants can compete on a common task, datasets, and evaluation metrics, which are also a great way to learn further if you want to deep dive into a particular field of NLP.

Summary

- Machine learning code is usually a small portion in real-world NLP/ML systems, supported by a complex infrastructure for data collection, feature extraction, and model serving and monitoring.
- NLP modules can be developed as a one-off script, a batch prediction service, or a real-time prediction service.
- It is important to version-control your model and data, in addition to the source code. Beware of train-serve skew that causes discrepancies between the training and the testing times.
- You can easily serve PyTorch models with TorchServe and deploy them to Amazon SageMaker.
- Explainable AI is a new field for explaining and interpreting ML models and their predictions. You can use LIT (Language Interpretability Tool) to visualize and interpret model predictions.

index